SMALL ARMS

⧫ AT ⧫

GETTYSBURG

Joseph G. Bilby

SMALL ARMS

AT

GETTYSBURG

INFANTRY AND CAVALRY WEAPONS
IN AMERICA'S GREATEST BATTLE

WESTHOLME
Yardley

Title page: Private George Thompson of the Fifteenth New Jersey Infantry poses with his Enfield rifle musket. Although his regiments commanding officer, Colonel Penrose, disliked his men's Enfield rifle muskets, and exchanged them for Springfields found on the Gettysburg battlefield, some men from the fifteenth parted with their Enfields reluctantly. (*John Kuhl*)

First Westholme Paperback 2023
Copyright © 2008 Joseph G. Bilby

Westholme Publishing, LLC
904 Edgewood Road
Yardley, Pennsylvania 19067
Visit our Web site at www.westholmepublishing.com

ISBN: 978-1-59416-390-6

Printed in United States of America

For Kate and Geoff, Meg and Jarrett, and John and Carol

CONTENTS

PREFACE

THERE ARE PROBABLY MORE BOOKS about Gettysburg than any other battle in history, certainly United States history. Gettysburg has been covered extensively, from general accounts to detailed histories of the action on particular days or portions of the battlefield, the role of particular arms of service in the fight, biographies of commanders down to regimental level, and the effect of the battle on civilians, property, and animals (and even the ghosts who allegedly haunt the field) in a seemingly ad infinitum catalog of subjects. There are magazine articles dealing with almost every conceivable aspect of Gettysburg and even an entire magazine dedicated solely to examining the details of the three days of fighting there and the events immediately leading up and following it.

To date, surprising as it may seem, there is no detailed book-length study of the firearms used at Gettysburg. This work is an attempt to remedy that absence. In the conventional wisdom of the Civil War, Gettysburg has traditionally been cited as a turning point, a high-water mark. Recent scholarship has revealed that much of that view is rooted in retrospective. There was no doubt in the immediate aftermath that Gettysburg had been a great battle, and a significant one, among Northerners, and the Army of Northern Virginia certainly knew it had suffered a setback. There was no immediate general view that the battle was either the beginning of the end or the end of the beginning of the war, however.[1]

Even shortly afterward, though, it was clear to the most casual observer that Gettysburg was indeed a small-arms watershed. By the time of the battle, the infantry of both the Army of the Potomac and the Army of Northern Virginia, which had begun the conflict largely armed with obsolete smoothbore muskets, had been almost entirely rearmed with rifled arms. At Gettysburg, however, some soldiers were still carrying smoothbores, somewhat surprisingly even by choice, while others shouldered transitional-technology separately primed breechloaders like the Sharps, and a small number of Yankee cavalry-men brought single-shot and repeating breechloaders firing advanced self-contained metallic cartridges to the fight. Thus Gettysburg meld-ed, for the first time in a major battle, small-arms technologies past, present, and future, all on the same field.

This book reviews the origins of those technologies and traces them down the years to those climactic July days, investigating how they were actually used by soldiers at Gettysburg. Although designed to be read in its entirety, it is not intended to be a chronological account of the battle, since that narrative is abundantly available elsewhere. It can be read in its entirety or sampled by topical chapter, or in the case of the rifle-musket, a three-chapter section, as each tells the story of a par-ticular arms technology, its history, and use in the battle.

Chapter 1

BREECHLOADING CARBINES

———◆◆———

SECOND LIEUTENANT MARCELLUS E. JONES would remember that morning for the rest of his life—and so would the nation. It was around 7:00 AM when privates Elisha S. Kelley and James O. Hale, the advanced vedette of Company E, Eighth Illinois Cavalry, saw the Rebels in the distance, marching straight at them astride the Chambersburg Pike. Kelley spurred his horse back to the picket reserve post to spread the word. His breakfast interrupted, Lieutenant Jones led the rest of his detachment forward and deployed them as skirmishers.

Jones, convinced that a big fight was about to begin, borrowed Sergeant Levi S. Shafer's carbine, rested it on a fence rail, aimed at a mounted Confederate officer some 600 yards distant, and squeezed the trigger. The gun bucked and roared and sped a bullet on its way, which landed somewhere between the lieutenant and the enemy. Jones, who probably forgot to estimate range and raise his rear sight, hadn't hit his mark, but he had done what he set out to do: secure his place in history. It was July 1, 1863, and Marcellus E. Jones was sure he had just fired the first shot of the battle of Gettysburg.[1]

The instrument of Jones's fame, a .52 caliber Model 1859 Sharps, was considered the best carbine in Union cavalry service at mid-war. The first privately mass-produced breechloading weapon of the era, the Sharps had been steadily improved since its invention by Christian Sharps in 1848 and would assume a central place among the legendary arms of the American *Iliad*.

Before the war came, in the turbulent 1850s, Sharps carbines were cited by abolitionist leader Reverend Henry Ward Beecher as more efficacious instruments than prayer in preventing the spread of, and bringing an end to, slavery. As a result, they gained the nickname "Beecher's Bibles." The Sharps played an important role in the mini–civil war that erupted in "Bleeding Kansas" and also in John Brown's 1859 abortive raid on Harper's Ferry, rehearsals for the events of 1861 that would eventually lead two great armies down dusty roads to meet at a small Pennsylvania crossroads town.

The Sharps was one of a large variety of firearms that saw action in the hands of Civil War horse soldiers. By 1863, diversity of armament had long been a United States cavalry tradition. The first permanent American mounted force, the Regiment of Dragoons, was organized in 1833. Frontier patrol units capable of fighting on foot or horseback, the dragoons were initially armed with pistols, sabers, and short-barreled muzzleloading carbines, or "musketoons," with ramrods attached by swivels to prevent loss in mounted combat. The vast majority of small arms had, to that date, always been muzzleloaders, but the concept of guns that could be rapidly reloaded at the breech was almost as old as the weapons themselves, and the idea was an attractive one for a number of reasons to men in mounted forces.

Breechloaders, however, usually foundered in practice due to excessive powder gas escape at the breech joint, lack of durability, and high cost of production, especially when used with the flintlock ignition system. A flintlock gun was fired when a piece of flint held in the gun's hammer, or cock, scraped the "frizzen" and showered sparks into a priming charge alongside a channel hole in the barrel. The spark ignited priming that then exploded the main load in the gun's barrel. Although simple and durable, the flintlock was susceptible to failure in rainy or even damp weather and was difficult to design an effective breechloading system around. Although some flintlock breechloading systems, including the Chaumette and Ferguson, showed promise, they failed to materialize as effective firearms in the field.[2]

The breechloading idea, however, refused to die and was particularly attractive to mounted men. Rapid reloading was an obvious plus to often-outnumbered frontier soldiers. In addition, although dragoons

A .52 caliber Model 1859 Sharps carbine. Although earlier versions of the Sharps saw action in the Civil War, the most common, and the dominant cavalry carbine at Gettysburg, was the Model 1859. The Sharps used a combustible paper cartridge, which made it rapid to reload, but ammunition fragility proved a drawback in service. (*John Kuhl*)

usually employed their carbines in dismounted combat, breechloaders were also far easier to reload on horseback. At least as important, an over-bore-size projectile loaded through a gun's breech would not roll out of the barrel when slung muzzle down over a dragoon's shoulder on a horse trotting across the prairie, a not-uncommon occurrence with the under-bore-diameter muzzleloading balls. The ability to withstand horseback "jouncing," as we shall see, was an important consideration in evaluating the efficiency of otherwise seemingly satisfactory cavalry arms and ammunition, yet it is often overlooked by historians.

With these desirable attributes in mind, the dragoons were issued the Hall carbine, which used a lever to raise the breech for loading a chamber with a paper cartridge containing powder and a round ball. Although Hall flintlock rifles, the most successful of the flint ignition breechloaders, had been issued to selected American infantry and militia units for some time, the shorter-barreled Hall cavalry gun was a step further along the evolutionary path for firearms. In addition to being a breechloader, the Hall carbine was the first United States military firearm with a percussion ignition system, in which the gun's hammer hit a waterproof copper percussion cap containing fulminate to ignite the main charge. The Hall did, like its rifle antecedent, leak some gas at the breech and, like the common infantry musket, did not have a rifled barrel—so while the system increased loading speed and resistance to fouling, accuracy and effective range remained limited.[3]

In the years leading up to the Civil War, the cavalry was the army's primary firearm-testing service. By the late 1850s, the weapons mix in the mounted arm, in addition to handguns and sabers, included a bewildering array of long arms, all by then featuring percussion ignition. Some troopers were issued older smoothbore muzzleloaders and others the 1855 series of long-range .58 caliber muzzleloading rifles and carbines firing the hollow-base, conical Minié ball. Still others carried old Hall or new Sharps breechloading carbines. Small-arms technology was advancing rapidly, however, and in 1857 the army tested twenty different breechloaders for possible adoption.

All of these guns were "capping breechloaders," using unprimed semi-fixed ammunition with a cartridge containing powder and bullet that required an external percussion cap for ignition, and all had rifled barrels. Some, like the Sharps, used a paper or linen cartridge, which was fast becoming old technology. While the Sharps was easily loaded by working a lever to drop its breechblock to expose the chamber for loading a cartridge, it sealed against gas escape with a moveable breech face and, beginning with the 1859 model, a sliding chamber insert. Newer designs, including the Smith, used disposable or reloadable cartridge cases made of various materials to seal gas leakage. The most modern inventions, like the Burnside and Maynard, employed brass cartridge cases to achieve a complete gas seal but were still dependent on ignition by an external percussion cap. All of the newer ammunition was, however, more robust than the paper or linen cartridge. Ammunition durability was particularly important in the cavalry, due to the jounce factor, as constant horseback movement tended to break up fragile cartridges carried in a leather cartridge box.

In the 1857 trials, the Sharps, which was equipped with an automatic priming magazine propelling fulminate wafers under the gun's falling hammer and from which the shooter did not have to remove an expended cartridge case, proved the fastest firing (eighteen shots in fifty-five seconds) gun. The Colt five-shot revolving rifle (which loaded at the front of its cylinder using a combustible paper cartridge) was the most accurate arm tested. The Burnside, however, with its durable brass cartridge case, was chosen the best overall weapon for cavalry use, and a number were ordered for field testing.[4]

At the outbreak of the Civil War, Federal ordnance chief Brigadier General James W. Ripley was besieged by inventors of "patent breechloaders" seeking lucrative contracts. Although Ripley is often castigated for not showing enough interest in innovative arms technology, much of the criticism fails to appreciate the realities of his position. The general was committed to getting the largest quantity of proven muzzleloading Springfield .58 caliber rifle-muskets into the hands of hundreds of thousands of infantrymen in the shortest possible time—all else was secondary.

Brigadier General James W. Ripley. Although much maligned by some historians for his lack of progressive attitude towards innovative firearms at the outset of the Civil War, as Federal ordnance chief Ripley's arms acquisition policy proved effective in adequately arming the Union army through 1863. (Library of Congress)

Ripley was committed to breechloaders for the cavalry, but most inventors were in no position to rapidly manufacture a significant quantity of arms. In addition, the field durability of most of these guns was unknown, with ammunition resupply a potential logistic nightmare. The Sharps was a proven product and had a factory already dedicated to its manufacture, making it the understandable first choice of the ordnance department.

Early on in the war, it appeared that guns in storage and those rolling off an expanded Sharps production line would provide more than enough carbines to uniformly arm the Federal cavalry, initially limited to the five regular army regiments. When large numbers of volunteer cavalry units were authorized in the wake of Bull Run, however, the need for carbines increased exponentially. General Ripley opposed ordering Sharps rifles for elite infantry use because the factory could not produce both rifles and carbines at the same time and had to be retooled to make rifles, losing valuable carbine production time. When he finally caved in to political pressure to order Sharps rifles for Colonel Hiram Berdan's Sharpshooter regiments, carbine production fell significantly behind.[5]

The overall shortage of carbines inevitably led to contracts with inventors and entrepreneurs for a variety of guns of varying quality, which began to trickle into service in the spring of 1862. The best of these—the Burnside and Smith, as well as the more dubious Gallager—were purchased in fairly large quantities, as were lesser numbers of inferior arms like the Cosmopolitan and the Gibbs. Each of these guns required a unique cartridge and spare parts supply, however, complicating the work of ordnance officers.

While awaiting their breechloaders, many Union volunteer cavalrymen were issued whatever arms were available in America or scoured from the surplus armories of Europe. At the end of 1861, troopers of the Seventh Kansas Cavalry were armed with an assortment of guns, including obsolete Model 1809 Prussian "Potsdam" muskets, while the men of the First Kentucky Cavalry were given similar antiquated American arms. In the spring of 1862, the Third Wisconsin Cavalry was issued useless .71 caliber Austrian hybrid pistol/carbines, and the Eighth New York Cavalry rode into action in the Shenandoah Valley carrying obsolete Halls. Some new regiments remained almost totally unarmed for months, and the First Maine Cavalry was performing guard duty with axe handles as late as March of 1862.[6]

Early war Confederate horsemen were even more randomly equipped, with some carrying the latest Maynard and Sharps breechloaders and Colt revolving rifles and carbines from prewar state purchases. Georgia, for example, purchased 1,600 Sharps carbines in 1860. Other Rebel cavalrymen were limited to whatever was available, including old muskets, sporting rifles, and civilian double-barrel shotguns. Interestingly, the shotgun became a favorite weapon of some Southern horsemen due to the close-quarters shock effect of two rapidly fired loads of buckshot.[7]

A few breechloading designs were manufactured in very limited quantities in the South during the war. The most successful Confederate breechloader, a Richmond-made copy of the Sharps carbine produced by Samuel C. Robinson, had a reputation for poor performance. One complaint was that the gun's forearm occasionally exploded in a shooter's hands, although this problem might have been the result of poor training, ignorance, and careless handling on the part of troops.[8]

A dearth of modern Southern arms and ammunition-making machinery, save that captured at Harper's Ferry in 1861, assured that most breechloaders used by Confederate horse soldiers were captured Yankee guns for which Confederate industry could produce cartridges. Several prominent Rebel cavalrymen, including Lieutenant General Nathan Bedford Forrest and Brigadier General John Hunt Morgan, however, came to prefer muzzleloading carbines, rifles, and rifle-muskets, many of them imported British Enfields, which used readily available infantry ammunition and which they correctly believed had a longer effective range than breechloading arms. Since cavalry skirmishing usually involved dismounted troops, and many Confederate cavalrymen armed with muzzleloading rifles acted as mounted infantry, riding to battle but fighting on foot, the awkwardness of reloading on horseback was not necessarily an issue.

Part of the Confederate cavalry's preference for muzzleloaders may simply have been a need to do the best with what was available. By mid-war, when Lieutenant

Brigadier General John Buford. A Kentuckian with a brother serving as a general in the Confederate Army, Buford was perhaps the best cavalry division commander in the Federal army on June 1, 1863, so it was indeed fortunate that his division was the first to encounter advancing Confederates at Gettysburg. (*Library of Congress*)

Jones rested Sergeant Shafer's carbine on the fence post outside Gettysburg, the standard Union carbines were breechloaders, and the Sharps was the most desirable of the lot. Although Yankee horsemen in the western and Trans-Mississippi armies in 1863 were still indifferently armed, with many still carrying muzzleloaders, the men of Brigadier General John Buford's cavalry division of the Army of the Potomac, in which the Eighth Illinois served, were universally equipped with single-shot breechloading carbines. It was good they were well armed, since in the spring of 1863, the men of Buford's division (in fact, the whole cavalry arm of the Army of the Potomac) began to assume a far more aggressive stance toward their Rebel opponents. The war was moving into a new phase.[9]

In the wake of the Confederate victory at Chancellorsville in May 1863, it became clear to the Southern leadership that the military initiative in the east had, for a time at least, shifted to them. Although several ideas were advanced, including using part of General Robert E. Lee's Army of Northern Virginia to reinforce Confederate armies in the west while assuming the defensive in the east, Lee's plan of staging an invasion of the north with his army prevailed. Such an incursion would remove the seat of war from ravaged Virginia, allow the army's soldiers to feed off the enemy's larder, and strengthen the political hand of peace advocates in the North. A battlefield victory in the course of the campaign, envisioned as a great raid rather than an attempt to take and hold ground, might also have the effect of gaining the Confederacy the international recognition it needed to survive.

By June 3, Lee's veterans were sidling west from their camps at Fredericksburg, Virginia, toward the Shenandoah Valley, while Lieutenant General A. P. Hill's Corps remained in defensive positions along the Fredericksburg line, confronting the puzzled Army of the Potomac commander, Major General Joseph Hooker. Hooker's cavalry, under the command of Brigadier General Alfred Pleasonton, was tasked with finding out if the Confederates were moving and, if they were, where they were going.

On June 9, Pleasonton's troopers caught the vaunted Major General J. E. B. Stuart's Rebel horsemen by surprise at Brandy Station, Virginia. The ensuing fight was for the most part a slashing, shooting, stirrup-to-stirrup classic mounted melee, with sabers and handguns more in use than carbines. Although the battle ended in a draw, the morale of the formerly outclassed Yankee horse soldiers soared. Brandy Station proved to be the making of the Army of the Potomac's mounted arm.

As Pleasonton continued to probe toward the Confederate army in hopes of gathering intelligence on its movements, the cavalry of both armies clashed again at Aldie, Middleburg, and Upperville. In these fights, both sides used dismounted detachments to provide suppressive carbine fire while mounted squadrons charged at the proper moment in a version of the modern fire-and-maneuver concept.

Despite the Federal efforts, Lee's infantrymen, screened by their cavalry, moved steadily west and then north. By June 13, Confederate

Lieutenant General Richard S. Ewell was advancing his corps of the Army of Northern Virginia on the town of Winchester, Virginia, then occupied by Union forces under the command of Major General Robert H. Milroy. Ewell swept over Milroy's ineptly handled troops and kept on moving north.

Finally divining his opponent's course, Hooker peeled his own infantry away from the Rappahannock River line and headed north in pursuit, keeping his army between the Rebels and Washington. His cavalry were, as they should have been, out in front and on the move when Major General George G. Meade replaced Hooker on June 28. Meade preferred that Pleasonton manage his mounted corps from army headquarters rather than in the field but approved the cavalry leader's suggestion to shuffle subordinate commanders in the midst of the campaign. Making some dramatic leadership changes, Pleasonton jumped favored young officers into positions of authority, a move he believed would increase the mounted arm's aggressiveness. Among others, new assignments came to recently promoted controversial Brigadier General Judson Kilpatrick, who assumed command of Pleasonton's Third Division, and George Armstrong Custer, who moved from captain to brigadier general literally overnight and was assigned to command one of Kilpatrick's brigades.

The end of June found the Federal army concentrated around Frederick, Maryland, with the Confederates located, ironically, to the north, near Chambersburg, Pennsylvania. The three Union cavalry divisions—Kilpatrick's Third, Brigadier General Buford's First, and Brigadier General David McMurtrie Gregg's Second—pushed into Pennsylvania seeking to make contact with Rebel horsemen.

On June 23, Yankee horsemen skirmished with the enemy in the Keystone State, the first fighting of the war north of the fabled, albeit irrelevant, Mason-Dixon line. Kilpatrick's division engaged in the first significant action of the campaign a week later. On June 30, 1863, Brigadier General Elon Farnsworth, who, like Custer, had been catapulted from captain to general and command of a brigade under Kilpatrick only days before, encountered Rebel horsemen at Hanover, Pennsylvania. In fighting that included a long-range barrage from the Fifth Michigan Cavalry's Spencer repeating rifles, Custer and

Farnsworth fought Brigadier General Fitzhugh Lee's men to a stalemate, and the Confederates withdrew under cover of darkness.

As Kilpatrick's division battled at Hanover, General Buford's troopers, who had skirmished with Major General Henry Heth's Confederate infantry division on June 29 at Fairfield, occupied the town of Gettysburg. The citizens of the little Pennsylvania crossroads town were in a highly agitated state. On June 26, enemy cavalry had chased a militia defense force out of Gettysburg, gathered supplies, and left the following day. Buford's men arrived at midday on June 30 to the enthusiastic cheers of the locals, who were afraid nearby Rebels would return. Buford moved his division through the town and west along the Chambersburg Pike and sent out patrols and scouts, who returned to report that a large force of Confederate infantry was but a few miles away.

Buford took stock of the terrain he would have to defend should the Rebels move on Gettysburg and deployed his two brigades on the ridgelines west and north of the town, covering all of the approach roads. He dispatched an orderly to request that Major General John Reynolds, then at Emmitsburg, Maryland, who commanded the Army of the Potomac's First Army Corps as well as the whole army's left wing, move his infantry up fast. Buford knew the enemy was nearby in strength and appeared to be concentrating and that the ridgelines west of Gettysburg were as good a place as any (and better than most) to fight them.

Buford was anxious for Reynolds' men to arrive, as his mission was to find the enemy for the Union infantry, not engage them in an all-out brawl. The Yankee troopers would, however, do all they could to interdict and delay any Confederate advance toward Gettysburg. The cavalrymen were armed with sabers, revolvers, and carbines. Sabers and handguns were close-range weapons, but the carbines, although lacking the range of the infantry rifle-musket, were the best arms available to horse soldiers dueling with Rebel foot soldiers.

Colonel William Gamble's First Brigade was assigned to hold McPherson's Ridge, which ran in a generally north-south direction. The brigade's component units included Major John L. Beveridge's Eighth Illinois Cavalry, Lieutenant Colonel William L. Markell's Eighth

New York Cavalry, and a composite regiment formed from four companies of the Twelfth Illinois and six companies of the Third Indiana Cavalry commanded by the Third's Colonel George H. Chapman.

In keeping with prudent tactical practice, Gamble established a reserve force on Seminary Ridge, moved his main body to McPherson's, and then pushed a screen of vedettes, including Lieutenant Jones's detachment, another 1,300 yards west to Knoxlynn Ridge, where they covered the high ground on either side of the Chambersburg Pike. Jones's thirty-five men held the center of the advanced line, with troopers from the Eighth New York to his left and the Twelfth Illinois/Third Indiana to his right.[10]

The Eighth Illinois was armed with Sharps carbines and Colt .36 caliber Model 1851 or 1861 Navy handguns, plus Colt .44 Army revolvers, probably the streamlined Model of 1860, the most common cavalry handgun of the war. The regiment reported 291 Sharps carbines in service, but the reports for four companies—A, C, H, and M—are missing. Assigning the missing companies the average of the other eight gives the Eighth a total potential firepower of 435 carbines out of 446 enlisted men actually engaged.[11]

The Twelfth Illinois was armed with Burnside carbines and Colt Model 1860 .44 caliber revolvers, but the actual number of carbines the unit could field is similarly unclear. The second quarter of 1863 ordnance reports of only three of the five companies present—D (twenty), E (thirty-seven), and K (twenty-nine)—survive. An interpolation would leave, rounded up, an average of twenty-nine carbines per company for the missing companies for a total of 114. The six companies of the Third Indiana, merged for tactical purposes with the Twelfth, were armed with Gallager carbines but also some first-rate Sharps carbines and Colt .44 Revolvers.[12]

Colonel Thomas C. Devin's Second Brigade, composed of Major William E. Beardsley's Sixth and Colonel William Sackett's Ninth New York Cavalry, the Seventeenth Pennsylvania Cavalry under Colonel Josiah H. Kellogg, and a two-company squadron of the Third West Virginia Cavalry, commanded by Captain Seymour B. Conger, deployed to Gamble's right. Devin was tasked with picketing the north and east approaches to Gettysburg, beginning on Herr Ridge and ending at the base of Benner's Hill just beyond the York Pike. Maintaining most of his brigade in the vicinity of Oak Hill, Devin established vedettes screening the roads from Carlisle, Harrisburg, and York, while sending two companies of the Ninth to occupy the grounds of Pennsylvania College. In all, Buford's troopers covered a seven-mile-long arc on the north and west of town.[13]

Devin's Sixth and Ninth New York Cavalry were armed with Sharps carbines and Colt .44 caliber revolvers. Three companies of the Ninth— C, D, and H—carried Sharps and Hankins carbines chambered for self-contained metallic rimfire cartridges, the most modern arms on the field on July 1. The Seventeenth Pennsylvania was armed with a mix of Smith and Merrill carbines, Colt .44 and .36 caliber, and Remington .36 caliber revolvers. The Third West Virginia shouldered Smith and Gallager carbines and holstered Colt .44 and Remington .36 caliber handguns.[14]

Despite the temporary hiatus in production to fulfill Colonel Berdan's rifle order, almost 6,000 New Model 1859 carbines had been delivered to the Federal government by the end of 1861, with more than 17,000 more forwarded by December 31, 1862. The Model 1859 was eventually replaced by the New Model 1863, the same gun sans patch box on the buttstock. Almost 100,000 Sharps guns eventually saw service during the Civil War, most of them cavalry carbines. Aside from the repeating Spencer, the Sharps became the most desirable carbine issued during the war. It was the most common carbine carried by Union horse soldiers at Gettysburg, with, according to one tally, 4,724 in action over the course of the three days.[15]

If there was a weakness in the rugged, accurate Sharps, it was the gun's ammunition. The first breechloading carbines, like the 1833 Hall, were loaded with loose powder and ball or paper cartridges containing powder and ball; but ammunition suitable for more advanced breechloading arms like the Sharps became steadily more sophisticated, beginning with combustible paper cartridges. Paper cartridges, combustible or not, however, required that a gun's breech design include an effective mechanical seal to prevent the escape of powder gas. Escaping gas reduced velocity and accelerated the deposit of carbon-based fouling in the action, often jamming the gun after a few shots. Paper ammunition was, in addition, fragile and often broke apart in cartridge boxes. Although the Sharps gas-escape problem was resolved by 1859, ammunition continued to remain problematic, due to fragility exacerbated by the jouncing factor of moving soldiers.

Colonel William Gamble. A native of Fermanagh, Ireland, and veteran of service in both the British and American dragoons, Gamble was working as a civil engineer in Illinois when the war broke out and joined the Eighth Illinois Cavalry. Gamble, a colonel commanding a brigade at Gettysburg, was an experienced and solid officer, well prepared to play a major role in the delaying action of July 1. (*Library of Congress*)

The old technology of the Sharps paper ammunition could not, despite ingenuity and effort, be overcome. The first Sharps cartridges were paper tubes tied to the base of a lead bullet. As early as 1854, an officer in the Mounted Rifles serving on the frontier complained that ammunition shipped to him became "unserviceable in transportation" because "the conical Balls are so heavy that they are apt to break off from the cartridge to which they are attached." As a partial remedy to the problem and expense of shipping ammunition long distances, the army began to produce Sharps rounds at Benicia Arsenal in California.[16]

Despite all due care, the problem of Sharps ammunition durability had not been solved by the time of the Civil War, even though many cartridges by that time were made of sturdier linen with a paper base glued in place. In 1859, Captain Thomas J. Wood of the First United States Cavalry complained of the "very great wastage of Sharps carbine cartridges which unavoidably occurs in the field." According to Wood, this problem occurred for two reasons. First, he maintained, cartridges broke apart in soldiers' cartridge boxes due to poor manufacturing processes, although it would seem the very nature of the ammunition contributed to its fragility. His second complaint was that cartridges carried nose down in a soldier's cartridge box often came apart as the soldier removed a round, base first, from the box, due to the weight of the bullet causing it to separate from the paper. Wood maintained that an issue of twenty rounds per man would only last a couple of days before disintegration made an ammunition reissue necessary.[17]

Originally, Sharps ammunition was longer than the gun's chamber. On closing its action, the Sharps breechblock sheared off the paper tail of the cartridge to expose powder to the flame coming from the nipple once the gun's hammer crushed a pellet primer or standard musket percussion cap. With the introduction of the New Model 1859 series, the gun used at Gettysburg, however, the Sharps company produced paper-based linen rounds that fit into the chamber in their entirety and were reliably ignited by the cap's flash.

Civil War Sharps ammunition was purchased from private contractors as well as produced, at one time or another during the conflict, by seven different Federal government arsenals, although production at Leavenworth was minimal. Most government-made Sharps ammunition came from two sources: the Saint Louis, Missouri, and Watervliet, New York, arsenals. At least one state arsenal fabricated an unknown number of Sharps cartridges as well. It was generally believed at the time that the linen cartridges purchased from the Sharps Company itself were the gold standard in Sharps ammunition. Ordnance officers called for ending government arsenal production of paper cartridges in favor of linen ones, which were generally accorded as more sturdy, but paper cartridges were still in production well into 1864.[18]

Sharps ammunition durability problems persisted throughout the Civil War, however. Brigadier General August Kautz wrote in July 1864 that the "Sharps carbine is a favorite arm, but the ammunition in a few days' marching deteriorates so much as to be a serious objection, as ammunition trains can seldom be taken on cavalry expeditions, and therefore only a limited supply can be carried by the men. The same objection exists against all paper cartridges."[19]

Although some testimony indicates that the unique Sharps primers, which were stored in a magazine in the action and automatically propelled under the hammer as it descended on the gun's nipple, worked well, the endorsement came from infantry units. First Sergeant Wyman White of the Second United States Sharpshooter Regiment swore by them, calling his Sharps rifle "a breech loader and a self capper" that allowed him to shoot so fast he captured five Confederates at Spotsylvania in 1864. Overall, however, priming pellet purchases by the Union government were limited, with only two, in 1861 and 1864, for a total of 2,557,574 pellets, on record. It is unlikely that the pellets, which, when they worked, significantly increased the single-shot Sharps' rate of fire, were in use by cavalrymen at Gettysburg on July 1, 1863.[20]

Christian Sharps was represented at Gettysburg not only by his classic carbine but also by his newer design, the Sharps and Hankins guns carried by three companies of the Ninth New York Cavalry. In 1854, Sharps severed his connection with the company that bore his name in exchange for 400 carbines, a one-time cash payment, and a royalty deal. He then established a new business, C. Sharps and Company, in Philadelphia and made some small four-barreled pocket pistols chambered for the then new .22 caliber rimfire self-contained cartridge, with bullet, powder charge, and priming compound all held together by a waterproof copper case. In 1860, Sharps entered into a partnership with William C. Hankins, who provided a cash infusion significant enough to lead to the company's name change to Sharps and Hankins.[21]

By the advent of the Civil War, cartridge production technology had advanced to the point where rimfire ammunition could be produced in heavier calibers than .22. The Sharps and Hankins gun, based on a series of patents filed between 1859 and 1861, was chambered for these new technology rimfire cartridges detonated by a firing pin in the gun's hammer. Although produced in several experimental bore sizes, Sharps' final military version was a .54 caliber. His new gun was operated by a trigger guard/lever that when depressed, moved the barrel forward for loading, and when raised, returned the barrel to lock up with the breech for firing. Once fired, an extractor pulled the empty cartridge case out of the barrel as the depressed lever moved it forward into the loading position.[22]

The U.S. Navy was not as sorely in need of masses of small arms as was the army and was thus more prone to order newer interesting but unproven models. The navy tested the Sharps and Hankins in July 1861 and ordered 500 rifles with saber bayonets along with 50,000 rimfire cartridges. Deliveries did not begin until March of 1862, however. In May of that year, Sharps approached the army and, after negotiating a price reduction, received an order for 250 carbines, which were delivered in September 1862. The majority of these guns was issued to three companies of the Ninth New York cavalry in the spring of 1863 (the rest of

the regiment remained armed with standard Sharps carbines), but thirty-five were issued to Company C of the Eleventh New York Cavalry.
The Eleventh was in a sharp fight with Rebel horsemen at Fairfax Court
House on June 27, 1863, as the Confederate army moved north toward
Gettysburg. A number of troopers from the regiment were captured in
the skirmish, and it is possible that some of the new Sharps and Hankins
carbines may have passed into Confederate service for the Gettysburg
campaign, but there is no evidence confirming this.[23]

Captain Newel M. Cheney, the Ninth New York's historian, referred
to the Sharps and Hankins guns in the hands of his regiment on July 1,
1863, as "much more efficient and reliable than the Burnside or
Sharps" carbines. Colonel Sackett noted that his only recommendation
to improve the Sharps and Hankins was to strengthen the extractor.
Sackett reported that that the fact that "the ammunition never damp-
ens or breaks and no capping being required" led to "a rapidity of fire,"
making the gun "a very fine skirmishing weapon." This was in strong
contrast, no doubt, to the Sharps paper or linen ammunition most of
his men carried in their cartridge boxes.[24]

Shortly after Gettysburg, New Jersey Quartermaster General Lewis
Perrine requested Sharps and Hankins carbines for the Second New
Jersey Cavalry, a new unit then forming at Trenton. The Second's commander, Colonel Joseph Karge, was an experienced and highly regarded
officer who had served with the First New Jersey Cavalry in the Army
of the Potomac and was determined to acquire the best arms available
for his men. In the end, the Second was issued Spencer repeaters, but
the fact that Perrine and Karge requested Sharps and Hankins guns
speaks well of their reputation.[25]

There are several competing claimants to firing the first shot at
Gettysburg other than Lieutenant Jones. Most are easily dismissed,
save for Corporal Alphonse Hodges of the Ninth, whose case is the
strongest. Hodges, who was armed with a Sharps and Hankins, commanded a three-man picket on the Chambersburg Pike near
Willoughby Run. He claimed he saw Confederates advancing at 5:30
AM, ordered his men to notify his commander, and then fired several
shots at them from a bridge crossing the Run before withdrawing.
Although there is little doubt that Hodges was where he said he was at

the time he said he was, there is a problem with his claim. As David Martin points out, there is no evidence there were Confederates in the area of his post at the time he suggests he fired the shot. He may have been mistaken about the time or, as Major John Beveridge of the Eighth Illinois posited, fired at "some imaginary foe."[26]

If both Sharps guns were inarguably the best cavalry carbines on the field at Gettysburg on July 1, the Gallager, carried by some men in both Gamble's Third Indiana and Devin's Third West Virginia Cavalry, was arguably the worst. The invention of Mahlon Gallager, a Georgia native, the single-shot Gallager carbine was made in Philadelphia by the firm of Richardson and Overman. It was loaded, as with most breechloaders, by lowering its trigger guard lever, which moved the rear of the barrel forward and then raised it for loading with a .52 caliber brass cartridge holding both bullet and powder charge. The Gallager chamber, which held the round in place for firing, was divided between the breech and the barrel. Once the lever was raised, closing the breech to complete the loading process, the gun's hammer was brought to half cock and a percussion cap affixed to its nipple. Cocking the gun and pulling its trigger completed the firing cycle.

Although 18,000 Gallager carbines were purchased by the Federal government during the war, one officer whose regiment was issued these guns felt they were useless and requested double-barreled shotguns to replace them. The Gallager (often misspelled Gallagher), developed cartridge case extraction problems after firing and was detested by many of the troops to whom it was issued. Lieutenant Eugene F. Ware of the Seventh Iowa Cavalry, whose Gallager-armed regiment was rearmed with new Gallagers prior to being sent west to fight Indians in 1864, classified the gun as "an exceedingly inefficient weapon." Forty of fifty officers whose units were issued Gallagers and who responded to an Ordnance Department survey in 1863 and 1864 considered the Gallager "worthless." In an April 5, 1864, letter to assistant Secretary of War Peter H. Watson, Ordnance Department chief General George D. Ramsay urged that the gun be removed from future service.[27]

The Gallager's extraction problem was rooted in its ammunition design, although at first glance, this seems unlikely. The cartridge was drawn brass and had none of the problems of cartridge box deconstruction or susceptibility to moisture of paper or linen rounds. A semi-fixed metal case was a halfway step to the fully self-contained cartridge, a bridge technology between the paper cartridge old technology on the way to self-contained new technology rounds like that of the Sharps and Hankins. Unlike the Sharps, however, in which the paper cartridge case was destroyed on firing, or the Sharps and Hankins, which had a mechanical extractor to separate the fired case from the chamber as part of the reloading process, the expanded Gallager cartridge had to be removed with the shooter's fingers after firing. And there was the rub. The explosion that occurred on firing expanded the brass and often wedged it in the gun's chamber so securely that it could not be removed manually, rendering the arm useless.

Gripes about the Gallager were early and loud. Brigadier General Jeremiah T. Boyle telegraphed the War Department in July 1862, complaining that "The cartridge hangs in after firing; difficult to get the exploded cartridge out often with screwdriver; men throw them away and take musket or any other arm." The fiery Boyle opined that "the Gallagher [sic] carbine is not equal to a bar of iron." This situation—and the subsequent threat that his contract might be cancelled—caused George Richardson, one of the principals of Richardson and Overman, to travel to Kentucky, where he instructed soldiers in how to use the disassembly tool issued with the Gallager to remove a stuck case. The combination tool was nipple wrench, screwdriver, and circular cartridge wrench, all in one. The wrench was slipped over the protruding base of the stuck cartridge case, and then twisted to remove it. Although mollified by Richardson's demonstration, General Boyle was still concerned about the quality of the cartridges he was receiving, which he determined to be the problem.[28]

Problems with cartridge removal persisted, and in April 1863, Ordnance Lieutenant Horace Porter wrote from the Army of the Cumberland that the men of three cavalry regiments in that command armed with the Gallager—the Ninth Pennsylvania, Tenth Ohio, and Fourth Kentucky—were unhappy with their Gallagers. The soldiers complained that in addition to problems with broken screws and sights and burst barrels, "the metallic cartridge case can seldom be removed from the barrel without the use of the wrench, which the men can never find at the time it is needed."[29]

The invention of Mahlon J. Gallager of Savannah, GA, the .50 caliber Gallager carbine was plagued with cartridge case extraction problems, which limited its popularity. The Federal government purchased almost 18,000 Gallagers during the war. (*William B. Edwards*)

Porter reported that a telegram to the War Department resulted in another trip west by Mr. Richardson, who personally inspected and fired a number of Gallagers. Although Richardson resolved other issues in a "satisfactory" manner, he "required the use of the wrench to remove many of the cartridge cases." Porter's conclusion was that the Gallager, "in the hands of experienced and careful troops, each carrying a wrench in a convenient place for removing cartridge cases, would be a good cavalry arm. But, we have not such troops . . . ." He summed up the Gallager as "an inferior arm."[30]

In an attempt to save future contracts, Richardson and Overman began to print instruction cards on how to load, fire, and use the wrench tool to extract an empty cartridge case, should it stick, from the Gallager. Each gun was shipped with one in its patch box, and additional cards were packed in each case of carbines.

Over the last two years of the war, the government contracted with other cartridge makers for different styles of Gallager cartridge, including paper and tin, brass foil, etc. The best known is Silas Crispin's round, manufactured by Thomas Poultney, with a paper and thin metal cartridge case. These cartridges were produced long after the battle of Gettysburg, however. When the Third Indiana deployed on the skirmish line, its troopers would have had to keep their wrenches handy.

The men of the five companies of the Twelfth Illinois of Gamble's brigade carried Burnside carbines, which, like the Gallager, fired a metallic cartridge encasing powder charge and bullet, fired by a percussion cap placed on an exterior nipple. The gun was patented by Ambrose Burnside in 1856, after he had returned to civilian life following service in the Mexican War. Burnside's new carbine was taken seriously by the army, which ordered 200 of them for field trials from his Bristol Fire-Arms Company, located in Bristol, Rhode Island. The government bought and issued another 700-odd Burnsides prior to the carbine trials of 1860. The trials found the gun to be good, but not as fit for service as the Smith and Maynard designs. A prior panel in 1857, however, had found the Burnside the best carbine offered for consideration.[31]

The outbreak of war changed the ordnance department's minds, and in July 1861, even before Bull Run, the Union ordered another 800 car-bines from the gun's manufacturer, the Burnside Rifle Company of Providence, Rhode Island, which had replaced the defunct Bristol Company. An order for another 7,500 guns was placed the following month. Major General Burnside himself, for whom unluckiness became a way of life, had gone bankrupt, sold his patent, and no longer had an interest in the gun, which would prove fiscally unfortunate for him in the years to come.

The .54 caliber Burnside was durable, reasonably accurate, and pop-ular with most of the troopers who carried it. In 1862, a soldier in the Twelfth Illinois rhapsodized about his newly issued "celebrated Burnside patent" carbine. When the men of the Twelfth tried out their Burnsides they found they could "load and fire them 10 times per minute with care and take a very deliberate aim; in some target practice . . . a ball was shot 400 yards through a sheet iron car which is about 1/16 inch thick and almost through the other side."[32]

The Burnside, with a lever-controlled tilting breechblock that swiveled up for loading, was the only Civil War single-shot breechloader other than the Sharps and Hankins or Ballard, both of which fired self-contained cartridges, with an ejector of sorts. The Burnside ejector, which bumped the cartridge case free of the breech block on lowering the lever, was not foolproof, however, as evidenced by occasional complaints of sticking cases. Some soldiers apparently adopted the field expedient of inverting their Burnsides and giving them "a sharp rap on the bottom," which usually freed a stuck case.[33]

The First Model Burnside, which had no forestock under its barrel, saw limited service in the prewar regular army. A few Second Model Burnsides, also lacking a forestock, were in the hands of Union troops

Invented by Ambrose Burnside, who no longer owned the patent by 1861, the Burnside carbine was one of the "big three," single shot carbines, along with the Sharps and Smith. The Union purchased more than 50,000 .54 caliber Burnsides. The Burnside, with its brass cartridge case, was a sturdy and effective carbine, popular with the soldiers who carried it. (*John Kuhl*)

by late 1861. Addition of a forestock resulted in the Third Model Burnside, which began to be issued in March 1862. Most of the more than 50,000 Burnsides purchased by the government from 1862 on were the very similar Fourth Model guns. The Twelfth Illinois received its Third Model Burnsides in July 1862.[34]

When queried as to how they would rate their men's Burnside carbines in an Ordnance Department survey, which included the categories "best, good, fair, and poor," the overwhelming majority of officer respondents characterized the Burnside as a "good" weapon. One regarded the gun as "a very good weapon, second only to Spencers." Although Lieutenant G. T. Elgin of the First Texas (Union) Cavalry qualified his evaluation of the Burnside as an "excellent arm" by stating that it was "not quite strong enough for rough service," the men of the First New Jersey Cavalry were quite fond of their Burnsides, which were eventually replaced by Spencers. The troopers of the Second Ohio Cavalry actually grumbled when they exchanged Burnsides for Spencers because of the latter arm's greater weight. The Buckeyes were doubly doubtful about the exchange when their new repeaters failed to fire because of defective ammunition.[35]

The Burnside's brass cartridge case, unlike the straight-sided Gallager, was conical, tapering from the top toward the bottom, and is often compared in shape with an ice-cream cone. Independent ammunition contractors and government arsenals were turning out varieties of Burnside cartridges of varying quality by 1864, including a rolled thin-metal version by Poultney & Trimble of Baltimore, Maryland—a company that developed alternative ammunition for several different carbines, produced the Smith carbine, and was a large importer of foreign military goods and weapons. The rounds in the cartridge boxes of the Twelfth Illinois troopers and other cavalrymen at Gettysburg, however, were doubtless the original drawn-brass cartridges supplied by the Burnside Rifle Company, loaded with .54 caliber bullets backed by forty-five grains of powder.[36]

Another carbine design from the 1850s trials in service at Gettysburg on July 1 was the Smith, which was in the hands of the men of the Seventeenth Pennsylvania and Third West Virginia of Colonel Devin's Second Brigade. The gun was designed by Doctor Gilbert Smith of Buttermilk Falls, New York, who received patents for his gun and its unique cartridge between 1855 and 1857 and assigned his production rights to Poultney & Trimble of Baltimore.[37]

The Smith was a simple break-open-breech design, which, like the Gallager, split its cartridge chamber between barrel and breech. It was locked up for firing by a long spring latch extending over barrel and breech, which opened for reloading by pushing on a small lifter at the top of the trigger guard. It has generally been regarded as one of the best-designed Civil War carbines, especially among latter-day target shooters of Civil War weapons in the North-South Skirmish Association, but it did have its detractors. In numbers purchased, the Smith was one of the "big three" (along with the Sharps and Burnside) single-shot breechloading carbines used by the Union.

The Federal government bought over 31,000 Smith carbines, and captured Smiths were carried into battle by Southern cavalrymen as well. Nevertheless, horse soldiers who participated in Colonel Benjamin Grierson's famous 1863 raid felt their Smith carbines were not trustworthy firearms, but this may have been due to the fact that when Grierson's brigade served in the Department of the Gulf following the raid, there was no ammunition available for their Smiths. Likewise, an inspecting officer reported in April 1864 that the officers of the First Connecticut Cavalry reported that their Smith carbines were "entirely unreliable," and, in his opinion, "they are worthless, and should be turned in at once and replaced by others." Unfortunately,

Invented by Gilbert Smith, the .50 caliber Smith carbine used a unique rubber cartridge designed to expand on firing to seal the gun's chamber and contract after firing for easier removal with the fingers. The Smith was a popular gun, although some soldiers complained of its durability in service. (*John Kuhl*)

details on his conclusion were lacking. On the whole, though, the Smith got good reviews. The 1863–1864 carbine survey revealed that seventeen officers considered the Smith "the best carbine in service"; while forty-six rated it good; eleven, "fair"; four, "poor"; and eight, "worthless."[38]

As evidenced by the advent of the Burnside and Gallager, breechloader inventors of the late 1850s developed brass case ammunition to improve handling and weatherproofing and provide a more efficient gas seal over the previous generation of paper cartridges. After his initial pasteboard design proved unsatisfactory, Gilbert Smith used a different approach in ammunition bridge technology—an "elastic cartridge-case" of "india rubber cloth, or vulcanized india-rubber." According to Smith's patent application, the rubber cartridge would expand on firing to provide a gas seal and contract after firing so that it could be easily removed by the shooter's fingers. As with the Sharps, Gallager, and Burnside, the Smith cartridge was fired when the hammer hit a percussion cap on an external nipple, directing flame to a small hole in its base to ignite the powder.

Smith ammunition had an excellent performance record. According to Civil War small-arms ammunition historian Dean S. Thomas, there were "few complaints" about the rubber cartridges. One such was registered by First Lieutenant Francis J. Shunk in September, 1862. Shunk, an ordnance officer in the Army of the Potomac, wrote that the Smith cartridge's "powder, in riding, spills out of the hole in the rear end of the india rubber cartridge"—the jounce effect again. In all, the lieutenant thought the "arm . . . a good one," but believed a "change is absolutely necessary in the cartridge." Shunk's comments were forwarded to Poultney and Trimble, but there is apparently no record of the company's response. Thomas speculates that there were several potential remedies to the problem Shunk described, including making the hole smaller, plugging it with easily blown-out grease or thin paper, or using a coarser-grained powder. Since surviving Smith cases all have a fairly large diameter hole in the base, one of the latter three solutions, if any, was most likely arrived at. Another potential problem with the Smith was that the rubber cartridge cases occasionally stuck in the chamber "when the chamber got hot." This was apparently nowhere near as common a problem as with the Gallager, and the rubber round would have been easier to manipulate with the fingers than the brass one.[39]

The Crispin/Poultney metal foil and paper-type cartridge introduced in the Gallager carbine in 1864 was also adapted for use in the Smith, as ammunition made in that manner was less expensive than rubber cartridges. The new rounds were advertised as "soft metal cartridges." Poultney stated that these cartridges required an adaptation to the Smith chamber to reduce its size and that he could apply the new dimensions to the carbines then in production. There is some question as to whether this was done, and it appears the newer-style cartridges were used in any Smith carbine in service in 1864 and 1865. At Gettysburg, however, the Smiths of the Seventeenth Pennsylvania and Third West Virginia were fed the traditional rubber cartridge.[40]

About half the men of the Seventeenth were armed with an old-technology paper cartridge breechloader, the Merrill, patented by James H. Merrill, an experienced gun inventor and manufacturer, in 1856. Initially, the gun was found unfit for service after an army test, due to gas leakage and excessive powder fouling, and Merrill's subsequent adaptation of the Jenks carbine failed the carbine trials of 1860, due to a problematic gas seal and the delicacy of its paper cartridge. By July 1861, improvements in the gas seal plunger, based on the Jenks patent, seemed to solve the Merrill's previous problems. With cavalry arms in short supply, in the fall, the War Department ordered 600 Merrill carbines.[41]

The Merrill was loaded by placing the hammer on half cock, lifting a lever that ran along the stock behind the action and then over it and

Although it had a reputation for accuracy, the fragility of the Merrill carbine's paper ammunition handicapped it, although the government bought around 15,000, most of which ended up in service in the western theater of war. (*John Kuhl*)

abutting the rear sight, which retracted the breech plug plunger and exposed the chamber for loading. After a paper cartridge was inserted in the gun's chamber, the lever was pressed down, closing the breech. The hammer was then cocked and nipple capped for firing. During the Civil War, the Union purchased a total of 14,255 Merrill carbines, including the Old Model and slightly different Improved Model. The Merrills in the hands of the men of the Seventeenth at Gettysburg were Old Model carbines.[42]

How the Merrill held up in the field under combat conditions is problematic. The 1863–1864 rating survey of carbines brought responses from ninety-one officers. Five rated it as "best"; fourteen, as "good"; thirteen, "fair"; sixteen, "poor"; and a resounding forty-three rated it as "worthless." Problems apparently occurred regularly with parts wear and breakage. Although Colonel Samuel P. Spear of the Eleventh Pennsylvania Cavalry rated the Merrill as "best arm in the service," his division commander, Brigadier General Kautz, thought otherwise. In July 1864, Kautz wrote, "The issue of Merrill's carbine, made in this command just before commencing the campaign, seems to have been a very defective arm in the manufacture. The Eleventh Pennsylvania Cavalry started on the 1st of May with 280 carbines; they are now reduced to 117, and this reduction is due almost entirely to defects in the arm itself. The officers report that many burst in the barrel, and other parts give way." Further west, the troopers of the Eleventh Missouri Cavalry complained "bitterly of their arms [the Merrill carbine], and state Merrill's cartridge-box to be a nuisance that the service should be rid of."[43]

Much of the Merrill's paper ammunition was sold to the government by Merrill, Thomas, and Company, makers of the carbine, but additional cartridges were purchased from Johnston and Dow in New York City and still more produced by the Washington arsenal and perhaps the Saint Louis arsenal. Although nominally .54 caliber, firing a 400-grain bullet backed by forty grains of powder, Merrill bullet diameters from .537 to .560 are recorded. There is some possibility that heavier powder charges were loaded, especially for the rifle version of the Merrill, a few of which were in the hands of Massachusetts sharpshooters on Cemetery Ridge on July 2 and 3.[44]

How well the horse soldiers of Buford's Division could handle and shoot their diverse lot of carbines was yet another question. A distinct lack of marksmanship training was a hallmark of American Civil War armies. In the prewar regular army, far more professional than the force produced by hordes of wartime volunteers, there was no extensive target-shooting program either, and efforts varied by regiment. A cavalryman in the Second Dragoons noted that "I have but twice been at target practice, and we are not allowed to use our rifles on any other occasion."[45]

The flood of volunteers who rallied to the colors at the outbreak of the Civil War got even less firearms training than the regulars of the previous decade, as marksmanship instruction took a decided back seat to solving more immediate organizational problems. The Twelfth Illinois' Cavalry's target practice involved taking potshots at an abandoned railroad car at a range of 400 yards. Even later in the war, cavalry marksmanship training was, if anything, more haphazard that that offered the infantry. A veteran of the Seventeenth Pennsylvania Cavalry of Devin's Brigade recalled that the regiment had only been issued their Smith and Merrill carbines on the march to Gettysburg and fired them for the first time on July 1.[46]

Disregarding, for a moment, whether their men could hit what they fired at, how many actual carbines Gamble and Devin were able to put on the firing line is not represented by the number of men on their muster rolls. According to the best analysis, Gamble, whose units first made contact with the enemy, was able to field 1,600 men who were "engaged" in the morning's combat, including seventy-six officers.

Although Lieutenant Jones fired a carbine to open the fight, he had to borrow it from an enlisted man, and officers were more concerned with managing a battle rather than participating as combatants, save in emergencies. Deducting officers, then, the total of men available for combat in Gamble's brigade would be 1,524. When cavalry fought dismounted, every fourth man was detailed as a horse holder, so the maximum number of men Gamble could have put on the firing line was 1,143. As a prudent commander, Gamble had to hold back a reserve, further diminishing the brigade's firepower. Devin's Brigade, the Sixth and Ninth New York, Seventeenth Pennsylvania, and Third West Virginia, totaled 1,148 officers and men engaged, before similar draw-downs for horse holders and a reserve assigned to Gamble.[47]

The Rebels that Lieutenant Jones fired upon were the men of General Heth's Division of General A. P. Hill's Third Army Corps of the Army of Northern Virginia, led by Brigadier General James J. Archer's brigade of Alabamans and Tennesseans. Prior to Jones' opening shot, Colonel B. D. Fry of Archer's Thirteenth Alabama saw some Union soldiers across Marsh Creek, halted his regiment, deployed it in line of battle, then ordered his men to load their guns and shake out their regimental colors. Fry deployed three companies of his regiment and the Fifth Alabama battalion, a total of about 225 men, to his front as skirmishers. Skirmishers, individual soldiers loosely spread across a larger unit's front in the advance or defense, ideally worked together in groups of four, providing a reconnaissance screen in front of a main line of battle. They were intended to provide early warning of possible nasty surprises ahead and also deliver a steady individually aimed fire at enemy skirmishers and, eventually, the enemy's main defensive line, before either retiring or joining the main line of battle for the decisive firefight. As Fry's skirmishers advanced, Major John Pegram ordered the first gun in his artillery battalion, a rifled piece capable of long-range accuracy, unlimbered and trained on Federal horsemen he could see far to his front.[48]

Jones fired as Archer's skirmishers approached Marsh Creek. The Confederates held their own fire until they splashed across the creek and then began to shoot sporadically at the Yankees on the hill. As gunfire crackled along the line, Jones dispatched a rider to alert his company commander, Captain Amasa E. Dana, who led forward the rest of Company E of the Eighth Illinois as reinforcements. On arrival, Dana surveyed the scene and quickly dispatched a rider back to Colonel Gamble to request more men. The captain estimated that the advancing Alabama skirmish line, now reinforced by men from the First Tennessee, extended for a mile and a half, and noted that other Rebel units behind the skirmishers were moving from the road and into line of battle formations.[49]

Dana consolidated and then dismounted his company, withdrew it a few yards, and deployed the men (less a quarter of their number as horse holders) by dispersing them along the ridgeline roughly thirty yards apart and taking advantage of any natural cover available. Estimating the distance to the enemy, the captain ordered his men to raise the sights on their Sharps carbines to 800 yards. That they could hit, or even see, any targets like those presented by individual Confederate skirmishers, however, is extremely unlikely. An 1850s-era French study found a soldier could only distinguish "the movement of companies marching, advancing or retiring, the red color of infantry [uniforms]" at a distance of 650 yards.[50]

As small-arms fire began to intensify, Pegram's artillery began to hurl more shells at the Federal position. The Union picket line fought a delaying action back toward Herr Ridge, slowing down the advancing enemy infantry, which, when checked, would edge around the Yankee flanks, forcing the Federal horsemen to fall back once more. It was about 8:00 AM when Dana's men reached the ridge, where they were reinforced by two squadrons (four companies) from his own Eighth Illinois and two more from the Eighth New York. All were deployed as skirmishers. At this point there were around 450 fighting men on the Union line, which was soon stiffened by the addition of Lieutenant John H Calef's six-gun Second U.S. Horse Artillery's Battery A. Calef deployed four of his six guns across the Chambersburg Pike at McPherson's Ridge, the next high ground to the rear of Herr Ridge, and detached another two-gun section several hundred yards south to support Gamble's left flank regiment, the Eighth New York.[51]

As there were several claimants to the first shot at Gettysburg, there is also some confusion as to the first casualty. Excluding two dogs—one

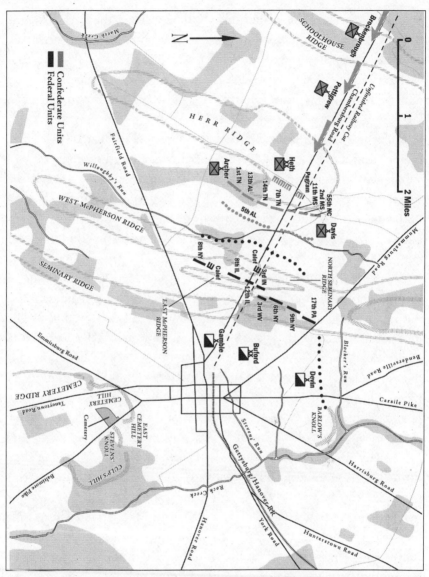

Map 1. Dispositions of Buford's cavalry division and advancing Confederate forces under Heth on the morning of July 1.

the mascot of the Fifth Alabama mortally wounded by a stray carbine bullet and another a farm animal shot by Confederate skirmishers—one candidate is an unnamed Yankee trooper some Rebels recall being shot off a white horse at about the time Dana was reinforced. This man may well have been the soldier that William T. Ivy of the Fifth Alabama Battalion, one of Archer's skirmishers, saw laying in his path as he advanced. According to Ivy, the soldier was riding a gray horse, and carried "what we called a Burnside carbine," which would have identified him as a member of the Twelfth Illinois, which did report one man killed on the line.[52]

What is known for sure is that Private John Weaver of the Third Indiana Cavalry was wounded by a shell fragment. Weaver's leg was subsequently amputated, and he died of his injuries. At around the same time, Private Columbus L. F. Worley of the Fifth Alabama Battalion was wounded, apparently by carbine fire. The twenty-year-old Worley lost his leg as well and ended the battle a prisoner of war but survived.[53]

As the skirmishers approached Herr Ridge, Heth ordered some of Pegram's guns to move forward and shell a woodlot, conducting a reconnaissance by fire that he hoped would reveal what was in it. The most comprehensive historian of the first day's battle, David Martin, asserts that Heth did not display a sense of urgency in deploying his men in the early stages of the fight. The Confederate commander kept most of his soldiers in column formation on the road while a relatively few companies were ordered out as skirmishers to spar with the cavalry vedettes. The pace of the fighting was not intense. Martin notes that "Colonel D. B. Fry's 13th Alabama, which was on the Confederate skirmish line from 0730 to 0930, lost only 7 men wounded during this time." After the war, Fry recalled that although he witnessed some instances of "individual gallantry" on the part of the Yankee horse soldiers, the overall resistance his men encountered was "inconsiderable." Indeed the firing seems to have been unhurried in the early part of the action. One trooper from the Twelfth Illinois reported firing only ten or twelve rounds in the entire morning.[54]

As the Rebels advanced, Archer's front was extended by the skirmishers of Brigadier General Joseph R. Davis' brigade, which included the Second, Eleventh, and Forty-second Mississippi and Fifty-fifth North Carolina Infantry. When the Confederates closed on them, Gamble's men abandoned the Herr Ridge line and fell back to McPherson's ridge, where they were reinforced by the remainder of their brigade. A speedy withdrawal at the last minute was possible for cavalry, who had but to remount and ride to the rear, far ahead of any pursuing infantrymen. Gamble ordered more dismounted skirmishers from the Eighth Illinois, Eighth New York, and Third Indiana to move down the forward slope of McPherson's Ridge, where they reinforced the withdrawing skirmish line falling back across Willoughby Run, while Buford ordered Colonel Devin to close up on Gamble's right flank to prevent it from being overlapped and turned. Devin deployed his Sixth and Ninth New York forward and then reinforced them with the Seventeenth Pennsylvania. He also continued to picket the roads from the north on a line now extending at a right angle from McPherson's ridge over to the rise of ground on the right, which came to be known as "Barlow's Knoll" in the wake of the events of July 1.[55]

Buford, with Reynolds' Federal infantry on the march to join him, was determined to hold McPherson's Ridge as long as possible and arrived at Seminary Ridge to assume personal control of the fight shortly after 9:00 AM. Gamble's troopers and Calef's gunners were now directing a fairly heavy fire on the enemy skirmishers advancing across the valley of Willoughby Run. As he observed the Union activity on McPherson's Ridge, General Heth noticed that the number of Yankees to his front had increased dramatically. In response, he deployed more of his infantry and shook out a line of battle to reinforce his skirmish line, all of which took around half an hour. The Rebel line of battle formation, with each regiment deployed in two ranks, passed through the skirmishers and began to close on the Yankee horse soldiers and their artillery supports, firing as it advanced. A regimental line of battle of, say, 300 men, would cover more than 150 yards of front. The formation was intended to deliver massed fire to achieve a decisive result and, if long enough, hopefully overlap the enemy's line, producing a tactical situation forcing a retreat.[56]

The record of the war includes numerous injunctions from officers to withhold fire until it could be decisive. In this case, however, the Confederate fire appeared to be a sort of "marching fire," at relatively long range, in which men loaded and fired individually as they advanced in line. It was not terribly effective, with one company of the Twelfth Illinois Cavalry reporting only one man killed and three wounded. Still, the length of the advance line threatened the whole position. The advancing Rebel lines of battle were longer than Gamble's defensive line, and they would eventually overlap it. It was clear to Gamble that he could not hold on much longer, but he did the best he could, since Buford's tactical task was to keep a grip on the good ground until Reynolds' Federal infantry could arrive. When Buford's signal officer, Lieutenant Aaron B. Jerome, spotted Yankee foot soldiers moving up the Emmitsburg pike, he knew his commander had succeeded—barely.

The Yankee infantry abandoned the road and moved diagonally at the double quick across the fields toward McPherson's ridge, arriving just in time. Most of Gamble's men withdrew, allowing the foot soldiers to pass through their lines. Some troopers from the Third Indiana Cavalry, however, continued to blaze away with their Gallagers alongside the Iron Brigade's infantrymen for a while. A couple of Hoosiers traded their carbines for dropped infantry muskets and continued the fight in the Iron Brigade infantry line. After the war, Thomas G. Day, a veteran of the Third, asked Will Rea, one of these men, if it was "pure bravery" that made him and the others advance into the maelstrom. According to Rea, the reasons were more prosaic. He was interested in removing the saddle and revolver from an officer's dead horse, and his comrade, Matt Glanber, who later became a Deadwood stage coach driver, wanted to acquire a horse that was wandering between the lines.[57]

The rest of the brigade moved behind and south of the infantry, continuing to screen the Union left flank. While Gamble made his fight, Devin's troopers, who protected his right, were steadily pushed back by Davis' skirmishers, and when they turned over their battle to the infantrymen of the I Army Corps, they were running low on ammunition. Like Gamble's brigade, though, Devins' men had accomplished their mission.

When the foot soldiers took over the battle, Gamble withdrew to Seminary Ridge, where he could observe the continuing action. Late in the afternoon, with the I Corps falling back toward Seminary Ridge and in danger of being overrun, The Eighth Illinois threatened the advancing Rebel right, forcing the Seventh North Carolina Infantry to deploy and temporarily paralyzing other advancing Confederate units. Some of the Eighth's troopers dismounted and opened a rapid fire at the enemy with their Sharps carbines while others maneuvered mounted, delaying the Rebel advance and assisting the Federal infantry's retreat. This timely harassment was the final service rendered by Buford's division to the Army of the Potomac at Gettysburg.

Some historians have asserted that John Buford's delaying action on July 1 at Gettysburg was successful due to the rapid firepower of his men's carbines. In truth, the rate of fire of most single-shot breechloading carbines, with the notable exception of the Sharps, was not dramatically higher than that of muzzleloading muskets. Rates of fire with the Smith and other single shots were limited by the need to cap before a shot and the need to extract a fired, occasionally jammed, cartridge case with finger power. In fact, if his men were armed with muzzleloaders, it is possible they would have achieved the same outcome. Buford's success that day was due to several factors, including his own grasp of critical terrain and resultant tactical dispositions, pushing as far west of town as practicable, Heth's dilatory deployment response after initial contact, and more than a bit of luck that Reynolds' infantry arrived when it did.[58]

In all likelihood the loose skirmish formation used by the cavalrymen was effective in limiting Union casualties while achieving the mission of delaying the Confederate infantry. The opposing infantry suffered light losses as well, most likely since their own forward elements fought as skirmishers in open formation. There is no evidence, however, that in the brief period as the Rebel line of battle closed in and before the Federal infantry were fully committed, breechloader firepower caused many Confederate casualties. The July 1 fight at Gettysburg provides no support for the postwar claim of a cavalry officer that "the mobile and elastic dismounted skirmish line with artillery supports was far superior in destructiveness to the infantry line of battle, on account of its rapidity and dash." A dispersed skirmish line, even armed with breechloaders, did not deliver decisive firepower on a line of battle, especially when faced with another intervening skirmish line, which was the normal course of events.[59]

Another widespread myth regarding Buford's fight that has been espoused by some historians is that his men used new Spencer repeating rifles or carbines to delay the enemy. Actually, no Spencer carbines were in service prior to October 1863, although longer-barreled Spencer rifles were first used in combat by Colonel John T. Wilder's mounted infantrymen at Hoover's Gap Tennessee on June 24 and six days later at Hanover, Pennsylvania, by Custer's Michigan brigade. The Wolverines employed their repeaters again at Gettysburg on July 3 when they battled J. E. B. Stuart's Confederate horse behind the main Union line at Rummell's farm.[60]

Thus, in retrospect (there were good guesses but no one knew for sure at the time) Gettysburg witnessed the high-water mark not only of the Confederacy but also of the old cavalry carbine. Buford's fight west of town was the last great stand of the breechloaders invented during the previous decade. Although the results achieved by the Spencers in the hand of Custer's Michigan horsemen two days later were inconclusive, largely due to the fact that no tactical doctrine yet existed for their employment, the new repeater and its metallic cartridge were in the war to stay.

The Yankee mounted arm, which began the Civil War as an ad hoc force armed with a hodgepodge of obsolete muzzleloaders, obsolescent breechloaders, and axe handles, was, by the time Lieutenant Jones fired his shot at Gettysburg, on its way to becoming perhaps the most powerful mounted force the world had ever seen. The cavalry not only fired the first shots at Gettysburg on July 1 but, two days later, when the horse soldiers of the Fifth and Sixth Michigan Cavalry blazed away with their Spencers at the stalwart Thirty-fourth Virginia Cavalry Battalion, launched the first shots of modern warfare as well.

Chapter 2

THE RIFLE-MUSKET, PART I

THE I ARMY CORPS INFANTRY SOLDIERS WHO cut across the fields from the Emmitsburg Road on their way to rescue Buford's beleaguered cavalrymen on July 1, 1863, carried a variety of small arms, including Springfield .58 caliber, Enfield .577 caliber, and Austrian Lorenz .54 and .58 caliber rifle-muskets, with a few old .69 caliber smoothbore muskets in the hands of some troops of the Eighty-eighth Pennsylvania Infantry.[1]

By mid-war, most infantrymen in both the Army of the Potomac and the Army of Northern Virginia were armed with muzzleloading rifle-muskets. The rifle-musket, combining the accuracy of the rifle with the overall length, bayonet reach, and relatively rapid loading of the musket, was a recent small-arms development, with widespread military issuance and use occurring only in the decade before the Civil War. Ironically, although a highly regarded new technology, as a weapon of war, the rifle-musket was on the verge of obsolescence by the time of Gettysburg and would be obsolete within two years.

Although the infantry standard for hundreds of years had been the smoothbore musket, some American soldiers were armed with rifles even before the official birth of the United States army. Spiral grooves cut in the rifle barrel's interior spun and stabilized a round ball projectile and gave it far more range and accuracy than the same type of projectile fired from a smoothbore musket, with its barrel, as the name indicates, reamed smooth, like a modern shotgun. Strange as it may seem to those nurtured on stories of American Revolutionary War riflemen, Europeans were the first to issue rifles to their soldiers. A rifled barrel dated 1547 may well be the earliest physical evidence of the practice that Europeans cut grooves in gun barrels to stabilize bullets, although there are references to rifles existing as early as 1520. One written source cites a 1594 description of a gun with "eight gutters [cut] somewhat deep in the inside of the barrel" to increase its accuracy.[2]

Rifled arms definitely saw some military service in the ranks of eighteenth-century elite troops, including Austrian and German *Jaegers* and French *Tirailleurs* and *Chasseurs*. King Christian IV of Denmark put rifles in the hands of his bodyguard detachment prior to 1622, some French cavalrymen were issued rifles in the 1670s, and Tsar Peter the Great introduced rifles for special-service troops in the Russian army in 1715.[3]

Many eighteenth-century Americans were actually ignorant of the rifle and its capabilities at the outbreak of the War for Independence, as evidenced by John Adams' surprised comment on the accuracy of "a peculiar kind of musket, called a rifle" carried by Virginians and Pennsylvanians joining the 1775 siege of Boston. Although riflemen certainly contributed to the Revolutionary cause on a number of battlefields, most notably King's Mountain (where Americans fought each other), their overall tactical importance has often been grossly exaggerated.[4]

Many larger-than-life tales of American riflemen can be traced to press propaganda designed to scare British soldiers scheduled to serve in America, as the stories were often reprinted in English newspapers. In the event, the British, although they may have been apprehensive at first, learned to deal with the rifle threat through spirited and rapid offensive movements. Captain William Dansey of the Thirty-third Foot's Light Infantry company noted that "they [American riflemen] are not so dreadful as I expected" after his unit routed and captured a rifle-armed unit on Long Island in 1776.[5]

General George Washington, a more perceptive analyst of his army's needs than latter-day commentators, actually rearmed some rifle units with smoothbore muskets in order to deploy them as conventional light infantry. Washington's disenchantment with riflemen may have begun early, since an account of the 1775 siege of Boston includes the observation that riflemen were an "undisciplined set of villains" and that "Mr. Washington is very sensible of this." Contrary to song and story, well-served artillery was more of a factor in Andrew Jackson's 1815 victory at New Orleans than were rifle-wielding Kentucky militiamen, most of whom actually arrived at the Crescent City ill clothed, barefoot, and unarmed.[6]

Despite the apparent problems of American riflemen—more attributable to lack of discipline than their weapons—the potential military usefulness of the rifle in special operations led to limited issue in the British army as early as the French and Indian Wars. Ten "Rifled Barrelled guns were delivered out to each regiment to be put into the hands of their best marksmen" in General James Abercromby's 1758 expedition to Fort Ticonderoga.[7]

In 1776, the crown contracted for 1,000 rifles for service in America. One officer reported that "the Highlanders who have many marksmen & Deer

Private Simon Creamer of the Twelfth New Jersey Infantry with an Austrian Lorenz rifle-musket. Shortly after this picture was taken in 1862 the men of the Twelfth were rearmed with US Model 1842 smoothbore muskets. Creamer was killed in action at Gettysburg on July 3 and is buried in the National Cemetery. (*John Kuhl*)

Killers amongst them are particularly desirous of having 5 of those pieces [rifles] per company." At least some of the British rifles, and perhaps all of the barrels used to make them, were imported from Germany, and the British hired German mercenary *Jaeger* riflemen for service in America as well.[8]

Although most early nineteenth-century American officers believed the smoothbore musket, employed in tactical formations that accentuated mass firepower, was the ideal weapon for infantrymen, the rifle did remain a limited-issue special-purpose weapon in the regular American army. In 1808, the United States War Department authorized an entire regiment of riflemen, akin to the British rifle units that fought against Napoleon's armies during the same period and wearing a similar green uniform. Although the contributions of the "United States Regiment of Riflemen" (later denominated the First Regiment of Riflemen) and three additional regiments raised for the War of 1812 were recognized as significant, the units did not long survive the end of the conflict. General Jacob Brown advised Secretary of War John C. Calhoun that riflemen were not an "essential arm of the peace establishment," and the First Regiment, the last in service, was disbanded in 1821, although designated companies within infantry regiments and larger numbers of militiamen were still issued rifled arms. Ironically, the British army retained its rifle units as a permanent part of its peacetime establishment.[9]

The rifle was a useful tool for a number of specialized tactical tasks, including skirmishing, in which groups of soldiers detached from the main line of battle and deployed in open order screened the advance of the line to "develop" the enemy's defenses, while enemy skirmishers contested their advance. Effective skirmishing required aimed fire against large enemy formations as well as individual enemy skirmishers. Accurate on individual man-sized targets up to and somewhat beyond 200 yards in the right hands, the rifle was loaded with a measured powder charge and an under-bore-sized round ball encased in a greased patch that engaged the rifling on firing and imparted a stabilizing spin to the ball. Prepared paper cartridges, including patched balls, were sometimes provided for riflemen, but even when using them, the rifle had a slower rate of fire than the comparatively inaccurate smoothbore musket. The rifle's rate of fire (at best a third that of the smoothbore musket) was its greatest detriment in the eyes of military professionals.

The musket, which had dominated the battlefields of the world for two centuries, was easily loaded with a paper cartridge containing an undersized ball (often supplemented by buckshot or a second ball) capable of relatively rapid fire and, unlike most early American-issue rifles, was equipped with a bayonet. Every general dreamed of sweeping his enemy from the field with a successful bayonet charge. To be successful, it should be noted, soldiers charging with fixed bayonets did not have to (and most often didn't) close with their opponents. The simple sight of bristling bayonets advancing was often enough to put a less-disciplined enemy to flight.

It has been asserted that the small number of bayonet wounds reported in the Civil War was due to the fact that long-range combat introduced by the rifle-musket made "cold steel" an obsolete weapon. In fact, during the Napoleonic wars, a British surgeon observed that regiments "charging with fixed bayonets, *never* meet and struggle hand to hand and foot to foot; and this for the best possible reason, that one side turns and runs away as soon as the other comes close enough to do mischief." Opinions of realistic officers had not changed by the Civil War, when Colonel Henry B. Carrington of the Eighteenth United States Infantry, a scholar as well as a soldier, wrote, "'crossing bayonets' is never done by any considerable force." Few well-authenticated cases are found in history."[10]

Bayonet charges aside, thoughtful military men on both sides of the Atlantic did, however, realize that a number of advantages would accrue from marrying the rapid-fire feature of a musket with the inherent accuracy of a rifle. In the years following the downfall of Napoleon Bonaparte, French army officers proved the axiom that innovation often follows in the wake of defeat. The French concentrated their research and development efforts on inventing a rifle/musket hybrid, which would use the relatively new percussion ignition method.

Alexander Forsyth, a Scottish country parson and avid wildfowler seeking a faster, more waterproof ignition system than the flintlock for his shotgun, developed the percussion system early in the nineteenth century. Forsyth, a scientist as well as a man of the cloth, based his idea on previously unsuccessful attempts that had been conducted in Europe using fulminates, or metallic salts. He eventually developed a system using a refined compound of fulminate of mercury powder as a priming compound. Joshua Shaw, a British artist and inventor living in the United States, refined the process by sealing a small amount of fulminate compound in a copper percussion cap. When hit by the gun's hammer, the cap exploded, and its flame detonated the main powder charge. By 1830, although most military arms still used the flintlock system, the percussion cap was in fairly common use on sporting arms.[11]

In 1826, Henri-Gustave Delvigne, a French infantry captain, developed a method of loading a rifled gun in which an undersized, unpatched, round lead ball was rammed down the gun's barrel and then "upset" to a larger diameter against the rim of a chambered breech by thumping it several times with a heavy ramrod. On firing, the expanded ball engaged the rifling. The *Tirailleurs de Vincennes* carried Delvigne-system guns to Algeria in 1840. Armed with the new rifles, the *Tirailleurs* gave a good account of themselves, and one reportedly dropped a mounted Arab at a distance of 600 meters. Variations in ramming pressure, along with powder fouling buildup and occasional lead fragments lodging on the chamber rim led, however, to inconsistent accuracy in the Delvigne rifles.[12]

Further experiments suggested that the chamber rim could be replaced as an expansion device with the *tige*, a one-and-a-half-inch spike projecting from the gun's breech plug face into the barrel. The *a tige*, or "pillar breech," rifles, invented by Colonel Louis-Etienne Thouvenin, were field tested with round-ball ammunition in North African colonial fighting in 1846. Accuracy was satisfactory, but the *tige* itself proved susceptible to damage and corrosion and complicated cleaning of the breech area as well.[13]

Captain Claude-Étienne Minié of the *Chasseurs D'Orleans*, an Inspector of Musketry at the French military school at Vincennes, assisted Colonel Thouvenin with the design of a solid-based conical bullet that improved the accuracy and range of the *a tige* rifles. Although Captain Delvigne also developed a conical-bullet version of his chamber-ring system, Thouvenin's system prevailed. Thousands of flintlock smoothbore Model 1822 muskets were subsequently converted to percussion ignition, rifled, and fitted with *tige* breech plugs. Many were still in use at the time of the Crimean War. Although most line infantrymen still shouldered smoothbore muskets, guns using either the Delvigne or Thouvenin systems were in widespread use in Europe by the early 1850s, with one observer reporting them in service "in France, Belgium, Russia, Sardinia, Austria, Prussia, and nearly all the states of the German Confederation."[14]

Variations on the Minié Ball, l-r. .58, .69 and .54 Burton design, smooth sided Pritchett style and Confederate Gardner. (*John Kuhl*)

Delvigne and Thouvenin established the conical bullet's long-range ballistic superiority, and Delvigne pushed the concept one step further in his 1842 patent of a hollow-based bullet design that bypassed both breech ring and *tige* and used gas from the exploding powder charge to expand an undersized bullet into the rifling. Although Thouvenin's manual expansion system was widely adopted, the colonel's assistant, Captain Minié, continued work on redressing its main problem, the *tige* itself, which hindered proper cleaning of the breech area. Following through on earlier experiments by Delvigne, Minié developed a hollow-based under-bore-sized bullet with a tapered iron plug in the base. The new conical ball needed no special chamber rim or spike to expand it, and was reliably upset into the rifling by the force of the exploding propellant charge, which drove the plug into the soft lead.[15]

The invention of progressive-depth rifling, which decreased in depth toward the muzzle, by Minié's colleague Captain Tamasier, enabled the expanded "Minié ball" to get a good bite into the rifling on firing and swaged it a bit as it spun down the barrel. Tamasier added grooves around the circumference of the Minié bullet, on the theory that like the feathers on an arrow, they would stabilize the slug as it zipped through the air. Although this theory was most likely incorrect, the Tamasier grooves did provide convenient receptacles for lubricant that kept powder fouling soft and also scraped some of it out of the barrel on firing, permitting more shots to be fired between cleanings.[16]

Despite all of the development work and progress on arms and ammunition at Vincennes, the French military establishment believed that advanced small arms should only be issued to elite troops. On an investigative tour of European arms-making establishments and military organizations in 1856, New Jersey Adjutant General Thomas Cadwalader was advised that in France only "the guns which are in the hands of the *garde imperiale*, and the *chasseurs a pied* are all grooved [rifled].[17]

In the years following 1815, the French filled the role of occasional ally and potential adversary to their former enemies across the English Channel. Throughout their research, the Gallic small-arms reformers had to buck older officers who believed the smoothbore flintlock was the ultimate military weapon and the round ball the only fit projectile for a firearm. Despite the opposition of many senior commanders, however, until the early 1850s, new weapons and tactical ideas gained more of an audience in France than Britain.

The British were not, as we have seen, unfamiliar with the rifle, and drew on their American experience in deploying riflemen as skirmishers during the Peninsular campaign in Spain and at Waterloo. Most British officers displayed little small-arms creativity in the post-Napoleonic period, however, and those who did were actively discouraged. Rifle enthusiast Captain John Norton experimented with a hollowed-base cylindrical bullet similar to Minié's eventual design as early as the 1820s. Norton discovered that the bullet would shoot accurately in the Baker rifle, then the issue weapon for British riflemen, but was rebuffed by the ordnance establishment. An 1860 British account notes that although "we have termed this the Minie [sic] principle; Captain Norton, however, undoubtedly has a prior claim (which has been allowed by the British government, we believe) to this invention. He was before his time . . . the shooting mania was not strong upon us." Norton, a prolific ammunition inventor and tinkerer, claimed that he first got the idea of an undersized projectile expanding to fit a barrel from observing Malays preparing ammunition for their blow guns.[18]

The Duke of Wellington, who headed the British military, believed that the .75 caliber smoothbore "Brown Bess" would serve his old soldiers' grandsons as well as she had them. Eventually, however, the duke was forced to concede that the percussion ignition system was the wave of the foreseeable future. The British army adopted a percussion smoothbore musket in 1842, and in his last years in office, the victor of Waterloo reluctantly agreed to trials of Captain Minié's new projectile.

The British trials of 1850 resulted in the adoption of an interim design, the .70 caliber "Minié rifle." The Minié rifle replaced both the standard percussion smoothbore Model 1842 musket used by line troops and the Brunswick rifle issued to rifle regiments, which had two grooves cut in its barrel to receive a patched round ball with a flange that fit in the grooves. In a nod to the ghost of Wellington, the new weapon's bore diameter was set at .702 so that undersized round-ball ammunition designed for the .75 caliber smoothbore could be fired in the new guns in a pinch. In the event, however, the old-style balls were only usable in a Minié rifle with a clean barrel. It was nearly impossible to ram them down a barrel fouled with powder residue. In actual combat, ammunition interchangeability proved to be a nonissue.[19]

Although many thought John Norton had an equal claim, the British government paid Minié £20,000 for the use of his patent. Another prominent British gun designer, William Greener, also claimed to have invented the hollow-base conical "expanding ball," and, being more of a self-promoter than Norton was, was awarded £1,000 by the British government for "the first public suggestion of the principle of expansion, commonly called the Minie [sic] principle."[20]

Many, including artists who have portrayed the conflict, believe the .577 caliber P53 Enfield rifle-musket, the Minié rifle's successor in British service, was the weapon of Her Majesty Queen Victoria's troops in the Crimean war of 1854–1856. Such was not the case. Although the first Enfields were delivered to the British army in the spring of 1854, three of the four divisions sent to the Crimea in that year carried P51 Minié rifles; the remaining division was armed with smoothbores. Supplies of new P53 Enfields did not arrive at Sevastopol until after much of the fighting was over and were issued to the smoothbore-armed troops. The British army fought the Crimean War largely armed with the big-bore Minié rifle.

The Minié rifle was sighted to 900 yards, and the British were quick to take advantage of the gun's long-range potential in the rolling, open Crimean terrain. At Alma, the British Light Division advanced, firing at will on the enemy, wreaking havoc on Russian formations at ranges up to 400 yards. On October 25, 1854, the Russian garrison of Sevastopol mounted a reconnaissance in force against the besieging British picket line. As the smoothbore-armed Russians advanced in dense column formations, the well-disciplined British regulars fell back firing, each picket force or skirmish line holding until its flanks were threatened. When the day was done and the enemy retreated, the pickets had inflicted far more casualties than they had suffered. The deadly .70 caliber Minié rifles, firing a projectile with great penetration power, even at long range, often killed or wounded several Russians per shot.

British infantrymen continued to use their rifled arms to good effect during the remainder of the Sevastopol siege. One young lieutenant, who viewed the war as a new type of sport, reported that he had hit three Russians out of thirty-five shots at a distance of around 800 yards. An Irishman in the Rifle Brigade claimed he took 600-yard potshots at enemy soldiers running to the latrine, averring that even if he missed, it "would be as good as a dose of opening medicine" for the terrified Russians. Although it is possible someone might have been calling shots through observation with a telescope or binoculars, the actual ranges cited in these examples may be subject to debate, considering the results of the French study that only "the different parts of the uniform" of enemy soldiers was only distinguishable at a distance of 325 yards.[21]

Following brief but distinguished service, the Minié rifle was replaced by the P53 Enfield rifle-musket. Although the P53 spawned a family of .577 caliber guns, the most important was the rifle-musket, a weapon with the weight, barrel length, and bayonet reach of a musket, yet rifled for greater long-range accuracy. The Enfield version of Claude Minié's projectile was a long, heavy .568 diameter bullet with the standard cast-iron plug developed by Minié inserted in its hollow base. When British ordnance people discovered that the Minié-style iron plug was not only unnecessary to assure proper expansion but occasionally drove through the bullet with unpleasant results, it was replaced by a boxwood or clay plug, which served to protect the bullet base from damage in transportation. The British did not adopt Tamasier grooves, and the projectile was smooth sided.[22]

Lubrication to cut powder fouling and prevent the deposit of lead in the Enfield's bore was provided on the Pritchett slug by the tallow and beeswax greased paper in which it was encased. The thickness of the

British .577 pattern 1853 rifle-musket. With minor variations in barrel band and sling swivels, this basic arm served not only the British army reliably for over a decade, but, manufactured by private contractors in both London and Birmingham, was sold around the world, from China to the Confederacy. The P53 was ubiquitous in the 19th century—the AK47 of its age. (*National Park Service*)

paper also acted as a patch, compensating for the difference between bore and bullet diameter. Such a system was common in European cartridge designs. Improved powder led to more efficient combustion and explosive force and a consequent reduction in bullet diameter to .550. Properly patched with lubricated paper, the Pritchett bullet proved remarkably accurate at extreme long range. It swabbed fouling from the Enfield's bore efficiently as well. In an endurance test of gun and ammunition conducted at the Tower of London between August 5, 1863, and May 5, 1866, one P53 was fired 16,000 times without cleaning![23]

Although in no way comparable in size, training or global responsibilities with the French or British armies, the American military kept close tabs on European developments. United States army weapons and uniforms were largely patterned on French models, and drill manuals attributed to American authors were mainly plagiarisms or adaptations of French editions. Brevet Major Peter V. Hagner visited France in 1848–1849 and reported extensively on small-arms developments, as did Major Alfred Mordecai in 1855 and 1856. Efforts to develop a rifle-musket began on Hagner's return, and by 1853–1854, Colonel Benjamin Huger was testing foreign muskets and a variety of experimental .54 and .69 caliber U.S. arms modified to use solid *a tige* bullets and hollow-based Minié-style slugs.[24]

France may have been in the forefront of mid-nineteenth century military matters, but Master Armorer James H. Burton of Harper's Ferry Armory introduced some design changes in what was coming to be called, generically, the "Minié ball." Like the British, Burton dispensed with Minié's iron base plug, but he deepened and widened the conical ball's base cavity to insure that pressure from the exploding powder charge alone would expand the slug. Unlike the British Pritchett, Burton's version used Tamasier-style grooves to hold lubricant rather than a greased paper patch. The Burton bullet, described as "the French cylindro-ogee ball, converted into a self expanding ball" was extensively tested at Harper's Ferry in 1854 and adopted for U.S. service the following year. Most of the millions of bullets issued to Union and Confederate forces during the Civil War are technically "Burton balls" not "Minié balls."[25]

Although Europeans were generally (James Burton being a notable exception) far ahead of Americans in firearms and ammunition development in the 1850s, arms production methods were much further advanced on this side of the Atlantic. Inspired by the exhibitions of Samuel Colt and Robbins and Lawrence at the famed Crystal Palace exhibition of 1851, British officers visited the Springfield and Harper's Ferry Armories in the early 1850s to study the American arms industry and purchase stock-shaping and lock-making machinery. They then hired Master Armorer Burton to supervise production at the British government armory at Enfield.[26]

Before the end of 1854, American troops armed with the .54 caliber U.S. Model 1841 "Mississippi" rifle (which had previously fired a patched round ball) were issued cartridges loaded with .54 caliber Burton Minié balls. While experiments directed toward the development of a whole new series of American small arms progressed, some 1841 rifles were fitted with long-range adjustable sights calibrated up to 700 yards and sent to the frontier, where the guns replaced smoothbore muskets in the hands of infantrymen.[27]

The .69 caliber Burton bullet proved more accurate than the .54 in the army's tests, but recoil from Model 1842 smoothbore muskets rifled for testing was deemed severe. In an attempt to compromise between the accuracy of the larger caliber and tolerable kick of the smaller, the ordnance department chose .58 caliber for the new family of firearms adopted in 1855. Although the 1855 models included a short, heavy-barreled pistol with detachable stock and a carbine, these arms were eventually dropped from production.

Benjamin Huger, left. The Charleston-born Huger, a West Point graduate, was a career ordnance officer in the US army. After serving with courage and honor in the Mexican War he commanded Harper's Ferry Armory, where he was responsible for the adoption of the Model 1855 series of arms. At the outbreak of the Civil War Huger, loyal to his native state, joined the Confederate Army, where he was commissioned a colonel in the artillery. Although promoted to general, his field performance was described as "lackluster" and he ended his career as Inspector General of Artillery. James H. Burton, right. A native Virginian, Burton went to work at Harper's Ferry in 1844 and rose from machinist to Acting Master Armorer. Burton developed the version of the Minié ball used by the U.S. Army, but left Harper's Ferry for Enfield in 1855. Throwing in his lot with the Confederacy, he was appointed superintendent of the Richmond Armory in 1861 and then superintendent of all the Southern armories. (*Library of Congress*)

The centerpiece of the Springfield development program was the Model 1855 rifle-musket, which was fitted with a Maynard primer magazine integral with its lock. Maynard primers were loaded into the magazine on a roll similar to that used in a modern child's cap gun. A cap was fed onto the gun's nipple (which could also be used with conventional musket caps) every time its hammer was cocked. The Maynard primers proved unreliable in bad weather, however, and the magazine was omitted from the subsequent Model 1861 rifle-musket lock. Private Philip H. Smith, issued the Model 1861 early in the Civil War, believed the new gun was "a far superior rifle altogether" to the 1855. Smith thought "tape locks is played out, some likes them the best but I can't see the edge. I have used them both and I know." Hammer, barrel band, and ramrod configurations underwent minor changes throughout the .58 caliber Springfield rifle-musket series, which included the Model 1863 and 1864 (also known as 1863 "second type") guns. Civil War Ordnance officers saw no significant differences in guns made between 1855 and 1865 and lumped them all into the same category on their returns. The dominant infantry arm among Federal troops on the Gettysburg battlefield was the .58 caliber Model 1861. A significant number of Springfields also fell into Confederate hands through capture, however.[28]

While Springfield and Harper's Ferry Armories were tooling up for the new models, a number of Model 1842 .69 caliber muskets were rifled, fitted with long-range sights, and issued as a stopgap measure. These guns are properly called rifled muskets, although the term was often used interchangeably with rifle-musket. Frontier soldiers put up with the heavier recoil of the rifled 1842 firing a Minié ball because of the gun's accuracy edge over the Model 1841 rifle with the new style ammunition. The Model 1841's deep-cut rifling, designed for shooting patched round balls, may have allowed gas blow by when shooting the Burton design, and consequent inferior accuracy.[29]

In another modernization effort, earlier model flintlock guns were converted to percussion ignition, rifled, and fitted with new "patent breeches" and Maynard primer locks at Philadelphia's Frankford arsenal. Most, if not all, of these conversions were issued to various states for militia use; New Jersey received several thousand of these guns in 1857. After 1855, some Model 1841 rifles were re-bored, re-rifled, and re-sighted for the new .58 caliber ammunition. All of these arms, plus unrifled smoothbore muskets, would see extensive use in the Civil War.[30]

The .58 caliber Model 1855 rifle-musket, which began to reach the field in 1857, had a nominal weight of nine pounds three ounces and a forty-inch-long three-groove barrel cut with progressive-depth rifling. Springfield Armory specifications allowed a bore dimension range from .580 to .5825. The rifle-musket's paper cartridge contained sixty grains of musket powder and a nominally .5775 diameter hollow-based Burton version of the Minié ball lubricated in Tamasier-style grooves with a combination of beeswax and tallow. To load the Model 1855, a soldier had to bite off the end of the cartridge, pour the powder down the muzzle of his gun, discard the paper, insert the bullet base-first in the muzzle, ram it down atop the powder charge, and place a percussion cap on the nipple. The Springfield, fitted for a triangular socket bayonet, was expected to shoot ten consecutive rounds into a four-inch bull's-eye at 100 yards. A "rifle" model, with a shorter, thicker barrel and sword bayonet, was also produced at Harper's Ferry Armory.[31]

By the outbreak of the Civil War, most regular army soldiers were armed with Model 1855 rifle-muskets or rifles, and a few had been distributed to the militia, which also upgraded obsolete smoothbore arms at state expense by rifling them and adding sights. The Montgomery Guards of Richmond, Virginia, for example, issued a drill order in January 1861 requiring members to assemble "with Regimental overcoats, cross belts, cartridge boxes, bayonet scabbards, cap-boxes, fatigue caps and Minnie [sic] musket." Supplies of rifled arms were limited, however, and the majority

A private with the 2nd Rhode Island Infantry holding a Model 1855 rifle-musket. (*National Archives*)

available, especially to state militias, were obsolescent Model 1841 rifles in both original .54 and re-bored .58 calibers and .69 caliber rifled smoothbores, the latter most likely the "Minnie musket" referred to. The New Jersey Quartermaster General reported in January 1861 that he had "465 rifles, serviceable and unserviceable" and "142 rifled muskets, new." The latter were most likely .58 caliber Model 1855s and not the recently adopted and slightly different Model 1861.[32]

Following the outbreak of war in April, 1861, Union Chief of Ordnance General James W. Ripley tried to restrict issuance of .58 caliber rifle-muskets to regular army units and then, beginning in May, the three-year volunteers, but his reserve supply was exhausted by August. Ripley's Confederate counterpart, Major Josiah Gorgas, had only 1,765 rifle-muskets at his disposal. One Confederate ordnance officer recalled after the war that the South had only "some 12,000 or 15,000 rifles" of all types on hand at the beginning of the conflict.[33]

As demand reached a crescendo, Ripley's attempts to control the trickle of Model 1861 rifle-muskets reaching his bureau from Springfield Armory—the only domestic source of new rifle-muskets since the Confederates seized the Harper's Ferry Armory—were undermined by politicians and officers using all available means and influence to secure .58 caliber arms for their regiments. Along with spiffy foreign drills, natty uniforms, and racy names, shiny new rifle-muskets became status symbols for the enthusiastic Yankee volunteers.

Secretary of War Simon Cameron, a Pennsylvanian, tried to funnel as many new rifled arms as possible to his home state's units. Governor Charles Olden of New Jersey lobbied Ripley for Springfields for the Ninth New Jersey Infantry. Perhaps because the Ninth was recruited as a sharpshooter regiment, the Chief of Ordnance relented and had a supply of newly manufactured weapons shipped straight from Springfield Armory to Trenton to arm the unit. The flamboyant and politically connected Brigadier General Philip Kearny managed to requisition enough rifle-muskets to arm several selected companies of his First New Jersey Brigade. The lucky Jersey riflemen became the brigade's elite light battalion.[34]

The obvious answer to the rifle-musket shortage, Union and Confederate, was to increase domestic production, an easier task in the industrialized north. The Federal Ordnance Department quickly contracted with a number of private firms to produce the Model 1861. Unfortunately, some of these contractors were mere paper entities, while still others depended on the same subcontractors for most of their parts. Many of these firms did not furnish firearms for several years, if ever. The first contracted Model 1861 rifle-muskets were delivered in the third quarter of 1862, when 4,500 were received. The total number of contract rifle-muskets delivered to the government by the battle of Gettysburg was 112,685. By mid-1863, the situation had stabilized and a weeded-out field of contractors began to produce an increasing number of new arms, supplementing a vastly expanded Springfield Armory operation.[35]

Some Southern states bought excellent firearms other than rifle-muskets from leading Northern gun manufacturers, including Colt, Maynard, Sharps, and Whitney, right up to the outbreak of hostilities, when the Federal government clamped down on the trade. With the exception of Richmond Armory, and to some degree Fayetteville Armory, both outfitted with machines and tooling captured at Harper's Ferry, Rebel rifle-musket makers never did get their production untracked. According to the best estimate of the most definitive researcher to date, Paul Davies, Richmond, the crown jewel of the Confederate ordnance department, produced a total of 37,736 small arms, including rifle-muskets, carbines, and "short rifles," the latter intended for mounted infantry use, between 1861 and 1865. Richmond also assembled guns from captured Harper's Ferry parts and acted as a rebuilding center for many damaged arms "from battle fields repaired," the latter accounting for most of its output. Although information is difficult to uncover, one recent researcher credits Southern arsenals and private contractors with a total production of around 100,000 rifles and muskets, with another 100,000 flintlock muskets converted to percussion ignition. The guns produced were of varying quality, but it can be argued that these manufacturers made more of a contribution to the modern collector's market then they ever did to the Rebel war effort.[36]

Josiah Gorgas. A Pennsylvania-born West Point graduate, Gorgas married the daughter of a former Alabama governor and left the U. S. Ordnance Corps for the Confederacy with the outbreak of war in 1861. Gorgas was appointed Chief of Ordnance for the Confederate Army, and proved an excellent choice for the position. Even though he lacked the industrial base of the North, and realized that advanced weapons technologies were not in the cards for the South, he did the best with what he had. Gorgas later recalled that the Confederate army never lost a battle due to lack or weapons or ammunition. (*Library of Congress*)

With large-scale arms production in its infancy in the North and not a significant factor in the South for the first two years of the conflict, both sides initially depended largely on obsolete small arms already in storage and guns purchased from private dealers, some in their original configuration and others hastily upgraded. These weapons were subsequently supplemented by large numbers of imports from Europe.

Although there were more muskets in Northern arsenals than Southern ones, many were, as a newspaper noted, "next to useless." Governor Olden of New Jersey informed his legislature that "there may be about 3,000 stand of arms in tolerable good condition for use in the hands of the militia, and about 4,000 stand of arms in the arsenal with flintlocks." New Jersey Quartermaster General Lewis Perrine quickly contracted with private firms, including Hewes and Phillips of Newark, to convert flintlock muskets to percussion ignition and rifle them for militia use as well as issue to the state's Fourth through Eighth Infantry Regiments sent to Virginia in late 1861. Employees at the state arsenal in Trenton were soon converting more flintlocks to percussion. Ammunition supplies were low as well. Perrine had to send an officer to a New York City gun store to buy cartridges for New Jersey militiamen leaving Trenton for the defense of Washington in May 1861. Things were slow to improve. Several months later, a Jersey volunteer was standing guard duty at Trenton's Camp Olden with "an old Harper's Ferry musket without a lock . . . in citizen's dress."[37]

The Confederate government realized early on that it would need far more firearms than would be available through domestic purchase, confiscation, capture, or contracting and dispatched Captain Caleb Huse to Europe to buy arms in April, 1861. Huse made a series of deals with private manufacturers of P53 Enfield–style rifles in Birmingham and London, which were reinforced by his superior, Major Edward C. Anderson, who arrived in Liverpool on June 22. Largely due to Anderson and Huse's efforts, as well as the desires of former Harper's Ferry and Enfield superintendent James Burton, who had thrown in his lot with his native Virginia at the outbreak of the war, the P53 Enfield became as close to a standard arm as the Confederacy possessed. Ordnance chief Josiah Gorgas later specified the Enfield caliber of .577 as the standard caliber for weapons manufactured in the Confederacy.[38]

Burton, who had returned from England to Virginia prior to the outbreak of the war, designed a new rifle-musket for the state's militia that was described as "a combination of the U.S. rifled musket and the British Enfield musket and it is hoped will possess the advantages of both." Although Burton had a prototype of the Virginia rifle-musket hand made at Springfield Armory, it never materialized as a production item. He was appointed superintendent of the Richmond Armory in June 1861, was subsequently commissioned a Confederate lieutenant colonel, and was given responsibility for all Confederate armories by the end of the year. During the war, he contracted in Britain for the tooling of an entire armory to produce Enfields, but the conflict ended with the machinery still in Bermuda waiting to be run through the Union naval blockade.[39]

The first Union overseas arms agent appointed, Colonel George L. Schuyler, had little technical knowledge of small arms, which, when the inspector detailed to accompany him fell ill, severely hampered his acquisition of first-class guns. Schuyler had to compete not only with Rebel arms buyers like Huse, whose British agent Archibald Hamilton was one of the most connected individuals in the Birmingham and London gun trade, but with other Yankees appointed by Federal and state governments as well as private Northern buyers like Herman Boker & Company. In many cases, Union agents bid not only against their Confederate competitors but also against each other, driving up the eventual price of the guns they sought to buy.[40]

Most of the small arms imported by the American combatants during the course of the Civil War were British Enfield-style rifle-muskets. These guns varied a bit in barrel band and ramrod style, but were generic P53 rifle-muskets. Smaller numbers of the shorter barreled Enfield rifles and still shorter carbines, or "musketoons," were also imported. Although guns made at the British government small-arms factory at Enfield were not sold to either side, private British gun makers located primarily in London and Birmingham were free to sell Enfields to anyone. In the end, the Confederates imported around 500,000 Enfields of various types, and the Union ordnance department purchased another 428,292.[41]

The first Rebel shipment, 3,500 Enfields and Austrian arms—a mix of Confederate government, private dealer, and state purchases—left

Liverpool aboard the *Bermuda* on August 18, 1861. In October, the steamer *Fingal*, purchased by Anderson, Huse, and fellow Southern agent James D. Bulloch on behalf of the Confederate government, set sail from England with 15,000 Enfield rifle-muskets, 500 revolvers, a million cartridges, two million percussion caps, artillery, and other military equipment. The *Fingal* made landfall in Savannah on November 15, and Enfields arrived in increasing numbers through 1862 and 1863.[42]

A typical cargo was that of the blockade runner *Modern Greece*, which ran aground off Cape Hatteras in June, 1862, and was subsequently sunk by gunfire from the Yankee blockading fleet. Archeological and documentary evidence revealed the *Modern Greece* was loaded with a variety of civilian and military supplies. Along with farming and carpenter tools, flatirons, and pocket and Bowie knives, the ship carried several advanced Whitworth artillery pieces and at least 500 Ward and Company Birmingham-made Enfields with bayonets, in rifle-musket, rifle, and carbine configurations. Also included in the cargo were thousands of rounds of British paper cartridges loaded with the distinctive Pritchett bullet with boxwood base plug, as well as percussion caps. About half the small arms were salvaged by the state of North Carolina shortly after the wreck. By the time of Gettysburg, the Confederacy had imported, not counting state purchases, around 180,000 foreign-made guns, the bulk of them Enfields.[43]

Most of the imported Enfields, with the notable exception of guns made by London Armory, were hand made or assembled of parts submitted to a general contractor by subcontractors in Britain or Belgium specializing in various parts, including locks, ramrods, barrels, etc. Each of these contractors had their own machining tolerances—or lack of them. The resultant lack of interchangeability of small parts is evident in surviving specimens, although standard rifle-musket barrel length was thirty-nine inches and average weight around nine pounds, and all Enfields looked pretty much alike.

The overall quality of hand-made Enfields varied with the rush to fill a huge new market, perhaps resulting in a drop in production standards. In the summer of 1861, the men of the Thirteenth Massachusetts Volunteer Infantry received "the Enfield rifle-musket—which has been pronounced by the officers of the regiment to be the most delicate, highly finished, and defensible weapon in the infantry service." The soldiers of the Tenth Massachusetts Volunteer Infantry, however, complained that "the Enfield received would not compare favorably with the Springfield musket, new pattern. The workmanship was rough and they were poorly rifled, and the parts would not interchange like the American gun. It was necessary to keep an armorer with the Regiment to fit such parts of the musket as were accidentally broken in service." Soldiers of the Tenth Illinois Infantry were issued Enfields whose mainsprings were "too weak to snap caps and the men of the Thirty-fifth Massachusetts Infantry complained that "the cones [nipples] of some [Enfields] snapped off at the base." This was, no doubt, due to improper case hardening of the nipples.[44]

The commander of the Fifteenth New Jersey Infantry was also less than delighted with his men's Enfields. Following the May 3, 1863, battle of Salem Church, the Fifteenth's Colonel William Penrose informed VI Army Corps commander Major General John Sedgwick that he believed the Enfields "now in the hands of the men of this regiment were refuse ones being purchased in a foreign country by the Government in the early part of the War and [have] evidently never passed inspection." According to Penrose, "the various parts of the pieces are badly finished and when a part from any cause is broken or lost it is with difficulty that another can be found to replace it."[45]

More important than parts finish or breakage were the problems the men of the Fifteenth had with their Enfields at Salem Church. After a few rounds the Jerseyans found it difficult to ram bullets down the barrels of their weapons. Some soldiers had to push their ramrods against trees to seat the Minié balls in their guns. Although Colonel Penrose opined that his men's loading difficulties were due to lead deposits caused by "imperfections in the grooving" of the barrels (and this is possible), the problems were most likely the result of powder fouling coupled with undersized bores and/or oversized bullets. Enfields came in two bore diameter sizes: the British .577 standard (twenty-five gauge) and the American .58 caliber (twenty-four gauge), the latter specifically intended for the American export market. Although ammunition originally intended for Springfields could be fired in .577

barrels, fouling buildup made loading difficult after a few shots. Inconsistency of available ammunition compounded this problem, which would raise its head again at Little Round Top on July 2, 1863.[46]

Similar situations occurred in the Confederate army. One Rebel brigade at Chickamauga was armed with Enfields in two bore sizes. Following the fight, an ordnance officer wrote that "caliber No. .57 was loose and never choked the guns, while the No. 58, after the first few rounds, was found too large, and frequently choking the guns to that extent that they could not be forced down, thereby creating some uneasiness among the men using that number of ammunition." Since Chickamauga was fought two and a half months after Gettysburg, and some of the same troops were engaged, it could be assumed that ordnance problems might well have been similar.[47]

Although Colonel Penrose's plea for Springfields to replace his Enfields was ignored, not all Yankee soldiers preferred Springfields to Enfields. When the men of Colonel Henry O. Ryerson's Tenth New Jersey Infantry turned in their Enfields for Springfield pattern guns in the spring of 1864, many of the new guns' mainsprings broke after they were cocked a few times. Regretting the exchange, Ryerson quixotically decided to "rely on the bayonet" in the upcoming campaign. He did not survive it.[48]

Despite the occasional complaints, the Enfield was generally regarded as highly as the Springfield by soldiers and was considered a firstclass firearm by the ordnance department. A soldier in the Forty-ninth Illinois proudly announced that his "regiment is armed throughout with the Enfield 'rifle with sabre bayonet' which is probably as good an arm as any in the country."[49]

With their own limited domestic production capacity, and the fact that most of the initial guns available to them were smoothbore muskets converted from flintlock to percussion ignition, Confederate infantrymen appreciated the British made rifle-muskets perhaps more than any Yankees. The soldiers of the Twentieth Tennessee, "a body of men that appreciated a good thing," were delighted when they received new Enfields to replace their "old flintlocks, squirrel rifles and shotguns" on the eve of the 1862 battle of Shiloh. Colonel Basil W. Duke of the Second Kentucky (Confederate) Cavalry noted that Enfields were

"unequalled weapons—the right arms for soldiers who want to fight."
Noted cavalry commanders John Hunt Morgan and Nathan Bedford
Forrest preferred the shorter "rifle" version of the Enfield. Morgan and
Forrest felt that the rifle was easier to carry on horseback than the rifle-
musket yet more accurate than the still shorter Enfield carbine. This
"medium Enfield" was the favorite weapon of the Second Kentucky
Cavalry "because of its ease of handling on and off horseback."[50]

The second most common imported rifle-musket in service at
Gettysburg was the Austrian Lorenz, both in its original .54 caliber and
also manufactured or re-bored into various approximations of .58 caliber for the American war market. The Lorenz, the invention of
Austrian army Lieutenant Joseph Lorenz, was introduced into
Hapsburg service in 1854 and was a sound weapon well regarded in
Europe. It had a thirty-seven-inch barrel, making it a bit shorter than
the Springfield and Enfield. Most Lorenz rifle-muskets were stocked
with beech wood, although some were apparently stocked with walnut.
Lorenzes have been variously reported as weighing between (depending on wood type and density) eight and nine and a half pounds. The
gun's quadrangular bayonet with unusual spiraling mounting slot in
the socket added almost another pound.[51]

Lorenz designed his gun to use a solid-based slug of the style originally designed by British arms inventor Henry Wilkinson rather than
the Minié-inspired bullets used in the British Enfield and American
Springfield. Wilkinson's bullet in the same .54 caliber (.537 diameter)
chosen by Lorenz had been a finalist in the 1852 British small-arms
tests conducted to find a replacement arm for the .71 caliber Minié rifle.
The Wilkinson/Lorenz bullet had two deep grooves designed to collapse and obturate the undersized projectile into the rifling on the
shock of firing. A greased paper patch wrapped around the slug provided lubrication.[52]

Both Yankee and Rebel buyers eagerly snapped up Lorenz-style
rifle-muskets; over the course of the war, the Union recorded purchases
of 226,924, and the Confederacy bought at least 100,000. Lorenz guns
were acquired from several sources, including the Hapsburg armories
in Vienna and private arms makers in Vienna and Ferlach. There were
two basic styles of Austrian rear sights: a nonadjustable "block," zeroed

at 300 *shritt*, or paces (approximately 250 yards), and an adjustable leaf with settings of 300, 500, 700, and 900 *shritt*. Theoretically the fixed, or "block," sight gun was intended for line troops and the adjustable-sight version for skirmishers. There was also a short *Jaeger* rifle designed for sharpshooters, bearing a unique leaf sight which slid in a track not unlike that used by the U.S. M-1 Garand of World War II fame. Some of the *Jaeger* guns were fitted with the Delvigne *tige* breech.[53]

Although Captain Silas Crispin, who inspected Lorenz rifle-muskets imported for the Union by Boker, described them in general as "fair arms in workmanship and finish, and in weight and caliber according more nearly with our established model than any other arms of Continental manufacture." Lorenz quality apparently varied. Crispin was impressed by one lot of Austrian rifle-muskets, "finished in some respects, in imitation of the Enfield rifle" as "somewhat superior, in every respect," to other lots of Lorenzes.[54]

Rebel Lorenz shipments apparently varied as well. Although Caleb Huse scored a coup with a purchase of 23,000 excellent rifle-muskets from the Vienna Arsenal in October 1862, he also bought Austrian arms from other sources. These were no doubt among the total of 27,000 "Austrian rifles" shipped by Huse to the Confederacy by the end of 1862. Unfortunately, not all of Huse's purchases measured up to his original acquisition. In 1863, Major Smith Stansbury, a Confederate arms inspector in Bermuda, classified a shipment of Austrian weapons as "a lot of trash, in horrible condition." After a thorough inspection and cleaning, however, most of these apparently well-used guns were found to be satisfactory. The bulk of them seem to have ended up serving in the Army of Tennessee and forces further west.[55]

In contrast to the Federal experience, the number of Lorenz rifle-muskets in Confederate service actually increased in the final years of the war. In April of 1863, the Army of Tennessee reported 663 Austrian small arms in service; by the following spring, thirty-two percent of that army's men shouldered Lorenzes. The Lorenz was among the weapons tested by the Army of Northern Virginia's sharpshooters in the spring of 1864 and was found to be fully equal in accuracy to the Springfield and Enfield up to 500 yards. [56]

Some Austrian gun dealers no doubt took advantage of the warring Americans' need for firearms and deep pockets to fob off guns of inferior quality. Among these may have been weapons rejected by the Austrian government or culled from some Balkan battlefield or the recent war in northern Italy, as well as copies of the Lorenz made elsewhere.

Exterior finish on the Lorenz rifle-muskets varied, with some guns blued or browned (the terms were used interchangeably) and others polished bright. Some Lorenz guns were re-bored, apparently in Belgium, on their way to America or here after arrival, in an attempt to make them conform to the standard .58 caliber, while others seem to have been purpose built to that caliber by Austrian makers. These conversions and adaptations were more or less successful, with actual calibers noted as varying from .577, .57, and .58 to .59. A hand-made product, the Lorenz suffered the same parts interchangeability problems as the hand-made Enfields

Despite these problems, the Lorenz was well regarded by some soldiers to whom it was issued, including those of the Fifth New Jersey and 104th Pennsylvania. Private Alfred Bellard of the Fifth praised his .54 caliber Lorenz for being "short, light and very easily cleaned," while Quartermaster James D. Hendrie of the 104th believed his outfit's Austrian guns to be "very superior weapons, although not so well finished as the American arms." The 104th's colonel remembered his regiment's guns as "rough but good and reliable." The men of the Twenty-third Pennsylvania were delighted to trade in their .69 caliber rifled muskets for Austrian arms, which they found to be "most efficient firearms." An Illinois officer regarded the Lorenz as "although a little heavy, a fine piece for service." Leander Stillwell of the Sixty-first Illinois considered his .54 Lorenz "a wicked shooter." Stillwell and his comrades "were glad to get the Austrians, and were quite proud of them." The Suckers of the Sixty-first carried their Lorenz rifle-muskets until June of 1863, when they exchanged them for Springfields.[57]

Other soldiers were not so enthusiastic about Austrian guns. In 1863, a Union inspecting officer condemned the Austrian weapons of the Forty-seventh Massachusetts Infantry. Lorenz rifle-muskets issued to western troops in the second year of the war seem to have been decidedly inferior to those issued the previous year. William E. McMillan of the Ninety-fourth Illinois' Company E wrote that his unit's Lorenzes were "not worth much," while the 100th Illinois reported that its re-bored .58 caliber Lorenz guns "are roughly and improperly made and cannot be called an effective weapon." The men of the 106th Illinois complained that the .58 caliber Lorenz was miserably poor" and "rather a poor excuse for a gun" and the 120th Illinois classified its .54 caliber Lorenz guns as "worthless."[58]

The 125th Illinois Infantry was issued Austrian rifle-muskets re-bored to .58 caliber of "which not over one half were perfect . . . many will not explode a cap." The 125th's regimental historian complained that some of the Austrian guns' nipples "were not entirely drilled out," and some could not mount a bayonet without hammering it on. The 130th Illinois reported that "one-third or three-eights of these arms [Austrian] are defective and the historian of the Ninety-fifth Pennsylvania, whose regiment was issued Lorenzes, recalled that "the utter uselessness of these latter arms was fully demonstrated by its [sic] frequent use in target practice." In January 1863, Lieutenant Colonel William S. Abert, Assistant Inspector General of the Department of the Gulf, inspected the arms of the Forty-seventh Massachusetts Infantry, armed with Lorenzes he determined were "made of poor material and badly constructed." Abert reported that he "examined eight hundred of these rifles and . . . do not consider one hundred serviceable."[59]

Historians like Edwin B. Coddington carried this dim view of the Lorenz into the modern era. Although Coddington, more than other historians of his era, provided a detailed assessment of the small arms carried by soldiers at Gettysburg, his conclusion that the Lorenz was the "most unsatisfactory rifle" in service at the battle is overdrawn. Some Lorenzes as well as other imported and contract arms surely had problems. It was not the case, however, as Coddington posits, that the "springs of the hammer lock [sic] were so badly tempered that in many pieces the trigger had to be pulled three or four times before the percussion cap exploded." Nor was it correct that "when the gun finally went off it had the kick of a mule."[60]

Lorenz guns may well have gained a bad reputation due to exaggerated veteran retrospective and confusion between them and older .71 caliber Austrian "Consol," or tube-lock, muskets, which were conversions from flintlock. These guns, some of which were rifled, others not, were converted by a method devised by Giuseppe Consol of Milan and improved by General Vincent Augustin of the Austrian army. The Consol/Augustin system replaced the flintlock pan and frizzen with a two-piece priming chamber and installed a new hammer.[61]

After muzzle loading, the main charge in the usual manner into its Delvigne chambered barrel, the Consol/Augustin was primed by bringing its hammer to half cock, lifting the top section of the priming chamber, inserting a small priming tube filled with percussion powder, and closing it. The gun could then be brought to full cock and fired. The hammer hit a firing pin device in the chamber, which, in turn, exploded the percussion tube and ignited the main charge. A number of these guns were converted to the standard percussion system before or after importation, but others, especially in the earliest days of the war, were placed directly in the hands of troops with their peculiar priming system intact.[62]

Continental European guns were more commonly issued and remained in service longer in the western armies. Major General John C. Frémont purchased 25,000 tube-lock muskets in his desperate search for weapons in 1861, and at least 3,000 .71 caliber Delvigne chambered Austrian "Garibaldi" rifles were issued to Minnesota troops. French weapons, as well as Belgian copies of them, were purchased in some quantity in the wholesale weapons bazaar of 1861 and 1862. The French saw the American war as an opportunity to unload surplus Crimean War guns as well as early, less desirable arms. The famed gun-making center of Liege in Belgium was a source for all types of weapons, including copies of French, British, and Austrian guns, as well as brokered obsolete German muskets. Although quality varied, Belgian weapons, like German arms, filled a vital gap in the Federal arms inventory in the first two years of the war. By mid-1863, however, most of these stopgap guns had been retired from active service in the Union army, especially in the eastern theater of war, as the Springfield and

Enfield rifle-muskets became the dominant infantry small arms, although large numbers of Lorenz rifle-muskets remained in service.[63]

Rebel ordnance officer J. W. Mallet recalled that in "the early part of the war" Southern infantrymen were armed with "Springfield and Enfield muskets, Mississippi and Maynard rifles, Hall's and Sharp's [sic] carbines and arms of English, German, Austrian and Belgian manufacture, of many different calibers." Mallet remembered that he had "at one time samples of more than twenty patterns of infantry weapons alone." Confederates, for the most part, however, avoided purchasing Continental arms other than the Austrian Lorenz, and most odd weapons in their service were captured from the Yankees. The South concentrated on getting as many Enfields through the Federal naval blockade as possible. Due to the blockade's porosity, this proved to be quite a large number. Adding captured arms and a small but steady production at Richmond Armory to those imports led to an Army of Northern Virginia that by mid-1863 was largely armed with the rifle-musket.[64]

Colonel Edward P. Alexander, General Longstreet's artillery commander, estimated that ninety percent of the Confederates who crossed into Pennsylvania in the summer of 1863 were armed with rifled arms in either .58 or .54 caliber, a percentage that dovetails with the known armament of the Union regiments at Gettysburg. On June 28, 1863, Lieutenant Colonel Arthur J. L. Fremantle of the Coldstream Guards, traveling as an observer with Major General William D. Pender's Division of Lee's army, noted that "the Confederate troops are now entirely armed with excellent rifles, mostly Enfields."[65]

In addition to the increasing number of imported Enfields, at least some of the Rebel army's guns had been gleaned from the Army of Northern Virginia's victorious battlefields of Chancellorsville and Winchester. According to the Army of Northern Virginia's chief of ordnance, Lieutenant Colonel Briscoe G. Baldwin, his men accounted for "nineteen thousand five hundred muskets and rifles (29,500 collected, 10,000 admitted dropped by our men, leaving 19,500 captured), 8,000 cartridge boxes, 4,000 cap-pouches, 11,500 knapsacks, 300,000 rounds infantry ammunition" in the aftermath of Chancellorsville. Many Rebel "dropped" arms were smoothbore muskets tossed away in favor of rifle-muskets found on the battlefield, as troops rearmed themselves as opportunity presented itself. Baldwin also noted that "every day small lots of muskets and rifles are brought in, and without doubt quite a number of arms, etc. are retained in regimental ordnance wagons for future contingencies and not reported."[66]

Lieutenant General Richard S. Ewell's Chief of Ordnance recalled that his scavenging activities had resulted in arming the entire corps with rifled arms, although several brigades may have had to wait until the mid-June battle at Winchester to complete the corps's rearmament. But rearmed they were, and the fight at Gettysburg would largely be a contest of rifle-musket against rifle-musket.[67]

Chapter 3

THE RIFLE-MUSKET, PART II

———◄►◄►———

MUCH HAS BEEN MADE BY HISTORIANS OF THE rifle-musket's accuracy, with assertions that its use in the American Civil War changed the nature of warfare on the tactical level. This belief has become conventional wisdom among popular and academic historians alike. One of the foremost scholars of the battle of Gettysburg asserted that a soldier shooting a rifle-musket "could easily hit a small target up to two hundred yards, and a much larger one up to five hundred yards." These conclusions are based on the arguments officers made for the adoption of rifle-muskets because they were believed capable of "close shooting" at ranges up to 500 yards and possessed of the potential to be effective on large formations at 1,000 yards. Some historians have suggested that the rifle-musket's deadly long-range accuracy shifted the battlefield balance of power decisively to the defense, not unlike the perceived role of the machine gun in World War I.[1]

A closer analysis, however, suggests that the rifle-musket seldom achieved the potential expected of it in United States or Confederate service. Actual battlefield performance was determined by the realities of combat and terrain, ignorance of junior officers, indifference of higher commanders, and poor or nonexistent marksmanship training. Even worse, many recruits, especially in Federal ranks, were totally unfamiliar with firearms. The historian of the Fourteenth New Hampshire Infantry freely admitted that many men in his regiment "cringed at every shot. Quite a number of them had never fired a gun in their lives;

and several of them, when commanded to fire, would shut their eyes, turn their heads in the opposite direction, and blaze away."[2]

Many veterans recalled nightmare scenarios with their first weapons, one writing that some of the imported Prussian muskets issued to his unit "burst at the first firing, and were more dangerous at their butts than at their muzzles." Another remembered that when he first pulled his musket's trigger, "the next moment I was on my back, kicking for all that was out." Needless to say, the years added much to these colorful stories, and all must be taken with the proverbial grain of salt, perhaps more, but they are instructive in that they accurately portray the ignorance of recruits regarding the tools of their new trade.[3]

Fear of one's own musket made a bad thing worse. The inherent accuracy a gun displays under controlled conditions does not predict combat accuracy. Soldiers in action, especially untrained ones, tend to fire high and often wildly. This tendency was graphically demonstrated at the May 12, 1864, fight at Spotsylvania's "Bloody Angle." One of the more astute observers of the Angle's aftermath was Lieutenant Colonel John Schoonover of the Eleventh New Jersey Infantry. Schoonover was a cool soldier in action and an excellent shot who often took a turn on the skirmish line with a rifle-musket. His observations are worth quoting in their entirety.

> The evidence of the continued fire at this point during the day and part of the night was everywhere apparent. The trees near the works were stripped of their foliage, and looked as though an army of locusts had passed during the night. The brush between the lines was cut and torn into shreds, and the fallen bodies of men and horses lay there with the flesh shot and torn from the bones. The peculiar whirring sound of a flying ramrod was frequently heard during the day. I noticed two of these that had fastened themselves in the oak trees nearby.
>
> While the great number of the enemy's dead and the terrible effects of our fire upon the logs composing the breastworks attested the general accuracy of our fire, the absence of the foliage from the top of the tallest trees made it evident that during a battle there is

much random firing. There is a large percentage of men in actual battle who load carefully, aim deliberately and shoot to kill. On the other
hand, it is not an uncommon thing for a soldier amidst the excitement
of battle, to load his gun, shut his eyes and fire in the air straight over
his head [emphasis Schoonover's]."[4]

Earlier in the war, Confederate sharpshooter Berry Benson made a
similar observation. After entering a woodlot where his regiment had
fought on the Rebel right at Fredericksburg, Benson noticed "the trees
spotted and scarred with the marks of bullets, most of them just overhead, which shows that the average aim is too high. In one tree we
found a ramrod which had been shot into it and wonderfully bent and
twisted it was."[5]

One officer recalled that men would "pop off their pieces long before
there [was] anything to aim at" and "drop their cartridges" and "load
and forget to cap their pieces and get half a dozen rounds into their
muskets thinking they have fired them off." His conclusion was that
"most of them just load and fire without any consciousness of shooting
at anything in particular."[6]

These observations lend credence to conclusions arrived at by
Captain John Gibbon's prewar *Artillerist's Manual*. While conceding
the potential of rifled arms to stop most any advance, Gibbon, who
became a Federal general and commanded the II Corps's Second
Division at Gettysburg, concluded that even "the very best disciplined
men will, in time of battle, fire with precipitancy and at too great a distance; from which results a great loss of ammunition and of effect upon
the enemy." In a similar vein, Admiral John A. Dahlgren noted that
"the excitement of the conflict, the noise, the smoke, the dust, the rash
haste of some, the dullness of others, prevent the soldier from aiming
and making the best use of his weapon."[7]

Wild firing is exacerbated when black powder smoke obscures the
target. Anyone who has fired or observed the live firing of rifle-
muskets at the North-South Skirmish Association's team musket
matches on the organization's rifle range near Winchester, Virginia, on
a humid, still day realizes how smoke hangs in the air with 400 or so
shooters on the line. To properly envision the haze of battle, one must
multiply that effect by 2,500 and add a heavy dose of three-pound

artillery powder charges. Connecticut Captain John W. DeForest recalled that on one occasion, his men, unable to see their opponents, volleyed into the "hostile line of smoke which confronted them." Soldiers blazing away at each other along Antietam's "Bloody Lane" in September 1862 caught only brief glimpses of their opponents.[8]

Heavy brush or forest as well as gun smoke often obscured enemy positions during the Civil War. These problems, coupled with the tendency noted by Gibbon of soldiers to fire uncontrollably once they began to shoot, led officers to control their men's fire until the enemy was very close, often well within 100 yards, especially in the first years of the war. This practice effectively negated the rifle-musket's range advantage over the smoothbore musket it replaced as the standard infantry arm. Much of the fire delivered by rifle-muskets was well within the effective range of the old-fashioned smoothbore's murderous buck-and-ball load, which, in the hands of the men of the Irish Brigade, was responsible for considerable carnage in Antietam's "Bloody Lane."

Military historian Paddy Griffith analyzed a number of Civil War firefights and found that the distance between opposing forces ranged from an average of 104 yards in 1862 to 141 yards in 1864–1865, with an average for the whole war of 127 yards. These distances were about the same, Griffith notes, as average musketry ranges during the Napoleonic Wars, when the smoothbore reigned supreme and caused horrendous casualties.[9]

Interestingly, the extension of engaged ranges in the last years of the war actually seems to have begun at Gettysburg, the first major battle in which the vast majority of soldiers on both sides carried rifle-muskets. The campaigns of 1862 had been fought with a large percentage of soldiers armed with smoothbore muskets. The more general issue of rifled arms by midwar seems to have provided encouragement to longer-range fire. Still, as late as 1864, some Yankee infantrymen of the Fifth New Jersey Infantry considered firing at the enemy at 200 yards "skirmishing and dueling at long range."[10]

According to Griffith, "decisive" Civil War musketry fights occurred at very close range—an average of thirty-three yards! It should be noted that in these and his other estimations, Griffith had to assume that the distances reported by those involved were accurate. In some cases at least, they were probably shorter or longer. Human recollection often fails, especially among those not trained to accurately estimate distance, which, for the most part, Civil War soldiers were not. In addition, this average includes early war smoothbore engagements, which skews the overall trend.[11]

On at least one occasion, a Federal division commander who had the opportunity to use the rifle-musket's superior range and accuracy to good tactical effect demonstrated an apparent ignorance of the gun's capabilities. At the Battle of Fair Oaks/Seven Pines, on May 31, 1862, the 104th Pennsylvania Infantry engaged a Rebel attacking force at a range of well over 100 yards. The Pennsylvanians, equipped with Austrian Lorenz rifle-muskets, were shooting their smoothbore-armed opponents to ribbons when Brigadier General Silas Casey ordered the 104th and several other regiments to charge the Rebels. As the Yankees came within fifty yards of the enemy, they were subjected to a murderous barrage of buck and ball, which drove them from the field.[12]

If Silas Casey, author of the Union army's standard tactics manual, had no real comprehension of the capabilities of the rifle-musket on the battlefield, then it is understandable that company and field-grade officers were even less enlightened. Then again, there is little evidence that most officers on either side displayed any significant degree of tactical innovation during the war. During the first two years of the conflict, American Civil War commanders, North and South, often ordered their men to hold fire until the enemy was within the old "whites of their eyes" range. Tactics were largely limited to attempting to overlap an enemy's flank. Individual marksmanship was a very low training priority.

By way of contrast, the British army's shooting instruction was organized and codified from the beginning of the official creation of rifle-armed units. In 1805, the British published a manual for their rifle regiments, providing information on the basics of loading, firing, and cleaning the Baker rifle, which was loaded with a patched round ball. The manual also included instruction in marksmanship basics, specifying that a tripod rest be used as a training aid to teach sight alignment. British army riflemen practiced with their Bakers, depending on individual marksmanship qualifications (there were three classes of marks-men) at ranges from ninety to 300 yards. All firing was at wooden tar-gets painted with bull's-eyes and human figures painted on canvas. In addition, unit quartermasters issued silhouettes of men six feet and five feet five inches tall to company commanders to use in training their men in distance estimation.[13]

By the mid-1850s, British soldiers armed with rifle-muskets had to qualify on an annual basis by completing a ninety-round course of fire. Fifty rounds were fired in company formation in the standing and kneeling formation and included volley, file, and individual firing as well as "ten rounds per man advancing and retiring between 400 & 200 yards." The remaining forty rounds of this course were expended in individual firing at ranges up to 900 yards.[14]

The soldiers who used the new rifled arms in the Crimean War received marksmanship training on their way to the Crimea. In March 1854, troops in transit engaged in considerable practice with their Minié rifles at Malta. The Guards fired at a target 250 yards away and "showed some excellent work, a large proportion of the balls going right through the target." Although officers possessed "stadia," or devices that when sighted on an object of known dimensions, indicated distances at 100-yard intervals, soldiers were also instructed in estimat-ing range by observing plainly visible uniform and equipment charac-teristics. A reporter noted that "to give the rifle fair play, the judicious course of training the men as to distances has been fully carried out. The officers of the Guards take out their men to the broken ground by the sea shore, and each captain instructs his company in estimating the distance of men who are sent out in front and placed at intervals."[15]

Even the British, who had developed a formalized doctrine regarding rifle-musket use that included training at range estimation and actual long-distance firing, and had at least some troops who used their guns to the extent of their capabilities in the Crimean War, apparently often failed in the event. One authoritative account noted that conservative officers

insisted on using the improved weapon with the same tactical methods which had been employed with the weapon it had displaced.

Thus, for instance, on the Crimean battlefields our infantry was armed with the long-ranging Enfield rifle, but it was brought into action against the Russians at the short range of the old Brown Bess. The effect on the enemy, who moved in massive columns, was deadly enough, but at the same time we incurred a heavy loss from Russian musketry fire—a loss which might have been considerably reduced if the officers of the day had realized the advantage the new weapon gave them, and had had enough imagination to prepare for the attack at close quarters by heavy rifle fire at medium ranges.[16]

Despite the approach of these officers, the Hythe Musketry School, established in 1853, had growing influence on the increasingly professional British military as the decade of the 1850s progressed. As in many such matters, the British were following the lead of the French reformers, who had been the first to use the new conical projectiles and had already established their own marksmanship institute, the *Ecole de Tir*. Hythe, scene of earlier marksmanship programs with the Baker rifle, is located on the Kent coast, where miles of beaches provided space for ranges allowing study of the effect and accuracy of long-distance small-arms fire. As with the new arms technology, the British expanded their new training regimen far beyond the limited service scope that its French originators had, appropriate in an army in which every soldier was issued a rifled arm.

Officers and men were detailed from their regiments to attend courses at Hythe and then return as instructors to their outfits. Since British regiments operated on the battalion system, with the depot battalion personnel serving as replacement training cadre, recruits were exposed to far more instruction than in the American system, where an infantry recruit was posted almost directly to his tactical unit and received whatever training he would get there, often "on the job."

Long-range rifle-musket work was taken seriously at Hythe, with emphasis on correct trigger pull, or squeeze, range estimation, and various firing positions. Standing or "offhand" was stressed as the most likely combat position, but kneeling, which the soldier could drop into quickly and provided a steadier firing platform, was also strongly emphasized. The British recruit was introduced gradually to his weapon, progressing on a path from dry firing an unloaded gun through snapping percussion caps to live fire. The preferred British army target in the 1850s was a six-by-two-foot cast-iron plate two to three inches thick, although iron frames of the same overall dimensions covered in canvas or other cloth were also used. The target had a centrally located bull's-eye eight inches in diameter. At longer ranges, a number of these targets were linked together to simulate the space occupied by an enemy unit. Soldiers fired at ranges up to 900 yards, when available space permitted.[17]

Unlike the American army, the British regular military establishment came to view its volunteer regiments of part-time soldiers, the British equivalent of America's "organized militia," created in 1859 when war with France seemed in the offing, as a significant potential adjunct in time of war. Rifle enthusiast and Volunteer Lieutenant Hans Busk lobbied energetically for the recognition of volunteer units, writing that "the whole of the rifle drill, together with tolerable proficiency at the target, is usually mastered in a few weeks by recruits of the intelligence of those who swell our ranks." By 1860, cadres from Volunteer regiments were cycling through the regular army marksmanship school at Hythe along with the regulars. Viscount Bury, a Volunteer battalion commander, was ecstatic when given the opportunity to attend a shooting course with some of his officers. According to Bury, the village of Hythe itself had become an appendage of the rifle-shooting movement. It was, he wrote,[18]

> redolent of rifle shooting. All day long either big guns or little guns were thundering or rattling on the shingles. Coles' Musketry Catechism, Field Exercise, Musketry Instruction, Hans Busk's Handbook of Hythe, The Rifle Lock Dissected—such were the titles of the works in the booksellers' shops; cross muskets for lucky first-class shots, belts and cartridge pouches, were in the tailors' windows; shingle boots at the bootmakers'; heel pads for those too stiff to sit in the "Hythe position," in the harness shop. The tradesmen who could not sell anything to do with rifle shooting—you cannot have rifle crockery, for instance—sold photographs of former distinguished pupils at the school.[19]

There was nothing like Hythe in America, and basic marksmanship training was virtually nonexistent in Civil War volunteer armies on both sides during the first two years of the war. The tactics manuals used by American amateur soldiers to train their commands—by Winfield Scott, William J. Hardee, and Casey—paid little attention to shooting other than to describe the method of loading a rifle-musket "by the numbers." All three manuals were largely plagiarized from French originals, with Scott's decidedly oriented to an army carrying smoothbore muskets. Hardee's effort replaced Scott's for evolutions up to and including brigade level in the regular army in the 1850s, but differed largely only in opening up skirmish formations and increasing the speed at which troops performed evolutions. Perhaps the most interesting aspect of Hardee was his assumption that since the battalions and brigades he envisioned would be entirely armed with rifled weapons, any company could be detached to perform as skirmishers without any special training. Although he made some minor deployment changes, including increasing the spacing between formations, Casey's work was essentially a "politically correct" Union version of the work of Hardee, who had become a Confederate general.

While paying lip service to a need to deal with "the revolution which has been wrought within a few years past in the weapons both of artillery and infantry," Casey's shooting instructions were limited to advising the soldier, after he loaded his gun according to the numbers, to "incline the head upon the butt, so that the right eye may perceive quickly the notch of the hausse [rear sight], the front sight and the object aimed at." To be fair, in advocating speed in the offense as a partial remedy to improved arms, Hardee and Casey were in line with the European tacticians from whom they drew their manuals, although they failed to offer case studies from European combat experience that might validate their points.[20]

Examples did exist, however. Although French officers led the way in research and development of the new rifled small arms, conservative French commanders were parsimonious in their issue; as late as 1860, only elite French troops were armed with rifle-muskets. The French and Sardinian war against the Austrians in northern Italy provided the first instance in which troops in the ranks on both sides had rifle-

The Battle of Solferino was fought in Italy on June 24 1859 between an allied French and Sardinian army under Emperor Napoleon III and King Victor Emmanuel II and an Austrian army led by Emperor Franz Joseph. Although both sides suffered heavy casualties, the allied victory was sealed by a bayonet charge, emphasizing the value of vigorous offensive action to counter the increased accuracy of the rifle musket to many observers. (*Library of Congress*)

muskets, although only the Austrians armed all their men with rifled arms. Most of the French infantry still carried smoothbores. Ironically, Austria, a major European power that had armed its men with rifle-muskets, apparently had less of a marksmanship program than the United States had at the time.

The French and Sardinians won the July 24, 1859, battle of Solferino with rapid advances and the steel-tipped bravado of a bayonet charge by elite troops in fine physical condition who were taught to shoot and think—revolutionary concepts for the day. The consensus was that firepower had not made the bayonet charge obsolete. Paddy Griffith notes that "The central fact of the Italian campaign was that charges with the bayonet were able to carry enemy positions more often than not." Although a bayonet charge usually did not result in actual bayonets being crossed at the point of collision, the influence of that story was pervasive enough a news event in both Europe and America to inspire poetic mention by William Cullen Bryant and, along with Magenta, another French victory in the war, a shade of color—Solferino blue to Magenta's red. Solferino also gave a name to eating establishments and saloons as remote from northern Italy as Richmond, Virginia. The victory itself may have overshadowed the fact

of Napoleon III's shock at its ghastly cost, which not only led him to
end French participation in the war with a negotiated peace but provided others with the rationale for establishing the Red Cross, although
that fact often went unnoticed.[21]

Almost 220,000 men were engaged at Solferino on both sides, with
combined casualties of 40,000 killed, wounded, and missing or captured. In numbers engaged and losses, Solferino was certainly comparable to the larger battles of the American Civil War, but it determined
the outcome of a short war, and perhaps gave American soldiers reason
to believe they could replicate its results on this side of the Atlantic a
few years later. Such a thought certainly occurred to an American in
Paris who wrote to the official publication of the New York State
Militia four days after Solferino, waxing eloquent on the decisive mer-
its of cold steel in the wake of the battle.

> Many people supposed that the long range of muskets and rifles
> would do away with the bayonet charge, but what a mistake! Ah!
> This deadly, this devilish weapon, how it has become the king of the
> battles! . . . Gunpowder, crossbows, long bows, rifles, revolvers, and all
> the missiles they can send, are cast into the shade. Hurrah for the
> bayonet![22]

Despite the less romantic judgment of Colonel Carrington regarding the actual use of the bayonet, the military frame of reference of
Civil War commanders was certainly colored by the offensive spirit of
Solferino, and such a perception was not, on the face of it, unreason-
able. The battle proved to many that the effective range advantage of
the rifle-musket could be countered by brisk movement, even by an
army armed largely with smoothbores. That these examples of quick
maneuvering had some validity is evidenced in the victorious Union
attacks at Second Fredericksburg and Rappahannock Station in 1863
and Colonel Emory Upton's successful, if brief, penetration of the Rebel
lines at Spotsylvania on May 10, 1864.

Casey's most useful small-arms employment suggestion, and one in
which he differed from Hardee, was abstracted from the tactical doctrine of the French *Chasseurs* who had proved so effective in the fighting in Italy. He recommended that two companies of every regiment,

"composed of picked men, possessing the highest physical qualifications, marksmen as well" be detailed as permanent skirmishers. Inexplicably, this portion of Casey's book was "suspended" by Secretary of War Edwin M. Stanton when the manual was published, in a reversion to Hardee's idea that any company, presumably in a regiment armed with rifled arms, could serve as skirmishers[23]

The armies of North and South in 1861–1862 were largely armed with smoothbore muskets. There is some indication that despite Stanton's suspension, many Federal regiments with smoothbores were, when possible, provided with enough rifled arms to arm two companies for flank protection and skirmish duties. In practice, equipping one or more companies in an otherwise smoothbore armed infantry regiment with rifles had been common practice since the early years of the century in the American army prior to the general issue of rifle-muskets. Special selection of or training for such men appears to have been rare, however. In 1861, the men of the Seventh Iowa Infantry were advised that "the flank companies, A and B [were] getting the Springfield rifle with tape self primers [Model 1855] and the other eight companies received the improved [either the Model 1842 or an earlier model converted from flintlock to percussion ignition] 'buck and ball' Springfield [smoothbore] musket." In September of 1862, the men of the newly raised Eleventh New Jersey Infantry were issued "a new Austrian rifle for our flank companies and the Springfield smoothbore, buck and ball musket for the eight center companies." The Eleventh's Colonel Robert McAllister, an experienced combat veteran, expressed himself "satisfied with this arrangement." At around the same time the Twelfth Rhode Island and Twelfth New Hampshire Infantry were issued the same combination of Austrian rifle-muskets and domestic smoothbores.[24]

Sometimes a rifle-armed regiment in a brigade otherwise equipped with smoothbore muskets was detailed for flank and skirmish duty. In the case of the famed Irish Brigade, in which four out of five regiments carried smoothbores for a longer time than most Union outfits, the Enfield-armed Twenty-eighth Massachusetts Infantry was detailed to permanent flank guard duties on the march as late as the spring of 1864. Likewise, the Fifth New Jersey Infantry was issued Austrian rifle-muskets in January 1862, while the other three regiments of the

Estimating distances was a vital aspect of training troops in the effective long range use of the rifle-musket. Due to the high trajectory of the projectile, accurate shooting beyond 100 yards was dependent on the shooter knowing the range of his target exactly and adjusting the sights of his weapon to bring it on target at that range. Placing live soldiers at various distances as visual aids was a common method of teaching this skill. (from *Manual of Target Practice* by G. L. Willard, 1862)

Second New Jersey Brigade remained armed with smoothbore muskets until the end of the Peninsula campaign. The weapons of the Fifth assured it would be assigned to skirmishing duty in the brigade's first fight at Williamsburg. In rifle-armed regiments, the selection companies for flank and skirmish duty seems to have occurred largely by happenstance. There is no indication that as in the case of the French *Chasseurs*, or as recommended by Casey, they were composed of physically fit "picked men" trained in the elements of marksmanship.[25]

With little else to go by, Union and Confederate regimental officers—largely military amateurs—buried their noses in Hardee's or Casey's work, learning and teaching drill evolutions, while their men often entered battle blissfully ignorant of the potential of the weapons they carried. The soldiers of the Eighth U.S. Colored Infantry had never even loaded their rifle-muskets with live ammunition before they went into action for the first time at Olustee, Florida, in February 1864. The situation of the recruits of the Thirteenth New Jersey Infantry, who fought at Antietam in 1862 with only the most rudimentary training, was similar. One man from the Thirteenth apparently placed the tompion, a plug intended to keep rainwater out of the barrel on the march, in his Enfield's muzzle after loading it. When he fired his gun for the first time, the brass-tipped muzzle stopper hit another Jerseyman in the back, mortally wounding him. Such a lack of weapons training was not unusual. A veteran of the Thirty-fifth Massachusetts Infantry recalled that "men learned their weapons in battle or by stealth," and the historian of the Forty-fifth Massachusetts Infantry wrote that "strange to say there was no target practice during our whole term so that surely not one in ten of us was a fairly good shot with his weapon." One writer on the subject quipped that "officers obviously lacked enthusiasm for this phase [target practice] of instruction in the art of war."[26]

Historian Bell Irvin Wiley, who examined hundreds of regimental histories for his classic study of the Union soldier, *The Life of Billy Yank*, came to the conclusion that

> One of the most grievous deficiencies of early training—and it persisted to an amazing extent throughout the war—was the lack of target practice. A few regiments did have systematic instruction in musketry, and one commander even had enough imagination to set up replicas of Jeff Davis for his men to shoot at, but references to marksmanship training are notable chiefly for their absence.[27]

As part of its preparations for possible conflict, in January 1861, the state of Virginia issued a sixteen-chapter "Manual of Instruction for Volunteers and Militia," authored by Major William Gilham, a West Point graduate and former commandant of cadets at the Virginia Military Institute. Gilham spent considerable time on drill and ceremonies, but his chapter on target practice had less information than the one describing bugle calls.[28]

Many soldiers apparently felt any lack of skill on their part would be compensated for by the inherent accuracy and power of their rifle-muskets. A Rebel in the Forty-fourth Georgia Infantry noted that his comrades "all seemed proud of their guns [Enfields] and seemed to think that they could knock over a Yankee over half a mile or more." Some of the Yankees were at least as optimistic. One marginally literate New Jersey soldier believed his Springfield would hit "secesh [at] 800 yards" and "kill stone ded through a stone six fot thick. And I can load it in the Twinck of an eie." An over-optimistic New Hampshire man, after reporting that his unit hit a target "the size of old Jeff" with 360 rounds at the unlikely range of 600 yards, noted, in an even more unlikely statement, that his Springfield "will range 1500 yards with considerable certainty."[29]

In some cases, prewar marksmanship training received by Yankee soldiers in foreign armies was put to good use. Although Brigadier General Thomas F. Meagher of the Irish Brigade was firmly wedded to the concept of a blast of buck and ball from smoothbore muskets followed by a rush with the bayonet, some of his men were not quite convinced. Many Irish soldiers in Meagher's ranks were combat veterans of the British army's wars in the Crimea and India and had been exposed to the Hythe system. When their brigade came under a heavy enemy skirmish fire while advancing at Antietam, some Irishmen "surreptitiously exchanged their muskets" for rifle-muskets and successfully sniped at opposing Rebel skirmishers.[30]

Suffice to say, the Irish skirmishers' success was not due to any instruction they received on this side of the Atlantic. Long after soldiers had mastered the intricacies of drill and even engaged in combat, Union army target practice was largely limited to occasional informal shooting matches. The historian of the Eleventh Rhode Island Infantry, armed with Enfields, reported that "target practice, by the various companies, went on for some time," and "five men put eleven out of fifteen shots into the target," the size of which, and distance shot at, went unspecified. In January 1862, a soldier in the Twenty-second Massachusetts Infantry wrote the homefolks that his friend "Cotton . . . . is the best shot in the company. We had a target shoot and he made the best shot; and if you believe me, I did the next at 150 yds. distant. We have the Enfield rifle; they kill at 1,000 yards."[31]

At another contest, following Washington's birthday celebrations in 1862, "after the regiments had been dismissed, they amused themselves in various ways. While daylight lasted, target shooting and numerous other outdoor sports were indulged in." At yet another match held among Union troops on duty at Newport News, Virginia, in November of 1863, "a shooting match took place with rifles, at two hundred yards distance, and with revolvers at thirty yards."

Interestingly, although men from the Ninth New Jersey, a regiment known for its marksmen, participated, the winner of both matches was "the chief bugler of [Captain James] Belger's Rhode Island Battery [F]." It is safe to assume that the bugler acquired his skill with the rifle and handgun in civilian life.[32]

Inattention to the rudiments of shooting was not universal. Although it was not an armywide practice, some Army of the Potomac regiments engaged in organized marksmanship programs prior to the 1863 campaign season. At the end of January 1863, the Twenty-first New York Infantry, just issued Springfield rifle-muskets to replace their old smoothbore muskets, began target shooting "almost daily." According to the regimental historian, "in their desire to outdo each other the men rapidly became good marksmen, which they were not likely to do with the old smoothbore pieces." The firing was at "one to five hundred yards," the latter being the longest range the 1861 Model Springfield sights were calibrated for. The Twenty-first's marksmanship program was initiated in response to an order instructing regimental commanders in their brigade to "pick out the best shots for sharpshooters" with the aim of creating a special unit intended for skirmishing duty. In the event, however, "the detail was never made, and when we finally took the field, the flank companies usually acted as skirmishers." Interestingly, the Twenty-first, which had been mustered out of service by Gettysburg, served in Brigadier General Marsena Patrick's Provost Guard Brigade, which filled a military police rather than infantry function.[33]

On March 12, 1863, the 121st New York Infantry, a regiment raised in the late summer of 1862, went "out today for the first time at target shooting" with their Enfield rifle-muskets. Sergeant John F. L. Hartwell reported that "owing to the wind we shot only three round apeace [sic] a 100 yards off at a bulls eye two feet in diameter. I put two balls inside the circle. 22 shots out of 90 hit the target 11 inside of the circle." On subsequent days, the 121st shot at increasingly longer range, firing at 150 yards on March 17, 200 yards on March 18, and 250 yards on March 19. A company commander noted that "Each man fired three rounds. It is quite [a] sport for the men." That same month, the soldiers of the Fifteenth New Jersey, another VI Corps unit, also engaged in the first target practice since they had enlisted the previous summer, firing a number of shots at predetermined distances. At best, this type of drill, although better than nothing, failed to teach range estimation (save by accident) or aiming and shooting techniques. Such training is properly called "familiarization firing."[34]

The Army of the Potomac's inconsistent pre-Gettysburg firearms training program did not prevent a number of armywide small-arms problems during the battle. Based on postcombat salvage figures, Paddy Griffith estimates that at Gettysburg "perhaps 9 per cent of all muskets [Union and Confederate] were misloaded." An April 19, 1864, circular order from Army of the Potomac headquarters instructed officers to "familiarize the men in the use of their arms." The order authorized "an additional expenditure of 10 rounds of small arms ammunition per man" and stressed that "every man should be made to load and fire his musket under the personal supervision of a company officer." The instructions were based on the belated discovery that "there are men in this Army who have been in numerous actions without ever firing their guns and it is known that muskets taken on the [Gettysburg] battle field have been found filled to the muzzle with cartridges." It was apparently more important that men learn how to load their guns than hit what they aimed at with them, however.[35]

Available evidence suggests that even when senior officers became dimly aware of its value, target practice throughout the Union army was haphazard and lacked preliminary basic marksmanship instruction. Sophisticated concepts like proper sight alignment and adjustment and range and trajectory estimation seem beyond the comprehension of most junior officers on both sides outside of a few special sharpshooter outfits. Even officers aware of the need for an important skill like range estimation had little faith that the average soldier could comprehend it. Colonel George L. Willard of the 125th New York Infantry fretted at the possibility of a "soldier's mind . . . perpetually occupied in guessing at distances." Willard, generally regarded as a die-hard proponent of the obsolete smoothbore musket, did actually recognize the potential value of the rifle-musket in the hands of men trained to use it—"thoroughly instructed 'light troops or skirmishers.'" However, he believed (quite correctly) that "in this character of soldiers, our army is certainly deficient." Willard made no assumptions as to whose fault that was or how it could be remedied.[36]

The deficiency was real but not innate, and the blame lay largely in the hands of the leadership of the army, rather than its "deficient" soldiers. The groundwork had been laid, but in the rush to war, ignored. Regular army marksmanship training had been erratic until the mid-1850s. The need for such training was evident, however, as early as the Jamestown settlement of 1607, when "a mark at which each soldier would twice fire his weapon was set up within the court of guard, the first time at the beginning of his watch and the second at the end of it." Commanders in colonial Virginia were admonished to allow Indians to see only "your best marksmen shoot, for if they see your learners miss what they aim at, they will think the weapon not so terrible, and thereby will be bold to assault you."[37]

Although some fired rifle balls (along with smoothbore musket balls) have been found at a Valley Forge archeological site, indicating that target practice may have been part of a training agenda, it appears that Revolutionary War riflemen were generally assumed to bring marksmanship skills to the service with them. In 1813, Colonel William Duane, former commander of the United States Rifle Regiment, tried to sell his *Handbook for Riflemen*, which one can assume had some mention of marksmanship training, to the Federal and various state governments without success. Absent a manual, training may well have been ad hoc and improvised. The historian of the Rifle Regiment reports that "it could not be ascertained . . . as to which system War of 1812 riflemen were drilled."[38]

In 1856, the newly formed Tenth United States Infantry Regiment put its men through a relatively thorough fifty-shot familiarization course of fire with their arms (probably Model 1841 rifles resighted for the Minié ball projectile) at ranges up to 700 yards. This contrasts with the Sixth Infantry Regiment's program in the same period, in which targets were shot at eighty and 150 yards, without very many hits. Colonel Joseph Mansfield, later a Union corps commander, reported that only about a third of the rounds fired at 100 yards by another unit at a target eight feet tall and eighteen inches wide hit it. Incredibly, Mansfield noted that some companies conducted this exercise using blank ammunition![39]

By 1857, as the Hythe movement caught on in England, it became abundantly clear to the most casual observer that American army marksmanship was deplorable. In an attempt to remedy the deficiency, Captain Henry Heth (The same Henry Heth who would, six years later, lead his Confederate infantry division against Buford's Yankee horsemen at Gettysburg.) of the Tenth Infantry, who had served on a board testing breechloading rifles, was assigned to come up with a comprehensive shooting instruction program. Heth complied and produced his training regimen in March 1858.[40]

Heth's manual was comprehensive and would not be out of place as a modern guideline to shooting instruction. In a plan cobbled together from European sources and his own ideas, he began with the basics, recommending that soldiers be introduced to their firearms and taught how to disassemble and reassemble them as well as practice correct sight alignment, trigger control, and simulated firing before going to the range. Heth emphasized distance estimation, using live soldiers placed at different distances as training markers. The program culminated in live-fire exercises at ranges from 150 to 1,000 yards, although actual qualification firing was limited to a range of 400 yards. As a method of recognition intended to attract interest and improve morale, he created designated classes of marksmen, their rank based on qualifying scores. Shooting prizes were awarded from company level on up, with prizes of a brass or silver visual rangefinder "stadia" worn as both a badge and practical shooting aid. Unlike the British plan, which established a permanent school to train cadres, Heth's method depended on the enthusiasm and participation of individual unit commanders, which varied considerably. Marksmanship training was often ignored in units fragmented on various frontier assignments, but there is some indication that his efforts resulted in an increase in regular army small-arms proficiency prior to the Civil War.[41]

Another prewar marksmanship advocate was First Lieutenant Cadmus Wilcox, also a future Confederate commander at Gettysburg. While on convalescent leave in Europe in late 1857, Wilcox spent a good deal of time in France observing the marksmanship program developed at Vincennes, the home of the *Ecole de Tir*, and studying French small arms, ammunition, and tactical innovation. He was also

Confederate Generals Henry Heth (left) and Cadmus Wilcox (right), both commanders at Gettysburg, were also the authors of pre-war marksmanship manuals. Their actions at Gettysburg do not, however, reflect any particular attention to the problems of marksmanship in their respective commands. (*Library of Congress*)

very impressed by the British musketry school at Hythe. On his return to the United States, Wilcox summarized his conclusions in a book: *Rifles and Rifle Practice: An Elementary Treatise upon the Theory of Rifle Firing, Explaining the Causes of Inaccuracy of Fire and the Manner of Correcting It.*[42]

Much of his work was a translation from French sources, describing basic rifle-musket marksmanship techniques and the effectiveness of long-range rifle fire on heavy columns as exemplified by the British use of Minié rifles against Russians in the Crimea. Wilcox advocated troop dispersion as a necessity in the age of the rifle-musket and suggested that soldiers should receive some basic individual training in marksmanship before joining their units. Although the War Department published a thousand copies of Wilcox's book, there is no evidence it had a significant influence on troop training until the spring of 1864, when it was adopted as a manual by the brigade sharpshooter battalions created in the Army of Northern Virginia.[43]

Any progress that had been made, real and theoretical, toward establishing a successful marksmanship program in the prewar United States army was obliterated by the massive infusion of volunteers of 1861. By 1862, the War Department publicly admitted that "the inaccuracy of the soldiers of our army in firing has been a matter of surprise and regret to many officers." In response the department published *A System of Target Practice for the Use of Troops When Armed with the Musket, Rifle Musket, Rifle or Carbine, Prepared Principally from the French*. This pamphlet, which included chapters on aiming, trigger control, and range estimation, was a composite of the ideas Heth and Wilcox had taken from European sources. In the event, there is little evidence the manual was put to use. As in the case of the April 1864 order from the Army of the Potomac's headquarters, target shooting in the Army of the Potomac continued to be viewed mainly as familiarization firing.[44]

Colonel Willard produced his own rifle-musket marksmanship manual in February 1862. Willard, a major at the time, combined the basics of disassembling and cleaning the rifle-musket provided in a government pamphlet with the translated French marksmanship basics described in *A System of Target Practice* and his own observations on the subject. The latter included some interesting statistics on shots fired to hits incurred in various pre–Civil War battles in the smoothbore era. Willard claimed that at the 1813 battle of Victoria in Spain, British troops fired 800 balls to record one of the enemy "touched." According to Willard, the Americans did better in the Mexican War, with one hit for every 125 rounds fired at Cherubusco in 1847. The French fared the worst in Willard's accounting, as their soldiers in the Crimea, who used both smoothbore and rifled arms, "are said to have used 25,000,000 cartridges, to disable 25,000 Russians—one ball in 1000 hit." To be fair, there is no real statistical norm for any of these figures, and they are, at best, guestimates.[45]

At least some senior officers were aware of the necessity of marksmanship programs early in the war, even though they did not get around to implementing them. Brigadier General Erasmus Keyes, an Army of the Potomac division commander who had no doubt read and implemented Heth and Wilcox before the war, testified to this before Congress in January 1862.

> I think the efficiency of the regiments in my command would be doubled if I could instruct them for six weeks in the use of their small

arms. I would wish them all to have the proper arms first [most were then armed with smoothbore muskets], and then instruct them. I once put a regiment in order that way, after they had been thoroughly drilled, in six weeks. But I instructed them six hours a day. I taught them to estimate distances and had them fire every day. In that way they had very great facility. I find the good of teaching the men, in that way, the use of these long range guns with elevated sights, for long distances.[46]

Later in the war, the idea that soldiers should know how to shoot began to take hold across the North even among the militia. Henry Lee, Jr., a writer on militia reform, quoted the veteran British officer Sir Charles Napier, who noted "let the target practice be constant" and "subscribe for premiums to those who are the best shots." Lee also approvingly cited Louis Napoleon's comment on the Swiss military system that "the object would be to train them [the infantry] as sharp-shooters." This movement, which had its origins in the failure of marksmanship in the Civil War, culminated in the formation of the National Rifle Association in 1871 and subsequent emphasis upon long-range target shooting that became such an important feature in the National Guard training schedule for the rest of the century.[47]

A notable exception to the general rule of indifferent marksmanship training in American Civil War armies was the case of Major General Patrick Cleburne's command in the Confederate Army of Tennessee. Cleburne, an Irish-born veteran of enlisted service in the British army, was well aware of the Hythe musketry school and its course of instruction. The general used men armed with rifle-muskets effectively as early as the April 1862 battle of Shiloh, when he called for volunteer sharpshooters to pick off Yankee artillerymen supporting Brigadier General Benjamin Prentiss' position in the "Hornet's Nest." Following that fight, Cleburne personally visited each regiment in his brigade to select men who were good shots and formally organized them into a company of sharpshooters. By early 1863, Cleburne had acquired a copy of the British *Regulations for Conducting Musketry Instruction in the Army*, published by the instructors at Hythe, and began to train his men in such concepts as range estimation using the British cadre system. Years later, a veteran of the Army of Tennessee correctly reflected that "the secret of marksmanship is not in the practice alone, but in the perception and education as to distance . . . . It takes judgement from position and experience as to the inflection and deflection of a ball from the force that propels it, to perfect one in this science." However, as with the Army of the Potomac, there was no such training on a large scale in either the Army of Tennessee or the Army of Northern Virginia.[48]

Considering the presence of Henry Heth and Cadmus Wilcox, it is perhaps surprising that there seems to have been no comprehensive marksmanship program in the Confederate army as a whole or the Army of Northern Virginia in particular. One reason for this seeming indifference may be that prior to the battle of Chancellorsville, there were far more smoothbore muskets than rifles or rifle-muskets in the ranks of Southern forces. In early 1862, General Robert E. Lee, concerned about the serious lack of such arms in the Confederate army, advocated that they be distributed "to the flanking companies at least" of experienced regiments. Lee believed that "fine rifles [imported Enfields] will be more efficient in the hands of tried troops."[49]

In an attempt to counter Yankee sharpshooters taking potshots at his men in the Williamsburg lines in the spring of 1862, Major General John Magruder decided to form a special counter-sniper unit. Out of the twelve regiments, approximately 120 companies, in his command, he was, however, only able to come up with four companies armed with rifles. Likewise, Colonel Archibald Gracie, tasked with training and employing a five-company "Special Battalion" for skirmishing duty and flank protection in April 1862, had to make do with men armed with smoothbores. The brigade from which he drew his companies was commanded by none other than Brigadier General Cadmus Wilcox.[50]

A dearth of rifle-muskets in the ranks could also very well explain, along with the inexperience of officers, the lack of interest in marksmanship in Union ranks early in the war, and General Keyes's testimony supports such a view. For soldiers armed with smoothbore muskets, as most were in the first year of the war, occasional familiarization firing at an old barrel could be deemed sufficient. There was also a mythology at work on both sides regarding the existence of a natural skill with the rifle, particularly of Southern troops, that did not require formal military training for effectiveness. One Federal officer maintained that Confederate armies were "composed mainly of men who had been trained to the skillful use of the rifle in that most perfect school, the field and forest." What he neglected to realize is that ability with one's short-range squirrel gun while a civilian was not necessarily a guarantee of marksmanship skills in a military venue, as some might assume. While the attributes of sight alignment, breath control, and trigger squeeze are indeed comparable skills in both hunting and war, most squirrels are shot at twenty-five yards or less, requiring no precise range estimation—and they don't shoot back.[51]

In May 1862, the Confederate Congress passed legislation calling for a sharpshooter battalion of from three to six companies, "armed with long range muskets or rifles" in every brigade in the army, as a way to use the limited long-range firepower available. Selection, organization, and training were left up to local commanders. A long season of fighting and marching from the Peninsula to Second Manassas, Antietam, and Fredericksburg further delayed any sort of effective implementation in the Army of Northern Virginia as well as in the west. It was not until late December 1862 that Brigadier General Robert E. Rodes assigned Major Eugene Blackford of the Fifth Alabama Infantry to organize and train a battalion of "trained skirmishers" for his brigade.[52]

Unlike the similar project the Twenty-first New York was involved in at around the same time that died aborning, the Rodes/Blackford Confederate version succeeded. Blackford was an enthusiastic and competent officer interested in good shooting. Arming himself with a Sharps breechloader, he selected "the Springfield long range rifle" to arm his battalion. He may have been referring to the early pattern Model 1855, with its sight adjustable to 900 yards or so, as opposed to the later Model 1855 and Model 1861 production, only sighted to 500 yards, or possibly the shorter barreled Model 1855 rifle, with its stiffer barrel and potential for more accurate shooting, although this was a Harper's Ferry product. The major trained his men to respond to bugle calls on the skirmish line, an essential control feature for a dispersed command. He also stressed elementary marksmanship techniques and, most important with the rifle-musket, range estimation and actual firing at targets at ranges up to 800 yards, at which distance his men achieved a thirty percent hit ratio—shooting offhand! With training and practice, Blackford noted, the skill his sharpshooters achieved was "wonderful."[53]

And so the rifle-musket-armed line infantry units of both sides who marched down the web of roads toward Gettysburg that July 1 had a mix of men in the ranks displaying a wide variety of training, familiarization, and skill with the small arms they carried. As shooters, soldiers on both sides ranged from Hythe taught Irishmen to New Yorkers and Jerseymen who had some sort of idea where their bullets landed at ranges out to several hundred yards to the proficient long-range marksmen of Eugene Blackford's Alabama sharpshooter battalion. They would all soon have a chance to exercise their skills, to a greater or lesser degree, on each other across the fields and farmlands and through the village streets of the small Pennsylvania town their respective armies were rapidly closing on.

Chapter 4

THE RIFLE-MUSKET, PART III

THERE WERE SOME FORMER SMOOTHBORE .69 caliber rifled muskets in the ranks at Gettysburg, but the majority of infantry small arms on the field were purpose-built rifled arms in .54 (U.S. Model 1841 and Austrian Lorenz), .577 (Enfields), or .58 (Springfields, Enfields, and Lorenzes bored for the American market) calibers. In his in-depth study of the types and amount of ammunition used by both sides in the battle, Dean Thomas concluded that "about two thirds" of the Union infantrymen at Gettysburg were armed with Enfields or Springfields. The most common bullet design loaded into the paper rifle-musket cartridges for both of these arms—as well as the .54 caliber U.S. Model 1841 rifles, .54 and .58 caliber Lorenzes, and .69 caliber rifled guns— was the variant of the Minié projectile designed by James H. Burton at Harper's Ferry Armory in the mid-1850s.[1]

Reports on actual ammunition availability and usage at Gettysburg are sketchy. Employing available information, however, Thomas interpolates that a sixty-round-per-man issue prior to the battle meant that "theoretically . . . the [72,000] Union infantry were marching to Gettysburg with 4,320,000 rounds of ammunition." When combat was imminent, the forty-round capacity of the standard infantry cartridge box was usually supplemented with an additional twenty-round issue. This extra ammunition, in ten-round packages, was carried wherever it could be crammed: in knapsacks, haversacks, and pockets. There is strong suspicion, however, that much of it, an extra weight burden on

the march, may have simply been thrown away at the earliest convenient moment. The Union Burton/Minié ball weighed approximately
500 grains, or a little more than an ounce, with powder and paper
adding a bit more. Sixty rounds would add around five pounds to the
soldier's burden. Thomas calculates "another eighty to ninety rounds
per man" carried in the Army of the Potomac's ammunition wagons,
for a total of more than 11,000,000 cartridges on hand for the action.
How many of these were actually "expended" by firing them is
unknowable. Thomas' educated estimate of about seventy-five rounds
per man total expenditure, including ammunition fired, captured, accidentally dropped, or simply tossed in the bushes, is about as accurate a
number as we are ever likely to have.[2]

Conversely, in a postwar analysis of Rebel cartridge consumption,
Confederate ordnance chief Josiah Gorgas wrote that by Gettysburg
the usual supply, including that carried by soldiers and in the ammunition train reserve, amounted to a total of "about eighty or ninety
rounds" per man. Gorgas' estimate, when compared with that of
Thomas, indicates that the Union infantryman at Gettysburg had
access to about a third more rifle-musket cartridges than did his
Confederate counterpart. Gorgas recalled that "at Gettysburg the
reports of a few days before the battle and a short time after showed a
difference of twenty-five or twenty-six rounds on the average," significantly lower than Thomas' expenditure estimate of seventy-five
rounds per man for Federal forces. In the event, however, ammunition
supply was not responsible for the battle's outcome.[3]

Neither estimate accounts for the actual disposition of cartridges
"expended" by firing or, for that matter, who expended them. Some
soldiers did not even get into the fight, while others shot away all their
ammunition and looted the cartridge boxes of dead and wounded comrades and enemies for additional supplies. Yankees who tossed away
ammunition as excess baggage often had cause to regret it. Union
forces, acting in a defensive mode in most engagements over the three
days at Gettysburg, were more likely to use more cartridges than the
Confederates, who were usually on the offensive. Confederates (as well
as Union troops) did often fire on the move, but it is a more difficult
task to load and fire a muzzleloader while advancing, thus slowing the
rate of fire somewhat.

The Springfield Model 1861 .58 caliber rifle-musket. Springfield Armory and various private contractors supplied almost a million and a half of these guns to the Federal army between 1861 and 1865. The Model 1861 was the most common small arm in Union ranks at Gettysburg. (*National Park Service*)

In addition to shooting less at some phases of the battle, Confederates drove the Federals from a number of positions on July 1 and 2 and had access to any ammunition remaining on the Union dead and wounded as well as captured from prisoners. Lieutenant Colonel Baldwin stated that at Chancellorsville, "the army generally helped themselves from the cartridge-boxes of the enemy," and there is reason to assume this conduct continued at Gettysburg. This was certainly the case with Rebel sharpshooters deployed in the town of Gettysburg itself on July 2 and 3, who fired hundreds of rounds per man from static positions and rummaged through bodies and dropped equipment in the streets to replenish their ammunition supplies. Shooting up scrounged cartridges would have lessened demand on the Rebel supply train and given the appearance that less ammunition was consumed than was the actual case.[4]

There is no doubt some Union units in defensive postures did a lot of firing. On assuming command of Brigadier General Strong Vincent's V Corps brigade following the general's mortal wounding on Little Round Top on July 2, Colonel James C. Rice was immediately advised by his subordinate commanders that their men were out of ammunition. Rice recalled that he "immediately pressed into service every officer and man in the rear not engaged in the action, whether known or unknown, and made them pledge their honor that they would deliver in person every order that I should send by them. I sent four of them, one after another, with orders for ammunition. The ammunition came promptly, was distributed at once, and the fight went on."[5]

Even promptly delivered, ammunition was on occasion problematic. Bullet diameter for the .580-bore Springfield at the outbreak of the war was a nominal .5775, which, early on, necessitated a smaller diameter bullet in cartridges intended for imported Enfields, many of which, especially early in on the war, were of .577-bore diameter. In July 1861, General Ripley requested that Watervliet Arsenal begin loading Enfield specific ammunition with .574-diameter bullets. In January 1862, the standard bullet diameter for all nominal .58 or .577 caliber ammunition was reduced to .574 so it could be used interchangeably in Enfields and Springfields as well as Austrian Lorenz rifles in .58 caliber.[6]

The standard production method for Union Minié balls was swaging, in which lead slugs were pressed into proper form by a large machine (although some bullets were cast in molds) and then forced through a sizing die, or swage. Bullets, both pressed and cast, were made at U.S. arsenals and purchased from at least eighteen different contractors. As such, they often varied to some degree from officially specified weight and diameter. There were similar problems with Confederate ammunition.[7]

After forming, bullets were lubricated with a beeswax/tallow mix and then wrapped into cartridges. The rifle-musket cartridge was composed of a separate paper cylinder filled with a measured powder charge, with the bullet placed on top of it, and the whole wrapped in a second piece of paper. To load his rifle-musket, a soldier bit off the tail end of a paper cartridge with his teeth, poured the powder down the barrel, separated the remaining paper by striking the empty cartridge tube across the gun's muzzle, inserted the naked lubricated bullet, and rammed it down atop the powder charge before priming the nipple with a percussion cap.

Although the larger bullet diameter cartridges should have been out of service by the spring of 1863, there were still complaints from the Army of the Potomac about the poor fit of issue ammunition. Colonel Penrose's post-Chancellorsville annoyance regarding his men's difficulties ramming bullets after a few rounds that he attributed to "imperfections in the grooving" of their Enfields may have been attributable to old stocks of the .5775 ammunition coupled with a buildup of powder fouling that interfered with loading some more tightly bored Enfields after a few shots, but, just as likely, it was the result of being issued cartridges with oversized bullets supplied by a contractor that slipped through the inspection process.[8]

Similar complaints surfaced after Gettysburg. Lieutenant Jonathan R. Edie, acting Chief Ordnance Officer of the Army of the Potomac, reported to then–Chief of Ordnance Ramsay in October 1863 that he had conducted a series of tests as a result of assertions of poor ammunition quality at the battle. Colonel Rice had complained to the Ordnance Department that during the Little Round Top fight, his men's "ammunition fouled the guns [a mix of Springfields and Enfields] to such a degree that not more than twenty-five shots could be fired without cleaning or changing them [the guns]." Rice had not mentioned this problem in his July 31 after-action report, and it is not clear whether he was speaking of his own regiment or the entire brigade he assumed command of when General Vincent was wounded. In his own Gettysburg report, Colonel Joshua Chamberlain of the Twentieth Maine, one of Rice's regiments, complained that his men's Enfields "did not stand service well" but did not otherwise elaborate. Other officers argued that the ammunition issued their men had a "want of force in the powder equal to that used by the enemy" at Gettysburg. The general consensus, according to Edie, was that "the Rebels had better ammunition than furnished them."[9]

To investigate the complaints, Edie selected a six-man firing party armed with Springfield rifle-muskets and issued them ammunition manufactured at Watervliet, Watertown, and Frankford Arsenals randomly selected from the army's ammunition train. Despite the order to cease manufacture of .5775-diameter Minié balls in favor of .574 bullets the previous year, Edie described the Frankford bullets as .577 and those from the other two arsenals as .57 in diameter, although it is probable that he trusted the information written on the ammunition box rather than subjecting individual bullets to a micrometer test. The lieutenant conducted firing tests at 100 and 200 yards, using a target made by "covering a four inch plank of red pine, which was very hard and tough, with a white pine board one inch in thickness." Edie noted that at 100 yards, the .57-caliber bullets penetrated the board and "two to two and a half inches" of the plank, but "fell short" of the target at 200 yards, while the .577 bullets drove completely through board and plank at 200 yards.[10]

Edie's testing crew fired several captured Confederate cartridges as well. His conclusion was that the Rebel ammunition, although it failed

to hit the 200-yard target, was loaded with a powder that was more regular in grain and better glazed and that he thought the bullets were
"thrown with greater force than our own." In an attempt to discover
the cause of the loading problem, Edie had one musket fired twenty-
nine times without cleaning but experienced no difficulties. It should be
noted that his test guns were Springfields, not the Enfields that seem
to have been the source of loading complaints. Edie's overall conclusion
was that a combination of sloppy powder measuring during manufacture, smaller-than-needed bullet diameters, and soldiers loading cartridge paper with their bullets instead of discarding it was at the root of
the multiple problems of inaccuracy, "want of force," and difficult loading. The lack of Enfields in his test arms selection, however, must cast
some doubt on the total validity of his experiments, and his assertion
regarding loading cartridge paper along with bullets is pure specula-
tion. As a result of Edie's and other investigations, however, the powder
charge in musket cartridges was raised from 60 to 65 grains in 1864.[11]

The Confederate cartridges referred to as superior to Federal issue in
the complaints and fired by Edie's test team were no doubt loaded with
Gardner bullets and powder probably made at the powder mill run by
Colonel George C. Rains at Augusta, Georgia—a plant constructed to
the standards of the best English powder mill, Waltham Abbey. The
Gardner bullet, patented by North Carolinian Frederick J. Gardner in
1861, was of the general Burton/Minié type, but with a split base making it appear, when initially cast, as if it had a wing or lip of sorts sticking out around its circumference near the base. The cartridge paper was
attached to the base by inserting it between the lip and side of the bullet
and then compressing the lip to the bullet to hold the paper in place.
The cartridge was then inverted to receive the powder charge and
twisted shut at the base. When a fired Gardner bullet is viewed from
the base, the two layers of lead the paper was compressed between
make it appear that a smaller bullet has been inserted inside the base of
a larger one. Gardner cartridges, with their bullets in plain view, unlike
the paper-shrouded bullets in other cartridges, were (and are) easily
identified, and the two lubrication grooves and thick base band makes
the Gardner bullet instantly recognizable.[12]

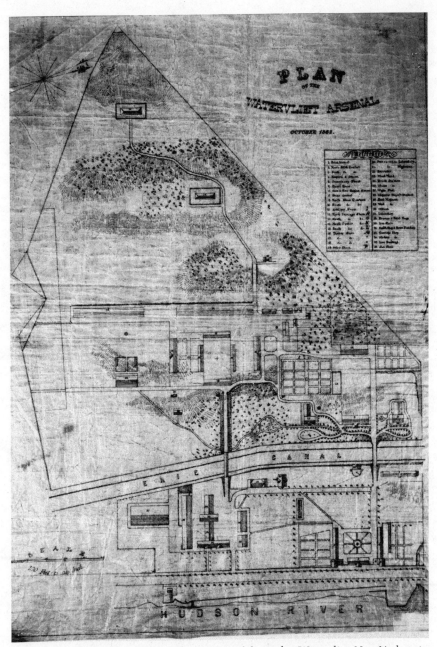

Watervliet Arsenal. Founded in 1813, the arsenal, located at Watervliet, New York, near Albany is still a functioning military facility. During the Civil War it produced millions of rifle musket and other cartridges. (*Library of Congress*)

The Gardner bullet, patented by North Carolinian Frederick J. Gardner in 1861, was of the general Burton/Minié type, but with a split base making it appear, when initially cast, as if it had a wing or lip of sorts sticking out around its circumference near the base. The cartridge paper was attached to the base by inserting it between the lip and side of the bullet and then compressing the lip to the bullet. The cartridge was then inverted to receive the powder charge, and twisted shut at the base. Gardner cartridges, with their bullets in plain view, unlike the paper-shrouded bullets in other cartridges, are easily identified, and the two lubrication grooves and thick base band makes the Gardner bullet instantly recognizable. (*Bill Adams*)

The Gardner design was a unique and effective way of making a cartridge and probably reduced loading time slightly. The Confederates also imported large numbers of high-quality paper-patched Enfield bullets and loaded cartridges from England, and a number of distinctive Enfield Pritchett bullets have been found at Gettysburg. Many English cartridges, however, were apparently "overhauled," or disassembled and reassembled, at Southern arsenals as rounds shorter in length to better fit existing cartridge boxes.[13]

Despite the Augusta Powder Mill's excellence, however, all was not perfect in the world of Confederate ordnance. Although Josiah Gorgas' order of June 9, 1862, was intended to standardize all Confederate manufactured ammunition to the proper bullet size for the .577 Enfield, one Rebel ordnance officer reported after the September 1863 battle of Chickamauga that "caliber No. 57 was loose and never choked the guns, while the No. .58 after the first few rounds, was found too large, and frequently choking the guns to that extent that they could not be forced down, thereby creating some uneasiness among the men using that number of ammunition."[14]

Some Southern-made cartridges were over bore size for either caliber. This situation, which, as we have seen, existed in the more industrialized Union, also surfaced time and again in the Confederacy, largely due to improper gauges and poor production control. Oversized ammunition became such a problem that at one point, a Rebel ordnance

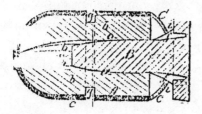

The Williams bullet (left), with a zinc washer attached to its base, was intended to scour fouling from the bore when fired. The Wilkinson bullet (right), unlike the Minie style hollow base slug, was intended to expand to fit the gun's bore by obturation on firing.

officer reported that a general in the Army of Northern Virginia informed him that "the men have repeatedly sought Miss.[issippi] rifle ammunition (cal. .54) for their Enfield rifles and rifled muskets (cal. .577 and .58)."[15]

Numerous minor variants of the standard Union "three-ring" Burton/Minié bullet and the "two-ring" Confederate Gardner were the most common rifle-musket bullets fired at Gettysburg. A variety of other rifle-musket projectiles have been discovered on the battleground in much smaller numbers, among them the odd three-part Shaler bullets in Union positions and .54 caliber Wilkinson-style solid-base, deep-groove expanding bullets, probably designed for the Austrian Lorenz, on the Rebel side.[16]

Probably the most common Gettysburg relic bullet aside from the Union Minié and Confederate Gardner is the Williams "cleaner" bullet. The 1861 invention of Elijah D. Williams, the bullet, made in two variations, had a solid base with a zinc washer attached. On firing, the washer would flatten, stabilizing the bullet and also serving to scour powder fouling from previous shots out of the barrel grooves as it exited.

Williams' design was highly touted by his agent, the entrepreneur Cyrus W. Field of Atlantic Cable fame, and was tested several times in the summer of 1861 with mixed results. Some officers saw no appreciable advantage for the Williams over the standard service bullet, while others believed the Williams to be considerably more accurate than the Burton/Minié. To resolve the matter, the Williams was tested in December 1861 by Springfield Armory's Master Armorer Erskine

Allin, who concluded that it did prove significantly more accurate than the issue bullet and "evidently keeps that part of the barrel through which it passes free from foul and lead."[17]

Williams and Field angled to get their projectile declared the official bullet for all U.S.–made .58 caliber cartridges, which would have generated considerable royalties without the responsibility of production, but instead they were granted contracts to furnish a number of manufactured bullets to be loaded into cartridges at various Federal arsenals. Williams continued to work on his invention and made improvements in its basic design in 1862. This Type II projectile featured a tapered base cavity with a corresponding pin that passed through the zinc disc and into the cavity. On firing, the pin drove forward into the cavity, expanding the washer by pulling it flush with the bullet base. Starting in November 1862, two cartridges loaded with Williams bullets were included in each package of ten musket cartridges issued. In April 1863, the number was raised to three, and it was officially noted that they were "not only more accurate in flight but keep the bore of a fire arm freer of dirt than any other."[18]

By the middle of 1864, the recommended proportion of Williams cartridges to standard ones had risen to six in ten. Following the unexpected death of Williams himself in May 1864, however, the quality and accuracy of the bullets produced by his company dramatically declined, leading to a halt in Federal purchase and issue by September of that year. It is safe to assume, however, that from twenty to thirty percent of all .58 caliber cartridges fired by Union soldiers at Gettysburg were loaded with Williams bullets.[19]

Some Southerners, on first examining Williams slugs, came to the conclusion that they were "a poisoned contrivance of the enemy." A more rational Rebel figured them out, however, and in 1864, he assured the readers of the Augusta, Georgia, *Daily Constitutionalist* that the Williams, an "excellent invention," was merely a "cleaner." Correctly describing the construction and purpose of the bullet, the writer reported that in the Army of Northern Virginia, Williams rounds were "eagerly sought after by our men when they get hold of captured ammunition." He did, however, concede that while use of the bullets kept a gun clean, "as accuracy of shooting is concerned, they are useless, as they fly exceedingly wild." This assessment accurately reflects the Yankee conclusion on the Williams bullet produced in 1864.[20]

Another odd, and to many, much more sinister, projectile used by Union forces at Gettysburg was the "musket shell," designed by New Yorker Samuel Gardiner, which had an internal time fuse in its base that ignited on firing and caused the bullet to explode several seconds later. In November 1861, Gardiner solicited sales of his

The Gardiner exploding bullet, or "musket shell" was intended to explode in enemy ranks when fired. In practice it proved a failure, with erratic, inaccurate performance and even dangerous to carry in a cartridge box in combat. (*Bill Adams*)

bullet from the War Department, maintaining that it was "a perfect shell, & so arranged as to explode at any given time within the enemies ranks, making a second report at the explosion almost equil [sic] to the first."[21]

Exploding rifle-musket balls were not new, and there had been considerable experimentation in Europe with such ammunition in the 1850s. Perhaps the most significant development was that of British Colonel John Jacob, who developed a unique double-barreled rifle accurate at extreme ranges. Jacob was also credited with inventing "a very effective rifle shell." Jacobs' ammunition, however, depended on "great accuracy of manufacture, and was somewhat complicated to produce." Gardiner, on the other hand, proposed to mass produce millions of his "shells."[22]

Despite some earnest correspondence, Gardiner was unable to attract any serious attention from the government until his friend Benjamin B. French exploited some political contacts to arrange a meeting with Assistant Secretary of War Watson. The interview gained Gardiner a test of his projectile at West Point in May 1862. Although all the musket shells fired in Captain Steven Vincent Benet's West Point test exploded (with varied results), General Ripley, his ordnance office besieged by inventors with harebrained war-winning ideas, expressed little interest. A moral revulsion on the part of army officers did not help Gardiner either. Benet's observation that "a Minié bullet would put a man out of action just as surely and less brutally" led to a conclusion that the "musket shell" had "no merit as a service projectile." Ripley concurred.[23]

Despite Ripley's lack of enthusiasm for the Gardiner bullet, in September 1862, Assistant Secretary Watson instructed him to order 10,000 rounds of Gardiner ammunition to be delivered to the Washington arsenal. A shipment of 200 cartridges was consigned for further test to the XI Corps, whose ordnance officer, Captain L. Schirmer, was far more enthusiastic than Benet had been. Schirmer concluded that he would "recommend them to be used in the army of the United States." French, now acting as agent for Gardiner, used the Schirmer report to persuade Watson to order more cartridges. Watson complied in December, instructing Ripley to order another 100,000 rounds. Ripley did so, but on their arrival in February 1863, he promptly placed them in storage. French continued to lobby to have the ammunition actually issued, petitioning General Hooker in March 1863 to request that the stored Gardiner cartridges be issued to the Army of the Potomac.[24]

Perhaps as a result of French's letter, Major General Daniel Butterfield, General Hooker's chief of staff, ordered a panel of officers to test and report on the Gardiner bullet. The results were not favorable. According to the panel, the "musket shells" did not meet expectations. They were inaccurate even at ranges within 100 yards, not all of them exploded, some that did exploded prematurely, and they had poor penetration power. According to Dean Thomas, there is archeological evidence of the use of some Gardiner bullets in areas occupied by the XI Corps at the battle of Chancellorsville, but no battlefield evaluation of the results exists.[25]

While it is possible that there were still some "musket shells" in XI Corps cartridge boxes at Gettysburg, nothing is known of their use by that unit. It is, however, certain that the Second New Hampshire Infantry went into battle at Gettysburg fully supplied with explosive ammunition. When the Second was camped at Washington in May 1863, the regiment's officers were apparently convinced by Gardiner, French, and/or Watson that they needed Gardiner cartridges for both their rifle-muskets and Sharps breechloaders. Shortly afterward, the

Attack by Louisiana troops on the XI Corps on East Cemetery Hill. The XI Corps was issued a large number of Gardiner cartridges prior to Chancellorsville and some may have still been in use at Gettysburg. (*Library of Congress*)

Second joined Colonel George Burling's brigade of the III Army Corps and fought at the Peach Orchard on July 2 after the brigade was deployed piecemeal along a line extending from there to Plum Run.

The effect of the musket shells on the attacking Rebels is unknown, but they were pretty deadly to some men in the Second New Hampshire. The Second's historian recalled that "several cartridge boxes were exploded" by enemy fire, with horrifying results. According to the unit history "one shell struck square upon the cartridge box of Corporal Thomas Bignall, of Company C, driving the cartridges into his body, where they exploded one after the other, with a popping like that of a bunch of fire crackers." When Sergeant James M. House's box exploded "he tore off the infernal machine hanging by his side," and "escaped with only a severe wound." In the wake of Gettysburg, the *New York Daily Tribune* published an account of an exploded bullet picked up on the field at Gettysburg after the battle by a Union artillery officer. This "fiendish missile" was, not unexpectedly, attributed to Confederate inhumanity.[26]

Pioneer ammunition historian Berkeley Lewis was certain that the Confederates not only apparently made some efforts to duplicate the Gardiner but were using some explosive bullets of their own design at

Vicksburg in 1863. Following the war, however, this was vigorously denied by, among others, Jefferson Davis, who indignantly dismissed such stories as "slander" in an 1879 letter to Reverend Horace Edwin Hayden. In his article for the partisan *Southern Historical Society Papers*, Hayden sustained Davis' view, but he, like the former Confederate president, conceded that Rebels probably fired captured Gardiner bullets back at their former owners. Hayden claimed "the distinguished officer who commanded the 143rd Pennsylvania volunteers" [Edmund L. Dana] told him that "during the last day of the [Gettysburg] battle, he and his men frequently heard, over their heads, amid the whistling of the minnie [sic] balls from the Confederate side, sharp, explosive sounds like the snapping of musket caps." According to Hayden, an ordnance officer advised Dana that explosive musket balls captured from Union soldiers and fired by the Rebels caused the noise. The bullet recovered at Gettysburg was undoubtedly a Yankee projectile. Who fired that particular round, however, seems up in the air. Following the Civil War, the world concurred with Captain Benet, and explosive small-arms ammunition was banned for use in war at an international convention held at Saint Petersburg, Russia, in 1868.[27]

While explosive rounds played only a very minor part in the battle of Gettysburg, the standard Springfield or Enfield conical bullet was the predominant projectile of any kind fired in the battle. In terms of small-arms usage, Gettysburg was, first and foremost, a rifle-musket fight—one of the first major encounters in the Civil War in which the vast majority of the infantry on both sides carried rifled arms. It is a less complex task, within the context of the battle, to cover breechloading carbines, smoothbore muskets, revolvers, sabers, and sharpshooter rifles, simply because the numbers of men carrying them were limited, and their particular roles in the overall struggle more easily defined. In recognition of this reality, and since the present work is not intended as a chronological or wide-ranging tactical narrative of the entire battle of Gettysburg, it would be impossible to cover all of the separate rifle-musket fights as they merge into the big one of the battle itself.

Editorial necessity has thus limited detailed examination and discussion to one clash within the larger framework of Gettysburg, selected to demonstrate typical rifle-musket use by troops in the field at mid-

Brigadier General Lysander Cutler (left) led his brigade across the unfinished railroad cut to engage the Confederates on the morning of July 1. Cutler had a reputation as a fighter, but seemed confused as to the effective range of musketry. His unit was the first infantry brigade in combat at Gettysburg. Cutler relieved Colonel Thomas A. Devin's cavalrymen. A New Yorker, Devin (right) was another of Buford's tough Irish brigade commanders. (*Library of Congress*)

war. The July 1 struggle of Brigadier Lysander Cutler's brigade with General Davis' Confederate brigade, coupled with the Sixth Wisconsin Infantry's attack against Davis' men in the railroad cut, is illustrative of a number of aspects of commanders' ideas regarding, as well as actual combat use of, rifle-muskets. Readers will no doubt be able to cite equally significant examples in other phases of the battle, and they would not be incorrect in doing so.

Rifle-muskets certainly came to the rescue on July 1. When Colonel Campbell's cavalrymen caught a sideways glimpse of blue-coated infantry marching up the Emmitsburg Road toward Gettysburg late that morning, they breathed a sigh of relief. The first Federal foot soldiers to appear at McPherson's Ridge were the brigades of Generals Solomon Meredith and Lysander Cutler of Brigadier General James S. Wadsworth's First Division of General Reynolds' I Corps, then under the leadership of Reynold's senior division commander, Major General Abner Doubleday.

Cutler's soldiers could see the smoke from the cavalry fight in the distance as they trudged north and were not surprised when they met Reynolds in the vicinity of the Codori farm. The general ordered them to leave the road and cut cross-country toward McPherson's ridge, where the cavalry was hard pressed. The men of Cutler's lead regiment, the Seventy-sixth New York, double-quicked through "fields, gardens and yards," knocking down and clambering over fences, dropping heavy knapsacks, and loading their Springfield and Enfield rifle-muskets on the run in a "wild rattle of jingling ramrods."[28]

General Wadsworth, who rode ahead of the division toward the sound of the guns, directed Cutler to take his Seventy-sixth and 147th New York and Fifty-sixth Pennsylvania across the Cashtown Road and an unfinished railroad cut running roughly parallel to it into the wheat fields beyond to engage Davis' Rebels, who were steadily pushing back Colonel Thomas C. Devin's dismounted cavalrymen. Wadsworth ordered Cutler's remaining regiments, the Fourteenth Brooklyn (Eighty-fourth New York) and Ninety-fifth New York, under the Fourteenth's Colonel Edward B. Fowler, to deploy on the left of the railroad cut in a defensive mode facing west. Wadsworth ordered the five regiments of his other brigade, General Meredith's "Iron Brigade" of Midwesterners, who were following Cutler on the run *en echelon*, to form on a line to the left of Fowler's demi-brigade.

General Cutler, riding into the wheat behind Colonel J. William Hoffman's Fifty-sixth Pennsylvania, spotted the Fifty-fifth North Carolina, which had drifted off to the left of Davis's brigade, to his front and ordered the Pennsylvanians to engage the Tarheels with rifle-musket fire. There was some question as to the distance between the enemy and the Fifty-sixth. In a November 5, 1863, letter to Pennsylvania Governor Andrew J. Curtin, Cutler recalled that "the enemy at the moment advancing, was within easy musket range." In the next sentence however, he seemed to contradict that assertion, implying that "at the moment" the enemy was far enough away to make it difficult to determine even whether the enemy was "the enemy." According to the general, "the atmosphere being a little thick, I took out my glass to examine the enemy. Being a few paces in the rear of Colonel Hoffman, he turned to me and inquired 'Is that the enemy?' My reply was 'Yes.' Turning to his men, he commanded 'Ready, right oblique, aim, fire!' and the Battle of Gettysburg was opened"—a contention General Buford's horse soldiers would no doubt dispute.[29]

Cutler further declared, somewhat surprisingly considering his initial assessment of "easy musket range," that "when Colonel Hoffman gave the command 'aim' I doubted whether the enemy was near enough to have the fire be effective, and asked him if he was in range; but not hearing my question, he fired . . . ." The Fifty-sixth's volley, if that's what it was, rather than a "fire by file," which was often the first fire delivered on engagement, was not successful, only wounding two members of the Fifty-fifth's color guard. While the range between opposing lines of battle was not specified, and exact positions are not easily determined by a modern survey of the landscape compared with the available information, it appears to have been around 500 yards.[30]

The Springfield rifle-muskets with which the Fifty-sixth was armed were sighted to a maximum distance of 500 yards, providing the proper sight leaf was raised. Even considering that, it does not appear that anyone in charge ordered sights to be raised from their point-blank settings. If they did so, they never saw fit to mention it. Although Hoffman was praised by his brigade commander as "one of the best officers, brave, faithful and prompt, and a most excellent disciplinarian," he, and Cutler as well, appear to have been ignorant of the importance of range estimation and the capabilities of their men's weapons.[31]

What the Fifty-sixth received in response to its ineffective fire, according to Cutler, was "a shower of Rebel bullets, by which many of the Colonel's men were killed and wounded. My own horse, and those of two of my staff, were wounded at the same time." This well-directed fire, in strong contrast with the inept Yankee musketry, was probably delivered by the sharpshooters or skirmishers of Davis' Brigade, perhaps hunkered down in the wheat, closer to the Union line and quite possibly more conversant with the range and sighting capabilities of their rifle-muskets. In contrast, Hoffman does not appear to have advanced any skirmishers to his own front.[32]

As the Pennsylvanians and Carolinians began their firefight, the Seventy-sixth New York, still marching in column, was hit by heavy small-arms fire from Davis' Second Mississippi, "lying down concealed from view in a wheatfield" and firing at a range "about 30 rods"[165 yards] away. The New Yorkers unscrambled and returned the fire but were hit in the flank by the Fifty-fifth North Carolina. The firefight was intense, but the Confederates continued to advance, shooting as

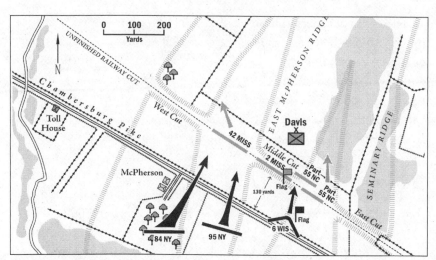

Map 2. The successful attack of the 6th Wisconsin, 95th New York and 14th Brooklyn on the Railroad Cut on July 1, 1863.

they moved, and drove the two Yankee regiments, along with their brigade command element, from the field.[33]

The 147th New York, meanwhile, got into its own battle with elements of Davis' Brigade as it advanced alongside the railroad cut to the left of the Fifty-sixth and Seventy-sixth. One New Yorker remembered seeing "innumerable heads of rebels bobbing up and down across the wheat." Another estimated that the Rebels were "not more than 30 or 40 rods [165 to 220 yards] off when the fighting began, although a soldier from the Forty-second Mississippi recalled that his unit encountered the Yankees at "not more than 100 yards" and hit the ground to avoid a volley from the 147th, which, despite the prompt evasive action, wounded several Mississippians. Another New Yorker supported that claim, estimating engagement range at "not over 10 or 12 rods." After the initial volley, the Yankees took partial cover behind a ridge-line and continued to blaze away. The fight turned into a close-range brawl, and despite their favorable position, the New Yorkers, who brought 380 soldiers to the fight, began to waver under the fire of the Forty-second's 575 men, aided by Rebels from the right wing of the Second Mississippi. The Confederates worked their way forward until some were within 100 feet of the Yankee line, and many New Yorkers were hit as they rose up from behind the ridgeline to fire.[34]

The front began to come apart. With the Fifty-sixth and Seventy-sixth driven from the field, the 147th provided covering fire for the withdrawal of Captain James A. Hall's Second Maine Battery, which had replaced Lieutenant Calef's guns in the Federal defensive line on the other side of the railroad cut to their left. Finally the men of the 147th, in danger of being completely overrun by Davis' whole brigade, took off for the rear. Leaving everything behind but their Enfields and cartridge boxes, they scampered across the railroad cut toward the road. The cut varied in depth, from two feet to around fifteen feet, depending on where one engaged it. A number of New Yorkers got trapped in the steeper sections and were shot down or captured by Davis' men. The regiment lost 289 men,

Colonel Rufus Dawes. Between 1861 and 1863 Dawes rose from captain to colonel in the Sixth Wisconsin and led the regiment in its successful attack on the railroad cut, even though his horse was shot from under him. (*Library of Congress*)

many of them during its escape. The Rebels thought themselves triumphant and wheeled toward Gettysburg, determined to finish the job. They were to be surprised.[35]

The instrument of the surprise was Colonel Rufus Dawes' Sixth Wisconsin Infantry. When the Iron Brigade trotted up McPherson's ridge it left the Sixth, along with the 102-man "Brigade Guard"—a group of picked soldiers from all of the brigade's regiments—behind in a reserve role. The Sixth was armed with Springfield Model 1861 rifle-muskets, and the Guard men with a mix of weapons, including Springfields and Austrian Lorenzes in both .54 and .58 calibers, depending on which regiment they were detached from. As the rest of the brigade reached the ridge, General Meredith called for Dawes, whose force totaled 436 officers and men, to advance and deploy on his left flank. Along the way, however, General Doubleday, senior officer on the field after Reynolds was shot dead from his horse while directing the Iron Brigade forward, commandeered Dawes' regiment. Aware of the deterioration on the right with the collapse of Cutler's brigade, Doubleday ordered Dawes to attack Davis' triumphant Rebels.[36]

The Badgers wheeled right in a complex maneuver with the facility of veterans and began to march toward the enemy, who Dawes could see advancing along the other side of the railroad cut. Since he was moving toward their flank, he had the Rebels at a disadvantage. Some Confederates spotted the Wisconsin boys early on, though, and the Rebels began to turn to meet the Sixth. Sporadic fire peppered the Yankees. Although the range was well beyond 200 yards, it did have some effect, and Dawes' horse was wounded and threw him to the ground. His men parted formation around him and the mare, and after they passed, Dawes jumped to his feet, and the animal made its way to the rear. When the Wisconsin men reached the fence bordering the south side of the Chambersburg Road and could clearly see the wheeling Rebels to their front, Dawes, running to catch up, began to yell, "fire by file, fire by file," at a range he recalled was "40 rods" [220 yards]. (A modern measurement reveals the distance between the north side of the road as it exists today and the current railroad tracks along the Sixth's front as averaging 130 yards, so the actual range was probably closer to 180 yards.) The regiment was advancing in a line of battle two ranks deep, and each two men, one behind the other, but slightly offset to enable both to fire at the same time, was a "file." Dawes' command was intended to initiate and maintain a steady rate of fire, without the embarrassing and vulnerable silence that followed a formal volley as everyone reloaded at the same time. File firing assured that musketry rippled down the regiment as each two-man file shot immediately after the file to its right. As each file discharged its muskets, its men reloaded and fired at will as fast as possible.[37]

Many of the Wisconsin men in the first rank rested their Springfields on the fence rails to steady them and "carefully aimed" at the Rebels. The three Confederate regiments—the Second and Forty-second Mississippi and the Fifty-fifth North Carolina—were stunned but recovered from the fire, completed their turn, advanced toward the Yankees, and then seemed to vanish as they dropped into the railroad cut for cover and began to return a heavy fire. One Badger remembered that "their whole line disappeared as if swallowed up by the earth."[38]

Momentarily, at least, it was a standoff firefight. As evidenced by their use of available improvised fence rail rifle rests, the Wisconsin boys were more gun-wise than a lot of soldiers. One, Private James P. "Mickey" Sullivan, an Irishman who thought himself a gunsmith of sorts as well as a good shot, had decorated his Springfield "with some silver ornaments and fixed the screw in a stock against the dog [sear] so it worked almost as easy as a squirrel gun." Sullivan bragged he "could hit a canteen at one-hundred yards" because of the light trigger pull his alteration achieved. At the fence line, however, his gun misfired, and after calculating he had inadvertently loaded it twice he handed it off to a lieutenant and picked up another, which also failed to fire. Concluding his percussion caps were faulty, Sullivan then rolled over a man who had just fallen to Rebel return fire and took his cartridge and cap boxes.[39]

While Mickey Sullivan was looking for a gun that would go off, Dawes' men began to advance again, crossing the road and the fence on the other side, firing all the while. The Federals were reinforced by Colonel Fowler's New Yorkers, who changed front, advanced, and began to fire at the railroad cut to their left. The Rebels came under more pressure when General Cutler rallied some men of his other regiments who began to fire down the cut from the east.[40]

Some of the Rebels ended up in parts of the cut so deep and sharply sloped that they could not return fire, and although the overall fire seemed hot enough to the Wisconsin and New York men, Davis' brigade was also badly disorganized. As Dawes ordered a charge, Davis ordered his own men to pull out of what had become a deteriorating situation. The Sixth surged toward the Rebels, firing on the run, and the New Yorkers joined them in a mad rush for the railroad cut, into a fire one soldier described as "fearful." A survivor recalled that "men were being shot by twenties and thirties and breaking ranks by falling or running. But the boys . . . crowded in right and left towards the colors and went forward."[41]

The Sixth lost a total of 165 men in its more-than-200-yard charge, and the Brigade Guard another thirty to thirty-five, most in the 130-odd-yard interval between the road and the railroad cut. The Wisconsin boys captured the Second Mississippi's flag and its Major John Blair

McPherson's Woods from the Chambersburg Pike. Taken on July 15, 1863, this Mathew Brady photo is a view looking south and shows the woods where the Iron Brigade attacked and General Reynolds was killed. (*Library of Congress*)

and a number of other men from that regiment and the Fifty-fifth North Carolina. The prisoner bag included seven officers and 225 enlisted men. Other Rebels had scrambled out of the ditch in headlong rout, many leaving their muskets behind.[42]

Although small as these things go, the attack of the Sixth Wisconsin, Fourteenth Brooklyn, and Ninety-fifth New York was a successful charge in the grandest tradition, evocative of Solferino. Some called it a bayonet charge, although Dawes stated afterward that he had never ordered bayonets fixed. It appears that some men fixed bayonets, while most did not. There was some brief hand-to-hand fighting at the end, and a few bayonets and clubbed muskets were apparently used, but, in general, the Rebels surrendered when they were put in an untenable position.

Interestingly, in their comprehensive account of the Sixth Wisconsin's fight, Lance J. Herdegen and William J. K. Beaudot specifically note a number of wounds suffered by the Badgers specifically attributed to buckshot and others that were probably the result of buckshot, indicating a fair number of smoothbore muskets in Rebel ranks. One Wisconsin soldier recalled that as he struggled for the

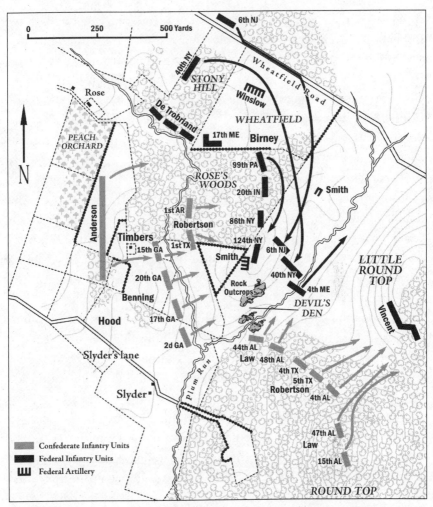

Map 3. Fighting around Devil's Den, late afternoon of July 2, 1863. Effective engagement ranges for the Fortieth New York and Sixth New Jersey, two regiments that plugged the gap as the Fourth Maine retreated up the Valley of Plum Run, were around 200 yards.

Second Mississippi's flag, a Confederate fired at him at point-blank range, and "his charge, a ball and three buck-shot passed through the skirts of my frock coat in front and lodged in my left forearm and wrist." The I Corps list of captured weapons at Gettysburg, many of them likely taken in the morning of July 1 from Archer's and Davis' brigades, totals 2,958. Colonel Dawes estimated that "about one thousand muskets lay in the bottom" of the railroad cut after his men captured the position. Although 2,402 of the I Corps captured guns were Enfields, 212 were identified as smoothbores.[43]

During the course of the railroad cut fight, the remainder of the Iron Brigade moved, *en echelon*, into position on McPherson's Ridge to Cutler's left and encountered the advancing Rebel infantry of Archer's Confederate brigade. As Archer's men crossed Willoughby Run and began to ascend the ridge through Herbst's woods, the Midwesterners appeared in the trees to their front and flank.

The men of the Second Wisconsin rammed down charges and capped nipples as they rapidly advanced toward the woodlot on the double quick. Colonel William W. Robinson of the Seventh Wisconsin could not see the enemy, because the ravine in front, "about 200 yards" distant, was full of gun smoke. Once a staff captain pointed out a Confederate flag in the ravine, the men of the Iron Brigade opened fire. Engagement ranges seem to have varied, with the Confederates variously reporting that they began to fire when the enemy was around seventy-five yards away. In the end, the Union tide was unstoppable, and Archer's men were routed in a wild charge, with many, including the general himself, captured, although the Union victory was considerably dimmed by General Reynolds' death.[44]

The engagement range average of around 200 yards in the opening musketry fights of July 1 would hold throughout the battle, and it marks a decided change from the closer-range firefights of 1862. Although marksmanship training had not advanced much, the confidence of officers in the technical capability of their men's small arms, either smoothbore or rifle-musket, had apparently increased. On July 2, Brigadier General J. H. Hobart Ward, commanding the brigade covering the Houck's Ridge to Devil's Den line, ordered his regiments "not to fire at a longer distance than 200 yards." Surveys from current regimental markers and monuments indicate that the Fortieth New York Infantry, coming to Ward's assistance, engaged advancing Rebels at approximately 160 yards. The Sixth New Jersey Infantry, coming up on the Fortieth's right, opened up ineffectually at around 400 yards but quickly advanced to engage the enemy at approximately 225 yards. On July 3, the Seventy-first and Seventy-second Pennsylvania regiments opened fire at an average range of around 210 yards as the Confederate assault on the Federal center, popularly known as "Pickett's Charge," reached the Emmitsburg Road.[45]

During the comparative lull following the defeat and retreat of Davis' and Archer's brigades, the remainder of the I Corps and then Major General Oliver O. Howard's XI Corps arrived at Gettysburg. As senior officer on the field, Howard assumed overall command from Doubleday and, based on the large and increasing number of Rebels to his west and north, deployed the I Corps along its original line and then extended it north and east. Howard's own corps filed into place to the I Corps's right, north of town, facing elements of Lieutenant General Richard Ewell's Confederate corps moving south. By mid-afternoon Rodes' division of Ewell's Corps was fighting around Oak Hill, and Rodes saw an opportunity to overrun the Union right before the XI Corps fully extended it.

In a rushed attempt to turn the Federal flank, Brigadier General Alfred Iverson's brigade of Rodes' Division advanced without skirmishers deployed to its front and was ambushed by Federals hiding behind a stone fence, resulting in heavy casualties. On the other hand, Major Blackford's sharpshooters heavily engaged Union skirmishers in the vicinity of Oak Hill, inflicting far more casualties than they suffered, vindicating Rodes' and Blackford's tactical ideas.[46]

Despite Iverson's disaster, Rodes' division cracked the Union line, precipitating a general attack ordered by General Lee, who had arrived on the scene. This time the Rebels, who also overlapped the Union left, swept the outnumbered Yankees before them. Even the stubborn Iron Brigade had to fall back, and suffered so many casualties it was virtually destroyed as a fighting force. Driven from Seminary Ridge and through the town of Gettysburg, the Yankees consolidated a desperate patchwork defense on Cemetery Hill, and the Confederate advance ran out of steam, fighting done for the day. Winfield Scott Hancock, the II Corps commander, took charge of the defense. With the darkness, General Meade arrived, and more Federal soldiers came up. More were coming. The stage was set for a climactic struggle.

Chapter 5

THE SMOOTHBORE MUSKET

———◆◆◆———

THE EIGHTY-EIGHTH PENNSYLVANIA INFANTRY WAS the only regiment in the Army of the Potomac's I Corps marching to the rescue of John Buford's cavalrymen on July 1 partially armed with smoothbore muskets. The regiment's role in the ensuing fight included shooting up most of its ammunition, then charging and capturing prisoners and colors from the Twenty-third North Carolina and Sixteenth Alabama regiments. Later in the afternoon, the Eighty-eighth fell back through Gettysburg to Cemetery Ridge, where the regiment received an ammunition reissue. There were no specific references to whether the Pennsylvanians armed with smoothbores believed they were undergunned.

Most, but certainly not all, the soldiers of both sides on the field at Gettysburg would have felt disadvantaged had they come to the battle armed with smoothbore muskets. By the time of Gettysburg, the smoothbore was fast disappearing from the ranks of both the Army of the Potomac and the Army of Northern Virginia. Except for units like the Twelfth New Jersey Infantry and the regiments of the Irish Brigade (outfits with a quirky preference for the old technology), most units initially issued smoothbores were eager to dispose of them from 1861 on and, by early 1863, had done so.

As noted in previous chapters, target practice with the more modern and accurate rifle-musket was sporadic in Civil War armies. If anything, the believed inherent inaccuracy of the smoothbore musket no doubt made such efforts seem even less useful to many soldiers armed with that weapon, even though recent evidence suggests that that should not have been the case. Bell Irvin Wiley remarked that "perhaps one of the reasons for neglect of target practice early in the war was the notorious inaccuracy of the antiquated muskets with which many soldiers were armed at that time."[1]

In pre–Civil War America, militia target practice with smoothbores in both north and south was haphazard at best, as an account from a Pittsylvania Court House Virginia militia unit reveals. Militiamen were apparently given a choice as to whether or not they wanted to participate in the exercise.

> Company A, commanded by Capt. Wm. H. Werth, was out on last Saturday, to shoot for a beautiful medal. There were only 69 shots fired (many of the company not firing,) and 56 were in the target, distance 80 long yards, and this with the old-fashioned musket altered to percussion. When they get the Minute [Minié] muskets, they will take the prize from any of your city companies, for most of the men can cut the cross with a rifle off-hand nearly every fire. Lieut. J. D. Coles won the medal, his nearest shot being a quarter of an inch from the tuck in the centre.[2]

In the north, many militia companies seem to have disdained target practice altogether, but this was counteracted, at least in New York City, by paramilitary Target Companies armed with smoothbore muskets and often associated with volunteer fire companies and social and political clubs. At one point, the "Pocahontas guards" were deemed "the best shooters in the city," and by 1850, it was estimated that 10,000 men were enrolled in these units. To be sure, many members of Target Companies were more interested in social and political networking and drinking than in serious shooting (they even paraded with wooden muskets), but there was a solid corps of men familiar with firearms, some of whom would join the Union army at the outbreak of the war whereas others—in particular, the members of the infamous Black Joke fire company—would be found in the ranks of draft rioters in 1863.[3]

Although accounted obsolete by 1861, the smoothbore musket had a long and honored history. Rifled shoulder arms were available in central Europe by the sixteenth century, but smoothbores—cheaper to manufacture and faster to reload—remained in favor for military use for several hundred years. This did not save the musket from being disparaged by some military men. The gun's historical reputation for absolute inaccuracy rests, for many modern readers, on an oft-quoted passage by British Colonel George Hanger.

> A soldier's musket, if not exceedingly badly bored, and very crooked, as many are, will strike the figure of a man at 80 yards, it may even at 100 yards, but a soldier must be very unfortunate indeed who shall be wounded by a common musket at 150 yards, provided his antagonist aims at him; and as to firing at a man at 200 yards with a common musket, you may just as well fire at the moon, and have the same hopes of hitting your object.[4]

In fact, however, David Harding (whose four-volume study of the weapons of the British East India Company is a firearms history tour de force) found "no evidence to substantiate Hanger's assertion that either in the Royal or Company's service 'many' muskets were 'exceedingly badly bored, and very crooked.'" Harding notes that of 7,500 muskets sent to Bengal in 1799, only 0.61 percent were found, on inspection, to have "crooked barrels," a percentage that is probably similar to that of American-made muskets of the era. A well-bored smoothbore musket was, if properly loaded, aimed, and fired by a trained individual, capable of reasonable accuracy on man-sized targets at ranges up to eighty yards at least and effective on large formations at ranges up to 200 yards. Although this conclusion, on examination, does not materially disagree with Hanger's statement on individual target hit ratios, it recognizes the reality that large formations were routinely encountered in combat in the eighteenth and nineteenth centuries and that effective musket range on the battlefield was therefore longer than a first reading of Hanger might suggest.[5]

Much is often made of the stereotypical view that armies of the Napoleonic era engaged in combat by simply pointing guns and firing them in massive unaimed volleys at point-blank range, but the truth of the matter is, as with most such assumptions, more complex. Although "point and shoot" volleys were an effective way to deliver mass fire, this practice was far from universal. With the advent of the wars of the French Revolution, a desperate French revolutionary government, short on formally trained troops with the discipline to fight in line, initiated mass conscription and used loose swarm formations of musket-armed skirmishers to take a toll on better drilled enemies like the Austrians.

The British army realized the value of aimed fire as well, even with smoothbore guns, at the close of the eighteenth century. The British *Manual and Platoon Exercise* of 1800 advised the soldier to "look along the barrel with the right eye from the breach pin to the muzzle and remain steady. Pull the trigger strong with the forefinger." An 1803 directive gave further instruction on concentrating on proper trigger pull, "so as to avoid haste and spoiling the aim." At around the same time, Russian General Barclay de Tolly emphasized smoothbore marksmanship and designed a target "painted with horizontal stripes to assist in the elevation and depression of the musket according to range."[6]

French troops engaged in target shooting with smoothbore muskets at variable ranges as early as 1806, and one army corps held a championship match in 1813. By 1822, the post-Bonaparte French army issued specific directions for recruit target practice, including construction of a two-meter-tall target, with instructions as to aiming point, delineated by red stripes indicating an opposing line's waist, chest, head, and top of hat, at varied distances. Four years later, firing range construction details were provided to all French units, along with directions on the use of cast-iron targets. One nineteenth-century French test firing of smoothbore muskets at a large target resulted in hit ratios of forty percent at 150 meters and twenty percent at 300 meters.[7]

Admittedly, even the aimed musket was a relatively short-range weapon by today's standards. A British Government test conducted in 1846 found the maximum range of a smoothbore with a muzzle elevation of five degrees to be "about 650 yards, the point-blank range being 75 yards." Although an American calculation indicated that a ball fired from a smoothbore musket retained "sufficient force to pass through a pine board 1 in. thick" at 500 yards, the British concluded that "as a general rule, musketry fire should not be made at a distance exceeding 150 yards and certainly not exceeding 200 yards, as at and beyond that range it would be a mere waste of ammunition to do so."[8]

Admonitions about necessary sighting elevation at various ranges calculated by British army engineers were, however, based on calculations that David Harding has proven to be in error. That report suggested that a soldier hoping to hit a man at 200 yards with his smoothbore musket should aim five foot six inches over the target's head. In actuality, Harding, correcting erroneous assumptions regarding sighting and trajectory, concludes that the drop of a round ball at 200 yards was actually only fifteen inches from a musket's line of sight. This makes sense, as, despite the inferior ballistic shape of the round ball vis-à-vis the conical bullet, the round ball from a smoothbore musket starts off with a significantly higher muzzle velocity, due to its lighter weight and greater powder charge. An 1855 American test revealed that the muzzle velocity of the round ball fired from the .69 caliber smoothbore musket was 1,500 feet per second, while that of the .58 rifle-musket's conical slug was 963 feet per second.[9]

To get a rough idea of smoothbore musket accuracy and bullet drop, the author and a friend test fired an original U.S. Model 1842 Springfield .69 caliber musket in March 2007. In an attempt to replicate the ammunition of the era as closely as possible, the gun was loaded with cartridges rolled with masking paper and containing 100 grains of FFG black powder and a .648 diameter spherical bullet (original ball size was a nominal .650). As in the nineteenth century, the cartridge paper was rammed down with the ball, providing a stabilizing sabot for the projectile on firing. Three shots fired at a silhouette target from a standing position at a distance of fifty yards all hit the target in what would have been a vital area at the approximate point of aim. At 100 yards, three shots out of four hit the target, also in a vital area. The drop of the bullet from the line of sight at 100 yards, considering the aiming point and center of shot group, appeared to be about twelve inches. Another modern shooter, firing a British Model 1842 smoothbore, was "impressed by the results" of his own firing of that gun at 100 meters and came to the conclusion that "you wouldn't really want to stand there" at that range. He also observed that "ricochets flew straight, and . . . you could use this 'indirect fire' as a way of following the fall of shot, with the clear majority of short shots ending up through the target."[10]

Although never a precision weapon, the musket was intended to be effective on area targets presented by the large formations necessary to concentrate firepower in hopes of achieving a decisive effect on the battlefield. A nineteenth-century British work records a smoothbore musket trial result of thirty percent hits on a target representing a line of cavalry at 200 yards and twenty-three percent at 300 yards. A similar French study of smoothbore fire from a steady rest at a target one and three-quarter meters by three meters gave a twenty-five percent hit ratio at 225 yards and twenty percent at 300 yards. Another French test, in which 100 shots were fired at a two-meter-square target, resulted in ninety-eight hits at 100 meters, eighty-four at 150 meters, forty-four at 200 meters, thirty at 250 meters, and five at 300 meters. A German test at a six-by-100-foot target gave a fifty percent hit rate at 200 paces and a twenty-five percent hit rate at 300. As late as the Crimean War, British officers noted that in past sieges, men firing smoothbore muskets at ranges "not usually exceeding 200 yards from the enemy's batteries" were able "very commonly to silence absolutely the guns immediately opposed to them."[11]

Within its range limitations, the smoothbore musket was an awesome weapon. At the battle of Austerlitz in 1805, the defeated Austro-Russian Army lost 27,000 men killed, wounded, and missing out of a total strength of 85,700. At Borodino in 1812, Napoleon lost 30,000 out of his 130,000 men, while his Russian opponents suffered 40,000 casualties from a total force of 120,800 men. These losses, largely inflicted by smoothbore muskets and artillery, are quite comparable to those suffered in most Civil War battles, which, after 1862, were primarily fought with the more accurate rifle-musket. One analysis of smoothbore battles versus European pre–Civil War fights in which both sides possessed more accurate rifle-muskets suggested that casualty percentages in the earlier battles were considerably higher, according to one admittedly partisan analyst: "At Waterloo [smoothbore], French, 0.36, Allies 0.31. At Magenta [rifle-musket], June 4, 1859, French, 0.07, Austrians, 0.08." As Harding concludes, "smoothbores were accurate enough and could be loaded faster [than the pre-Minié ball rifle], and thus on balance were more effective than rifles in a sustained firefight."[12]

Swedish experiments conducted in 1845 produced some very interesting results on the potential combat results of smoothbores and rifles. The Swedes were investigating a new Norwegian breechloading rifle, similar to the raised-breech American Hall, and conducted tests involving that gun—the *kammerlader*—pitted against the old-style *Jaeger* muzzleloading rifle firing a patched ball and the smoothbore musket. Although the breechloader beat both of the older arms in both accuracy and rapidity of fire, the muzzleloading rifle trailed behind the smoothbore in effectiveness on large targets at ranges up to and beyond 200 yards. During a ten-minute period, nine smoothbore muskets fired a total of 134 rounds, while nine rifle-armed soldiers managed only eighty shots. Firing at a target six feet high and eighteen feet long at a range of 205 yards, the musket scored twenty-eight hits as opposed to the rifle's twelve. The rifle-musket, of course, increased the loading speed of rifled arms to that of the smoothbore and no doubt improved on the *Jaeger's* accuracy at longer ranges as well. The test is, however, instructive in that it verifies that the smoothbore was not, as it is often characterized, totally inefficient at ranges beyond 75 yards, especially on large-area targets, and that the rate of fire advantage of the smoothbore was indeed a significant factor at normal engagement ranges.[13]

Multiple projectile loads proved a way of making the musket even more deadly. Loading a single round ball seems to have been standard procedure in the very early days of firearms, but some people stuffed more than one slug down the barrels of their smoothbores early on. Samuel de Champlain loaded four balls in his arquebus before encountering Iroquois Indians in 1609 on the shores of the lake that bears his name. The French explorer's matchlock gun laid several Native Americans low with one shot. British General James Wolfe ordered his men's muskets double-shotted at the decisive battle on the Plains of Abraham outside Quebec in September 1759.[14]

Although Champlain and some colonial-era soldiers apparently used several full-diameter balls, by the time of the American Revolution, it was common practice to load smaller buckshot, averaging around .30 caliber, along with a musket ball in the paper cartridges used in .69 and .75 caliber muskets. New Hampshire Militiamen of 1776 were required to have "a pouch containing a cartridge-box that will hold at least fifteen rounds of cartridges at least, [and] a hundred buck-shot." In June 1776, George Washington recommended that his men "load for their first fire, with one musket ball and four or eight buck-shot according to the strength of their pieces." An October 1777 order specified that "buckshot are to be put into all cartridges which shall hereafter be made." The number of buckshot per cartridge used during the Revolution varied, and, in the 1775 American attack on Quebec, General Henry Dearborn carried a musket "charged with a ball and Ten Buckshott." Buckshot recovered from Nassau Hall in Princeton, where British soldiers were besieged by Americans in the January 3, 1777 bat-tle there, are on display in the museum collection of the Historical Society of Princeton, and fired buckshot have been recovered during archeological work at the site of the 1778 Battle of Monmouth.[15]

Some Revolutionary War cartridges were purchased from contrac-tors, while others were made by the soldiers themselves, who often cast their own bullets as well. One soldier wrote of doing his "Steant [stint] running ball" and "a quarter pound of buckshot or a pound of lead to be 'cast into ball to fit the bore' was a proper allowance for a man." Maryland issued troops bullet molds capable of casting both buckshot and musket balls, and a multibullet soapstone mold marked "1775" in the collection of the Monmouth County New Jersey Historical Association has numerous cavities for both musket-sized balls and buckshot.[16]

Single-ball, buckshot and ball, and straight buckshot loads of between twelve and fifteen pellets remained part of the American mil-itary ammunition inventory after the Revolution. Those men on the Lewis and Clark expedition who carried muskets were issued 100 balls and two pounds of buckshot each, and cartridges loaded with both buckshot and ball were standard issue during the War of 1812. Single-ball loads for the .69 caliber United States musket fired undersized .64 caliber projectiles to facilitate quick loading, at the expense of accuracy. The addition of buckshot made a hit more likely.

As the nineteenth century progressed, firearms theorists in both America and Europe demonstrated that the accuracy of the smoothbore musket could be improved by increasing the size of the ball and decreasing the weight and improving the quality of the powder charge.

In the 1840s, the diameter of the .69 caliber American musket ball was increased from .64 to .65 caliber, and the gun's powder charge reduced from 130 to 110 grains. Although accuracy improved somewhat, most military men continued to rely on multiple projectiles to improve combat hit ratios.[17]

Due to the limited effective range of straight buckshot loads, they were largely used as guard cartridges, but buck and ball became the military's favored combat cartridge. Between 1835 and 1840, three times as many buck-and-ball cartridges, loaded with a single ball and three buckshot, were issued as single-ball loads by the United States Army Ordnance Department.

Civilian shooters, especially eastern deer hunters who stalked their quarry in farm woodlots where ranges were short, also saw advantages in multiball loads. According to Ned Roberts, a New Hampshire hunter loaded his "smoothbore rifle" with buckshot in the 1840s because "When a feller has ter shoot nigh dark, or in a hurry, he has a better chance to hit with the smoothbore loaded with buckshot than with a rifle thet hes but one ball." Muskets loaded with buck and ball and buckshot were also favored for close in work and defense of forts by many civilian frontiersmen, who had similar requirements for a gun that was effective when shot "nigh dark or in a hurry."[18]

It was that "better chance ter hit" that inspired French military writers in the 1830s to extol the American-style buck-and-ball load. The French were predisposed to loading multiple projectiles, and Marshal Bugeaud had advocated double-ball loading in the musket as early as the Napoleonic Wars. As the French expanded their colonial empire in North Africa, they encountered Arab guerillas who wouldn't stand in compact formations to get shot, and they temporarily adopted buck and ball in the belief that they had a better chance to tag their elusive adversaries with a multiball load.[19]

Eventually, however, the French developed the Delvigne system and discarded multiple loads for the conical expanding Minié bullet, which allowed rifled weapons to be loaded as fast as smoothbores. The Americans followed the French lead this time, but the Model 1855 rifled arms were slow in getting to the troops. To fill the gap, some Model 1842 percussion ignition .69 caliber smoothbores were rifled,

U. S. Model 1842 .69 caliber smoothbore musket. The ultimate smoothbore musket, the Model 1842 was widely used in the first two years of the Civil War. Units like the Twelfth New Jersey and the New York and Pennsylvania regiments of the famed Irish Brigade came to prefer it to the more accurate rifle-musket. (*National Park Service*)

and Minié-style bullets were supplied for these guns and the .54 caliber Model 1841 round-ball rifles in service. Within a few years, no regular United States Army troops were carrying smoothbore muskets. Although many of the old flintlock smoothbores in state militia arsenals were converted to the percussion ignition system in the 1850s, most remained unrifled.

The droves of recruits who flocked to Federal and Confederate colors at the outbreak of the Civil War clamored for .58 caliber rifle-muskets, the most modern muzzleloading arms available, but supplies of these arms were limited. Of the 503,000 shoulder arms held in Federal and Northern state arsenals at the outbreak of the war, 400,000 were .69 caliber smoothbores, and 100,000 of the 135,000 small arms either held or seized by Southern states were smoothbores as well. The unrifled guns included Model 1816 Springfield and private contract flintlock muskets (the same weapons converted to percussion ignition by various methods) and Model 1842 smoothbore muskets from Springfield, Harper's Ferry, and South Carolina's Palmetto Armories originally issued as percussion guns.[20]

In late 1860, the arms in the Virginia state armory, which had unfulfilled ambitions of producing its own pattern rifle-musket, were mostly smoothbores, and the majority of these were flintlocks. According to one report "10,000 flintlock muskets, of the United States make . . . with flints in them, have been reserved by the Commissioners from the arms sold to Mr. Anderson, until 5,000 of the new rifle-musket have been manufactured. These reserved muskets are such as the Army used in Mexico [most likely the Model 1840], and are considered, by high authority, as not at all inferior to the percussion musket."[21]

A trickle of imported weapons, both rifled and smoothbore, which became a flood in 1862, eased the overall small-arms shortage on both sides by the end of the year. The majority of Union and Confederate regiments raised in the first year of the conflict were, however, issued .69 caliber smoothbore muskets, some of them with flintlock ignition. Among the arms captured by Federal troops following their February 1862 victory at Roanoke Island were large numbers of flintlock smoothbores. Some Confederates, especially those in the western armies, carried flintlocks as late as the April 1862 battle of Shiloh.[22]

In 1861, New Jersey militiamen were highly annoyed when the Federal government gave them bright-finished Model 1816 smooth-bores converted from flintlock—which they would have to polish assiduously for inspections—rather than rifled arms in exchange for their browned state-issue smoothbore weapons, which did not demand as much maintenance. Other units reacted more violently, and, in the case of the Seventy-ninth New York Infantry, a smoothbore exchange that turned out to be for more smoothbores rather than the hoped-for rifled arms caused a mutiny. One Illinois newspaper dismissed smooth-bores as "fit for nothing but drill." Given the opportunity, many men ditched their smoothbore muskets—often on the battlefield. Soldiers of the Eighth Illinois Infantry were "armed with the American Smooth-bore muskets . . . until after Shiloh battle, when a large number of the muskets were exchanged for Enfield and other rifles gathered from the field." After the capture of Arkansas Post in 1863, Carlos Colby and his comrades of the Ninety-seventh Illinois eagerly "threw away their old guns [smoothbore muskets] and took Enfield rifles captured from the enemy."[23]

Distaste for smoothbore arms was not universal, however. Prior to the war, a Virginia newspaper commented that

> Experienced officers of the regular service consider this [the smooth-bore] a better weapon for volunteers than the rifled musket. Although its range is less, and its accuracy when firing at small objects is not so great as the rifled musket in the hands of a good rifle shot, yet, in firing at masses at ordinary ranges and with unpractised troops, it is more efficient, inasmuch as it can be loaded with more

rapidity, does not foul or lead, carries both ball and buckshot, and is not so delicate and so liable to get out of order as the Minnie [sic] musket.[24]

Although the Virginia comments might be dismissed as a rationalization, since the Federal government was not releasing Model 1855 rifle-muskets to the militia in 1860, they make sense, and others shared a positive assessment of the smoothbore as a combat arm. A veteran of the Twentieth Illinois Infantry recalled that "although the boys were not very pleased" with the smoothbores they were issued in 1861, "they proved a very efficient and deadly weapon, and some of them were carried all through the service." Brigadier General Thomas F. Meagher, commander of the Irish Brigade, one of the best units in the Union Army, specifically requested smoothbore muskets for his men because he thought much of the brigade's fighting "would be at very close quarters." William O'Grady of the brigade's Eighty-eighth New York Infantry recalled after the war, however, that "sometimes our short range weapons were a disadvantage."[25]

Many officers, assuming that most fights would take place at relatively short range, however, agreed with General Meagher. As late as 1863, Colonel George Willard of the 125th New York, a well-known proponent of the smoothbore, flatly stated that "under certain circumstances, the arms formerly employed [smoothbores] were more effective than the new ones, particularly, when at close quarters." According to Willard, the necessity to change sight settings to compensate for the trajectory of the Minié ball during the course of combat, especially when infantrymen faced a fast-closing cavalry charge, was too confusing for average troops. He believed soldiers would do better to hold their fire until the horsemen were close and then deliver a decimating volley of buck and ball. Ironically, Willard was killed in action on July 2 at Gettysburg while commanding a brigade armed with rifle-muskets.[26]

In fact, throughout the Civil War, cavalrymen were generally very reluctant to charge organized infantry units armed with anything, but Meagher and Willard might not have been too far off the mark. British military historian Paddy Griffith has asserted that the types of small arms used by opponents in most Civil War battles mattered little, because the tactics (or lack of same) employed by officers on both sides led to essentially short-range firefights in which the accuracy of the individual or his weapon were largely irrelevant. If this is true, then the .69 caliber smoothbore may have had an advantage over the rifle-musket in most fights, as a buck-and-ball load gave the shooter four chances to kill or disable his enemy.

Most authorities thought buck and ball effective up to a hundred yards, which, according to Griffith, was the approximate distance of the average firefight during the first two years of the war. The buckshot in the cartridge apparently did serve as a hit multiplier within that range. In a test conducted in Texas in 1855, soldiers firing .69 caliber buck and ball at a six-by-eighteen-foot target a hundred yards away scored as many hits with their Model 1842 smoothbore muskets as a company armed with the much more accurate .54 caliber Model 1841 rifles firing patched round balls when each group fired a specified number of rounds. Although the lethality of buckshot at that distance can be fairly questioned, a wound does not have to be fatal to be tactically effective. In most cases, a wounded man will quickly leave the immediate scene of battle and may require one or more others to help him off.

The author conducted a live-fire buck-and-ball experiment in March of 1991. Four shooters fired both reproduction and original smoothbore muskets ranging from .69 to .75 calibers in both flintlock and percussion ignition. The loads were not exact replicas of Civil War–era buck-and-ball cartridges, using less of a powder charge, but firing one round ball and three buckshot pellets as did the original rounds. Both small and large targets were engaged. First, six full twelve-ounce cans of seltzer water were strung on a frame at fifty yards. Averaging two and a half shots each, the shooters quickly cleared the cans from the frame. Next, two full-size police silhouette targets were mounted on four-by-four-foot backers. Two men fired five shots each at each target, scoring eighteen hits (eight balls and ten buckshot) on one and thirteen hits (six balls and seven buckshot) on the other. Misses riddled the cardboard target backers and would have caused a number of casualties in a close two-rank-deep Civil War infantry formation.

Due to a lack of surgical antisepsis, minor wounds during the Civil War often proved fatal or disabling far out of proportion to the initial damage they caused. Lieutenant Joseph McDanolds of the Seventh New Jersey Infantry was put out of action by a buckshot wound at Chancellorsville. McDanolds was "shot in the head—the ball entering on the left side between the scalp and the skull, and ploughing from the back to the front, coming out near the temple. Had it been a Minie [sic] ball, it would inevitably have crashed through his skull, and probably caused instant death." The lieutenant had to return home on furlough to recover. A Fifteenth New Jersey Infantry soldier suffered multiple buckshot wounds in his right hand at the battle of Salem Church on May 3, 1863. Four buckshot were extracted by army surgeons, and the man was sent home to recover, where his family doctor discovered a fifth buckshot, flattened out to nearly an inch in diameter, in his wrist. He subsequently received a disability discharge.[27]

By mid-1862, some soldiers had modified their previously dim view of the smoothbore. After surveying the slaughter his regiment wreaked with buck and ball at the battle of Williamsburg in 1862, a New Jersey infantryman wrote, "At times, rifles would have been preferable, but as a general thing we did well with our smoothbores, as buckshot *tells* at short ranges." With rifle-muskets still in short supply, many new regiments raised in 1862, including the Eleventh New Jersey, Twelfth New Hampshire, and Twelfth Rhode Island, were issued a mix of smoothbores and rifles, with the latter arms going to companies designated for skirmishing duty. This policy coincided with Colonel Willard's belief that "*at short ranges, the buck and ball cartridge is certainly more effective*, and it is susceptible of proof, that it is a grave error, to adopt for an army, rifled, to the *entire exclusion* of the smoothbored arms [emphasis original]."[28]

Some outfits were still issued only smoothbores as late as the summer of 1862, however. The 116th Pennsylvania, which joined General Meagher's Irish Brigade after the battle of Antietam, was armed, no doubt to the general's delight, entirely with "the old pattern musket that was loaded with a ball, caliber .69 and three buckshot." In contrast to the policy in most units, however, the men of the 116th actually held "frequent [but apparently informal] target practice down by the riverbank, where the boys fired away at imaginary Confederates and filled trees full of buck and ball."[29]

Some regiments, entirely on the responsibility of their immediate commanders, engaged in limited target practice with smoothbores as early as 1861. This often occurred during guard mount changes. Lieutenant Benjamin D. Coley of the Sixth New Jersey Infantry's Company K "took the old guard out and they fired at a target with their smoothbore muskets." More formal, albeit limited, shooting was also encouraged in the Sixth, and Coley "went out with the company at target practice and they fired four rounds" on October 9, 1861. When the company couldn't get out to the range, Coley and his fellow company officers took muskets out themselves "and had a shot at the target." The lieutenant was proud that he "made the best shot." It should be noted that none of this target work included instruction of any sort other than loading and pulling a trigger. Even before the war, an inspecting officer posited that "the mere discharge of the guard of the previous day at the target to get rid of the load is not sufficient practice."[30]

Like Mickey Sullivan of the Sixth Wisconsin with his rifle-musket, some soldiers performed unauthorized freelance amateur gunsmithing on their smoothbores to increase their accuracy. Eugene F. Ware of the First Iowa Infantry recalled that his unit "drew a lot of [buck and ball] ammunition . . . and practiced a little shooting." The First's muskets "had no rear sight, only a notch, and we had to tinker them and change the front sight so as to get an approximation." Ware noted that "we could not make them shoot straight. But we understood guns and could get as close to it as anybody could or as the gun itself could be made to go."[31]

Confederate General Rodes, in addition to pooling his available rifle-muskets in an elite sharpshooter battalion under Major Blackford, encouraged marksmanship of a sort in his brigade's smoothbore-armed line companies. Rodes staged a shooting contest for his old Regiment, the Fifth Alabama Infantry, over the winter of 1862–1863. The Alabamans fired by company at a barrelhead a hundred yards distant. The winning company, treated to an oyster dinner by the general, hit the target nine times. Four other companies only managed ten hits among them.[32]

Despite the smoothbore musket's lack of long-range individual accuracy, many outfits were happy without rifles in the ranks. In 1862, the men of the Twelfth New Jersey gladly turned in their initial issue of Austrian Lorenz rifle-muskets for Model 1842 smoothbores. The Jerseyans of the Twelfth developed a sentimental attachment for their muskets, keeping them even when rifle-muskets became generally available. One soldier thought his 1842 was "as handsome a gun as was ever made." The Twelfth and its smoothbores would have perhaps their finest hour at Gettysburg, and some of the regiment's South Jersey farm boys proudly carried their smoothbores through to Appomattox.[33]

The Twelfth New Jersey monument on Cemetery ridge, shown here shortly after it was dedicated on May 26, 1886. The monument, a tribute to the men of the regiment and the "buck and ball" cartridge they fired in their smoothbore muskets is capped by a representation of one musket ball and three buckshot. (*Author*)

Close in, there was no arguing with the effectiveness of buck and ball. One veteran, remembering Shiloh in April 1862, recalled that early in the war "improved rifles were scarce, for my own regiment at that time did not have rifles, but old smooth bore muskets with buck and ball ammunition . . . . Of course we should have had no show against rifles at long range, but at short range, in woods and brush, these weapons were fearfully destructive."[34]

On August 10, 1861, the Third Louisiana Infantry encountered Union regular army infantry in a point-blank standup fight in a cornfield at Wilson's Creek, Missouri. The Louisianans were armed with smoothbore muskets and the regulars with rifle-muskets. After a lull following a desultory fight of around half an hour, "the dead lay thick along their [Federal] thinning line, and many of those still standing were visibly wounded, blood running down their faces from minor head wounds, suggesting, incidentally, that the Rebel infantry were firing 'buck and ball.'" Shortly afterward, the battle was renewed, and the smoothbore won the day.[35]

The Yankees of the Ninth New York Heavy Artillery, fighting as infantry, used their "old smoothbore muskets, with canister loads" to "make havoc in the Rebel ranks" in a fighting withdrawal at Monocacy, Maryland on July 9, 1864, a full year after Gettysburg. Even the ambivalent Captain O'Grady of the Eighty-eighth New York recalled that "the splendid [buck and ball] volleys of the [Irish] Brigade were conspicuous and effective," at Fair Oaks, Virginia, in 1862. He concluded that the brigade's Bloody Lane fight at Antietam proved "the efficacy of buck and ball at close quarters."[36]

An alternative load to buck and ball or single round ball in a smoothbore musket was a conical projectile known as "Nessler ball," which was widely used in the smoothbore muskets of European armies in the 1850s, including the Russians, Sardinians, and French, in varying configurations. By the end of that decade, Major Mordecai reported that the Russian army's "usual ammunition for the smooth-bore musket is the round ball; but of late much use has been made of the Belgian projectile known as the 'Nessler' ball." Mordecai described the Nessler as "of cylindro-spherical form, the cylinder being very short. The ball is hollow at the base, to make it expand, and has a projecting point in the bottom of the cavity. Its weight is 464 grains."[37]

Mordecai reported that the Nessler in use in the French army was said to extend the "accurate and efficient" range of the smoothbore to 300 or 400 yards, which may well have evened up the odds at Solferino. Nessler paper cartridges were made the same as those for round balls, but the bullet end was dipped in tallow, creating a lubricated paper patch. As with the Enfield Pritchett bullet, the Nessler cartridge paper was discarded in loading except for the lubricated portion surrounding the bullet, which helped keep powder residue fouling down.[38]

Nessler bullets, although proposed, did not catch on in the Union army, but were not uncommon in Southern ranks. In the spring of 1862, C. Shaler Smith, an engineer at the Confederate powder works in Augusta, Georgia, advocated what he called the "Nesler [sic] ball" for local militia use in double-barreled shotguns. Smith claimed that "its practice at 400 yards is not greatly behind the rifled musket, and much superior to the ordinary musket."[39]

Smith later elaborated on the Nessler, describing the bullet used in the French .69 caliber musket in the Crimea as "0.66 of an inch in diameter, 0.56 in length, rear cavity 0.20 inch depth and . . . weighs 463 grains . . . and was fired with a charge of 92 grains of powder." The hollow-base paper-patched bullet expanded against the musket's barrel walls in the same manner as the Minié ball. Although there was no stabilizing rifling in the smoothbore, the expansion, coupled with the sabot provided by the lubricated paper, did center the bullet in the barrel, providing satisfactory accuracy. In addition, the better ballistic configuration of the Nessler bullet over the round ball gave it greater stability at longer ranges. Smith, quoting Cadmus Wilcox's *Rifles and Rifle Practice*, claimed "the Nesler [sic] ball at 270 yards had twice the accuracy of the round ball; at 440 yards it had the same accuracy as the round ball at 270 yards; and at 550 yards it had one-half the accuracy of the round ball at 270 yards. Its trajectory was more flattened than the Minnie [sic] ball fired from a rifle."[40]

Civil War ammunition scholar Dean S. Thomas, who has made a detailed study of bullets from cartridges dropped and fired at Gettysburg, provides examples of Nessler-style slugs in Confederate service. Nessler bullets, along with round-ball and buck-and-ball ammunition, were found in an area occupied by General Heth's division—the unit that opened the battle against Buford's horsemen on July 1. Of the 242 Union infantry regiments that fought at Gettysburg, twenty-six, or 10.5 percent, were armed in whole or in part with various models of unrifled small arms. Overall, Thomas's study seems to indicate that probably around the same percentage of Confederates carried smoothbores into the battle. By mid-war, however, the once-common musket was becoming a rarity in infantry service. The Irishmen and the Jerseyans of the Twelfth still shouldered smoothbores at Gettysburg because they wanted to, but they were in a distinct minority.[41]

The smoothbore musket was not present in enough numbers at Gettysburg to make a distinct overall impression on the results of the battle. Loaded with round ball, buck and ball, or Nessler bullets, though, it was not the hopelessly ineffectual arm it has been often been characterized as. Smoothbore fire delivered on large-unit formations was certainly accurate enough to cause significant casualties at distances up to

200 yards, the range at which most Gettysburg combat was initiated, and Confederates using Nessler bullets could extend that capability significantly. The musket's most significant shortcoming would be on the skirmish line, where accuracy at individual targets was required, and it could not compete with the more accurate rifle-musket, especially in the hands of Confederate soldiers detailed to special sharpshooter battalions, who used their arms effectively at the ranges they were capable of.

Most of the smoothbore muskets in service in the Army of the Potomac were in the II Army Corps, and that unit did not get into the fight until July 2. When the II Corps, with the Twelfth New Jersey infantry in the van of its Third Division, trudged north toward Gettysburg on July 1, rumors of a battle in progress floated down the line and spurred the Jerseymen on. As the march continued, the Twelfth encountered stragglers and walking wounded men coming back from the front north and west of the town. The regiment halted at Taneytown, Maryland, three miles south of the battlefield, after dark. Here, amid the backwash of two battered Union corps, General Meade's Circular Order of June 30, calling for the summary execution of soldiers who failed in their duty, was read, and at 3:00 AM on July 2, the Twelfth double-quicked to the battlefield and deployed along northern Cemetery Ridge.

Federal guns opened up on the Rebel positions across the way at dawn, drawing a tremendous counter-battery barrage, and the Jerseyans hugged the ground as a maelstrom of shot and shell flew over them until they were ordered to move slightly further north along the ridge. The move provided no relief and subjected the Jersey boys to long-range rifle-musket as well as artillery fire. Yet another move ended with the regiment deployed behind a low stone wall, its right flank resting near the Bryan farmhouse. The Twelfth's left was connected to the rest of the II Corps, much of which was formed in mass of columns. Brigadier General Alexander Hays, the Third Division commander, deployed some skirmishers to his front and waited.

A large barn owned by the Bliss family stood about 600 yards in front of the Twelfth's line. Rebel sharpshooters had occupied the building and were peppering the Yankee formation with deadly long-range fire. Some sharpshooters, apparently from the First Company

The Bryan farm house, owned by Abram Bryan, a free black man who fled Gettysburg at the approach of the Confederate Army, stood on the right flank of the Twelfth New Jersey's final position on Cemetery Ridge. This view is from behind the house, with Cemetery Ridge in the distance. The Twelfth was deployed to the left. (*Library of Congress*)

Massachusetts Sharpshooters, were called up to try to silence the Rebels, since the Jerseymen's smoothbore muskets were useless at such range, and nearby line troops armed with rifle muskets (but untrained in their effective use) were able to perform little better. When the sharpshooters failed to stop the enemy sniping from the barn, the Twelfth's brigade commander, Brigadier General Thomas A. Smyth, ordered the regiment's Major John T. Hill to "send 100 men and take it!" Hill chose Companies G, B, H, and E of the Twelfth, actually close to 200 men, under Captain Samuel B. Jobes to do the job. Jobes' assault team formed up behind the Bryan barn on Cemetery Ridge in a column of companies and moved out at the double quick. The rifle-musket-armed Rebels in and around the barn immediately opened up on the trotting Jerseymen and took a heavy toll, especially since exact range estimation was not so necessary to hit a deep column formation. Six hundred yards is a long way to run under fire, and the force leaked casualties all the way to the barn. Captain Jobes was wounded but stayed on his feet as others fell around him. Captain Charles A. Horsfall was killed and Lieutenant Stephen G. Eastwick wounded. After what must have seemed an eternity, the Jerseymen got close enough to reply with their smoothbores. A blast of buck and ball cleared the Rebels from behind a fence row, and the Jerseyans swarmed into the farmyard, overrunning the Rebels and trapping many in the barn. The detachment sent back ninety-two prisoners from Brigadier General Carnot Posey's Brigade, including seven officers, held the position for an hour or so, and then retreated as a large enemy force began to advance.[42]

After returning to their Cemetery Ridge lines again, the Jerseyans readied themselves for an anticipated Confederate assault. The attack never came, however, and the regiment settled down for the night. The Twelfth's successful attack on the Bliss Barn proved the lesson of Solferino—that well-drilled veterans, even armed with smoothbore muskets, could carry the day in an assault against an equal number of rifle-musket-armed opponents, as long as the attackers moved quickly. The fact that the Jerseyans did not hold the barn was more a function of their small numbers and exposed position than their weapons.

Another smoothbore-armed II Corps unit, the First Brigade of the corps's First Division, better known as the Irish Brigade, was also in action on July 2. The brigade's three New York regiments—the Sixty-third, Sixty-ninth, and Eighty-eighth New York Infantry—had seen hard fighting since their 1861 enlistment and had been reduced to two understrength companies each. The 116th Pennsylvania, which had joined the brigade in 1862, was almost as weak as the New York Regiments, and all four regiments were armed with smoothbores. The only regiment in the brigade armed with rifle-muskets was the Twenty-eighth Massachusetts Infantry. It was also the largest Irish Brigade regiment. The usual tactical procedure in the Irish Brigade was to deploy the men of the Twenty-eighth on the skirmish line, where their rifled arms would be useful. That was not to be the case at Gettysburg, where the entire brigade mustered only 700 men, with a mere 532 of them available for combat.[43]

On the morning of July 1, as General Buford's horse soldiers began their fight on the ridges west of Gettysburg, the Irish Brigade, like the Twelfth New Jersey, began a march to Taneytown, Maryland, arriving there in late afternoon. When word arrived that General Reynolds had been killed and that the men of the I and XI Corps were fighting for their lives against a growing number of Rebels, II Corps commander Major General Winfield Scott Hancock sped north to assume command of the engaged Federal forces. His command continued its march on into the night, halting about three miles south of Gettysburg, where the First Division deployed across the Taneytown Road.

The men of Colonel Patrick Kelly's Irish Brigade were awakened at 3:30 AM on July 2 and, after a hasty breakfast, marched north for about a mile and halted again on the Taneytown Road until dawn. Around 7:00 AM, the II Corps moved again, this time to the west of the road and up Cemetery Ridge, where the corps deployed on the left of the battered I and IX Corps. Following the line of the gradually descending ridge, the II Corps's left flank linked with the right of the III Corps, which prolonged the Union position almost a mile to the south toward Little Round Top. The ground on the First Division's front sloped gently away toward Plum Run and, beyond, the Emmittsburg Road. Some Irishmen laid down to get some sleep as the sun rose in the sky, while others talked, played cards, or wrote letters. As the morning, and then the afternoon, slipped away, the heat increased, and a number of soldiers wandered down to Plum Run to refill their empty canteens.

Late that afternoon, Major General Daniel Sickles decided to improve his III Corps's position by moving the corps's two divisions forward toward the Emmittsburg Road. Sickles' corps eventually occupied a salient that ran south along the road and then doglegged across a peach orchard to a rocky ridge that bordered a wheat field and culminated in the helter-skelter glacial stoneyard of Devil's Den. The First Division soldiers watched Sickles' men go, and General Hancock, visiting his old outfit, predicted the advancing Yankees would soon come tumbling back.

Unfortunately for the Federal army, Hancock was right. Sickles' salient made the Confederate offensive plan to attack the Union left easier. Hit in front and flank with a heavy artillery barrage followed by advancing infantry as evening approached, the III Corps was severely shaken. General Hancock, who was ordered to bolster the endangered corps, directed Brigadier General John C. Caldwell to prepare his First Division to advance. As Colonel Kelly called his troops to attention, the

Irishmen heard a steadily increasing drumfire of musketry rolling across the fields beyond them. After a false start for the front, the brigade returned to its position. The tension increased.

With the brigade prepared to go into battle, Father William Corby, chaplain of the Eighty-eighth New York, stepped up onto a rock and the men fell to their knees. Corby, his statue still frozen in time, has gained eternal fame for absolving his Irishmen their sins at Gettysburg. The chaplain could see thousands of soldiers, however, and later said his general absolution was "intended for all—*in quantum possum*—not only for our brigade, but for all, North and South, who were susceptible of it and who were about to appear before their Judge." Even the profane Major General Hancock doffed his hat in reverence. The scene, which no doubt evoked memories of open-air masses and hedge schools in the days of the Penal Code in the "old country," remained with the participants all the days of their lives.[44]

With the arc of Father Corby's hand scribing a cross in the air still fresh in their minds, the Irish formed into column formation and moved out, following Colonel Edward Cross's First Brigade of New Hampshire, New York, and Pennsylvania regiments down the gentle slope of Cemetery Ridge due south, past the Weikert farm, toward Little Round Top. The division's remaining two brigades fell in behind Colonel Kelly's veterans. As Caldwell's division moved south, Colonel Samuel Zook's Third Brigade, the last in line, was detached by a staff officer and rushed into the Trostle Woods, off to the division's right.

General Caldwell's First Division of the II Corps may well have been, despite its diminished strength in comparison to other divisions, of 3,320 effectives, the finest division in the Army of the Potomac. It also had a higher proportion of smoothbore muskets, with one-third of its eighteen regiments, including the Irish, armed wholly or in part with smoothbores. One authority on the division's fight in the Wheatfield considered that this armament "reduced Caldwell's tactical choices." In his opinion, "regiments armed with smoothbore muskets could not break up Confederate formations with medium or long range fire; their only option was to close quickly to a range at which their weapons could be effective." In the event, however, this fact did not appear to pose any problems. The usual infantry engagement range at Gettysburg on mass

General John Caldwell and staff. The collapse of Caldwell's division in the Wheat Field, even though it was not his fault, was responsible for ending Caldwell's active career. Although an inquiry absolved him from blame, he lost division command in the 1864 reorganization of the Army of the Potomac and spent the rest of the war in non-combat posts. He had an extensive post-war diplomatic career. (*Library of Congress*)

targets, save for ineffectual barrages like that fired by the Fifty-sixth Pennsylvania on July 1, was around 200 yards, regardless of the weapons involved. Brigadier General Hobart Ward, whose brigade defended Houck's Ridge on the afternoon of July 2, instructed his men, all equipped with rifled arms, "not to fire a longer distance than 200 yards." As evidenced by the buck-and-ball barrage the Sixth Wisconsin suffered under in its advance on the railroad cut, smoothbores could indeed be deadly on mass targets within that range.[45]

Caldwell, who seems to have been unaware that his tail end brigade was gone, was ordered by V Corps commander Major General George Sykes to swing his division to the west, in an effort to restore the dissolved III Corps line, which had been reinforced earlier by V Corps troops, in the Rose Wheatfield. Caldwell pushed his brigades toward the enemy as fast as he could turn them.

The Irishmen splashed across Plum Run, moved northeast through Trostle's Woods and then southwest into the Rose farm's field of ripening wheat. Here Kelly shook his brigade out of column and into a line of battle and angled west, pulling away from Cross' Yankees. Kelly's men advanced toward Stony Hill, which overlooked the Wheatfield and dominated the ground stretching northeast from Devil's Den. Zook's brigade, which had passed through two battered V Corps brigades, reappeared out of the Trostle Woods advancing somewhat forward and off to the right of the Irish. Colonel John Brooke's Fourth Brigade, Caldwell's reserve, straddled the rear of Cross and the Irish. The Irish Brigade line advanced with the 116th on the brigade right, then the Twenty-eighth, Sixty-third, Sixty-ninth, and Eighty-eighth to the left of the Pennsylvanians. As the Irishmen moved forward, beaten V Corps soldiers passed through their ranks. Kelly, whose tiny brigade had no skirmishers out in front of its 150-yard-long line and no reserve element, had no idea how many Rebels lay ahead of his men. It was around 5:30 p.m.

Elements of Brigadier General Joseph Kershaw's South Carolina brigade occupied the Irish brigade's objective. The Carolinians of the Third and Seventh Infantry Regiments, with at least part of their vision obscured by vegetation and powder smoke, were concentrating on the advance of Zook's brigade, which threatened their left. As a result, the Confederates on the crest of Stony Hill were apparently unaware of the Irish approach. Conversely, Kelly's men did not know where the Rebels were. They would soon find out.

The men of the Irish Brigade entered the woods at the end of the Wheatfield and started up the hill, struggling to maintain their battle line amid a jumbled landscape of trees and rocks. Finally apprehending the threat, the Rebels fired a hasty, ill-aimed volley at a range of about fifty feet. Most of the Confederate bullets zipped over the Irishmen's heads. A soldier in the 116th caught a flash of gray uniform in the trees ahead and cried, "There they are!" And the brigade opened up with a blast of buckshot and musket balls.

Major St. Clair Mulholland of the 116th characterized the buck–and-ball smoothbore ammunition most of the brigade's men carried in their cartridge boxes as "a wretched ammunition for distant firing . . . [but] just right for close hand to hand work." And close work it was. "Little Jeff" Carl of the 116th shot a Rebel six feet from his musket's muzzle, and officers drew their revolvers and joined actively in the fight.[46]

For the Irish, it was payback time for their losses at Antietam and Fredericksburg, and the unlucky recipients were the men of the Seventh South Carolina Infantry, which had entered the battle with almost as many soldiers on its rolls as the whole Irish Brigade. The fight stalemated for about ten minutes of mayhem, but when other elements of Caldwell's Division swept across the Wheatfield and into the woods to the left, the Rebels on the hill broke under the barrage of close-range smoothbore fire. The Irish Brigade rolled over the enemy position, capturing a number of prisoners and driving the rest of the Carolinians off the hill and into the Rose Farm fields beyond.[47]

At least one of the Irish units, the Enfield-armed Twenty-eighth Massachusetts, descended the slope and moved toward the farm. Since the Twenty-eighth was customarily deployed in a skirmish line ahead of the brigade's smoothbore-equipped main line of battle, Kelly may have ordered the regiment to take the lead as the Irish broke out into the open. Unfortunately, the Massachusetts men were caught in a vicious crossfire as the tactical situation to their front and flanks deteriorated rapidly and fell back up the hill. Zook's brigade, which had merged with the Irish on the hill and spilled out to the right into an open field, was thrown into some disarray as well, and Zook himself went down mortally wounded as the attack began. As Federal forces abandoned the Peach Orchard and Union regiments strung along the Emmitsburg Pike north toward Gettysburg were pressed back, Zook's right regiment, the 140th Pennsylvania, found its right flank up in the air, exposed to any Rebels who might get around it.

As the Irishmen had approached Stony Hill, Colonel Cross' brigade became involved in a firefight with General George T. Anderson's brigade of Georgians several yards to the Irishmen's left rear. Cross himself was killed shortly after ending the fight and his regiments suffered severely, as they fought in the open Wheatfield while the Georgians had a stone wall for cover. If Cross' men fell back, the Irish Brigade would be as exposed as the 140th's right. The Irish position was, at best, tenuous.

General Kershaw hoped to make it more so. After rallying his men near the Rose house and barn, Kershaw rode for help from Brigadier General Paul Semmes' Georgia brigade. Semmes soon had other problems, though. As Kelly and Zook fought their way up Stony Hill,

Caldwell ordered Colonel John R. Brooke's brigade forward though the wheat to relieve Cross's beleaguered outfit. Brooke's Connecticut, Delaware, New York, and Pennsylvania men, last reserve of the II Corps' First Division, swept southwest across the Wheatfield with fixed bayonets, passed through Cross' position, and drove Anderson's Rebels from the stone wall into and through the Rose Woods. Brooke finally halted 150 yards forward of the Irish left, where his men engaged in a point-blank firefight with Semmes' Georgians, halting, and then pushing them back.

Although the First Division had swept all before it, and the smoothbore muskets of the Irish Brigade had proved deadly and decisive in chasing the Carolinians off the Stony Hill, trouble was in the offing. Both of Caldwell's flanks were now up in the air, and he no longer had a reserve. Then the III Corps position along the Emmitsburg Road and in the Peach Orchard completely collapsed. As Brigadier General William Barksdale's Mississippians cleaned out the Peach Orchard, Brigadier General William Wofford's brigade of 1,400 Georgians swept down the Wheatfield Road, picking up Kershaw's men and driving toward the 140th Pennsylvania's open flank. On the other end of the division line, Rebels began to lap around Brooke's position, which was dangerously in advance of the rest of Caldwell's brigades. The general desperately rode right then left in an attempt to find other units to protect his flanks. What he got was too little, too late. Caldwell felt that the radically changing situation forced him "to fall back or have my command taken prisoners." With the Confederates coming down on both flanks, his men anticipated his command and began to retreat on their own, as it became evident that the jaws of a trap were about to close around them.[48]

Of necessity leaving their dead and badly wounded behind, Colonel Kelly's Irishmen rapidly retreated down Stony Hill and into the Wheatfield, firing all the while. There they became mixed up with elements of Zook's and Brooke's brigades and suffered severely from Rebel crossfire. Although Caldwell's retreat saved his division from destruction, it left a bloody trail of dead and wounded across the Wheatfield and all the way back to Cemetery Ridge, where it was able to reorganize while other troops stopped the Confederate sweep short of its objectives and rolled it back, ending the fighting for the day.

Sporadic firing began before sunrise on July 3 as nervous pickets and artillerymen opened another day of combat at Gettysburg. The Rebels reoccupied the Bliss barn during the night and at sunrise started taking potshots at Cemetery Ridge again, causing General Hays to order the Twelfth New Jersey to recapture the barn. Five companies of the regiment, led by Captain Richard S. Thompson and supported by elements of the First Delaware Infantry, were detailed for the task. The Jerseyans moved out at a walk, then sped up to double-quick time as Rebel bullets began to fall among them. Lieutenant John J. Trimble went down wounded, and four others, including Corporal William Stratton, were killed before the force reached its objective.

This day the Rebels chose not to be trapped, and only a few were captured while the rest withdrew firing. Although the Jerseymen captured the barn, they were soon in trouble. While Rebel skirmishers kept up a steady fire on their front, some Confederates began to infiltrate around Thompson's right flank and take positions in brush between the crest of Cemetery Ridge and the Bliss building. Scouts dispatched by the captain to his rear reported that he was close to being surrounded. Facing isolation and capture, the Jerseyans delivered a Parthian volley of buck and ball into the encircling Rebels and fell back up the ridge in haste amid a blizzard of bullets.[49]

Following this sharp little fight, a temporary quiet settled over the battlefield. Anticipating a major infantry attack, the Jerseymen began to make last-minute preparations. Many broke open their buck-and-ball cartridges and created new charges containing ten to twenty-five buckshot pellets each and gathered up and loaded captured arms as well as those dropped by casualties.[50]

In the late morning, Southern sharpshooters occupied the Bliss barn yet again and started taking potshots at the Yankee line. This time, General Hays dispatched the Fourteenth Connecticut to clear the Rebels out. The Connecticut men not only chased out the sharpshooters but solved the problem by setting the barn afire. Following the Fourteenth's sortie, the Yankees settled down and waited in an ominous silence. Around one o'clock, a single Confederate artillery piece fired a shell that landed in the rear of the division. Shortly afterward, a Rebel gun from the left threw another shell, followed by one from the center, and then the entire enemy line opened fire. Soon the II Corps position was a screeching, roaring, smoking hell with exploding enemy shells and Union guns belching return fire. Infantrymen hugged the ground and crawled forward to avoid the impact of the incoming rounds, most of which were overshooting the front line. General Hancock rode back and forth serenely in the firestorm to set an example of courage to his troops. Then, as suddenly as it started, the shelling stopped.[51]

Almost a mile away, the Rebels emerged from the woods on Seminary Ridge and formed for their grand assault. Brigadier General J. J. Pettigrew and Major Generals Isaac Trimble and George Pickett spread out their 15,000 men in a front nearly a mile wide. Hays rode down his division line, shouting, "They are coming boys. We must whip them!" He paid particular attention to the Jerseyans, ordering, "You men with buck and ball, don't fire until they get to that fence," pointing at the border of the Emmitsburg Road. Seen in the light of the distances and weapons involved in the railroad cut fight of July 1, Hays' order makes sense. The distance from the Twelfth's position to the Emmittsburg road today is approximately 170 yards.[52]

The Rebels came on toward Cemetery Ridge with deadly steadiness while the Union artillery tore horrible gaps in their line. As the Southerners drew near, the men of the Twelfth New Jersey shook out their colors and checked their smoothbore muskets, stoked with heavy charges of buckshot and ball, as the Yankee artillery switched to canister. As the enemy approached the Emmitsburg Road, the II Corps regiments armed with rifled arms opened up, but the Twelfth, despite Hays' advice, held its fire until the Rebels were fifty yards away, in order to maximize the effect of their buck and ball and, perhaps more significantly, hand-crafted straight buckshot loads. The lack of fire coming from the Jerseymen's front appears to have caused some attackers to drift toward the quiet spot where the regiment waited. These Rebels, survivors of the railroad cut fight from Davis' brigade of Mississippians and North Carolinians and Brigadier General James J. Pettigrew's North Carolina brigade, had already seen hard fighting and been badly battered on July 1. When the Rebels reached the buckshot killing zone, the Jerseyans rose up, with their officers shouting "aim low" and delivered a crushing volley. The Confederates briefly continued to stagger forward into the blizzard of bullets and buckshot, but the attack quickly collapsed into bloody chaos. The Twenty-sixth North Carolina had arrived at Gettysburg with 840 men on its rolls. It lost 588 of them killed and wounded to the Springfield rifle-muskets of the Twenty-fourth Michigan on Herr Ridge on July 1 and more than half the survivors, many to buck and ball, on July 3.[53]

As the Carolinians went to ground, the Jerseymen turned their muskets on Pickett's Virginians, struggling to keep a toehold on the wall to their left front, and showered them with buckshot and bullets, helping to collapse that portion of the attack as well. It was a Confederate disaster, and the Union troops cheered and waved their caps in the excitement of victory. General Hays celebrated by riding up and down the line dragging a captured Rebel flag behind him. The general reported that his division captured "fifteen battle flags or banners . . . 2500 stand of arms . . . of the prisoners . . . cannot be less than 1,500." Of this haul, the Twelfth New Jersey's share was 500 prisoners, two colors, and 751 small arms.[54]

Soldiers of the Sixty-ninth Pennsylvania Infantry, a Philadelphia Irish unit, manned the II Corps line on Cemetery Ridge to the left of the Twelfth, right at the apex of the copse of trees that was the guide for the Confederate attack. The Irishmen were armed with a mixture of Springfield and Enfield rifle-muskets and rifled .69 caliber muskets. In the evening of July 2, however, the men of the Sixty-ninth picked up a number of .69 caliber smoothbore muskets and a quantity of buck-and-ball ammunition left scattered around their position from Confederate attacks earlier in the day. Like the Jerseyans of the Twelfth, the Irishmen of the Sixty-ninth "abstracted the buckshot from the ammunition and reloaded the spare guns putting 12 to the load, and almost every man had from two to five guns that were not used until Pickett got within fifty yards of the wall." John Buckley of the Sixty-ninth's Company K recalled years afterward that "the slaughter was terrible, to which fact the ground literally covered with the enemy's dead bore ample testimony."[55]

When the celebrating ended, many of the Jerseymen, their rancor drained, went over the wall to give succor to the Rebel wounded. Being practical soldiers, they also helped themselves to the contents of any full haversack whose owner was dead. The rest of the day was given to occasional long-range artillery duels and skirmishing. At nightfall the men of the Twelfth lay behind their wall and got some sleep. The next morning Hays sent out skirmishers, who discovered that the Rebels were still there. The two armies, however, were content to carefully watch each other. By the morning of July 5, the Rebels were gone and the battle was over. The Twelfth New Jersey had acquitted itself well but paid a heavy price, losing twenty-three men killed, eighty-three wounded, and nine missing.[56]

On July 3, the diminished Irish Brigade occupied a reserve position about 200 yards south of the famous copse of trees. Although Colonel Kelly's men did no close-range fighting with their smoothbores that afternoon, the men of the Twenty-eighth Massachusetts fired some long-range rifle-musketry volleys at the advancing Rebels on their right front. A number of Confederates came into the Irish Brigade lines with hands raised rather than risk life and limb retreating across the bullet- and shell-swept field to their rear.

At Gettysburg, many units took the opportunity of a weapon-strewn battlefield to exchange unsatisfactory issued arms for better ones. The men of the Twelfth New Jersey and the Irish Brigade, satisfied with the performance of their Model 1842 smoothbore muskets, declined, although it appears the Jerseyans kept two captured Enfields, perhaps for special-purpose duty. Although there were others, including in the ranks of the Pennsylvania Reserves who stiffened the Union line in the evening of July 2, the Twelfth New Jersey and the New York and Pennsylvania regiments of the Irish Brigade were the most notable units armed with smoothbore muskets at Gettysburg. They still shouldered smoothbores the following spring, by that time representing an extremely small percentage of the Army of the Potomac's regiments carrying guns then universally considered obsolete. By the fall of 1864, the Irish had been re-equipped with rifle-muskets. Jerseymen returning from convalescent leave and new replacements assigned to the Twelfth were also issued the more modern arms. At the beginning of 1865, however, seventy-eight out of the 309 small arms reported in service in the Twelfth New Jersey were still Model 1842 smoothbore muskets. The regiment was one of the last units in the Army of the

Potomac with any smoothbores in its ranks. The Jersey boys never forgot their old smoothbores and what they did with them at Gettysburg, and when the time came to dedicate their monument on Cemetery Ridge on June 30, 1888, they made sure the plinth was carved with the words "buck and ball."[57] The collapse of the Confederate attack on Cemetery Ridge, its last gasp extinguished by ball and buckshot from smoothbore muskets, heralded not only what came to be called the high-water mark of the Confederacy, a fact not noted except in retrospect, but also the high-water mark of the smoothbore musket.

Admiral John A. Dahlgren's 1856 observation that "in the excitement of the conflict, the noise, the smoke, the dust, the rash haste of some, the dullness of others, prevent the soldier from making the best use of his weapon," was a valid assumption. Likewise, his conclusion—that since the rifle-musket could be loaded and fired as fast as the smoothbore and proved much better for the occasional longer-range shot, the military might just as well issue rifled arms—was correct as well and became, despite some recalcitrant Irish and New Jersey dissenters, standard army policy by mid-war.[58]

Although the smoothbore musket was fast fading as an infantry weapon earlier in the year, Gettysburg proved to be the end of its day as a significant military arm. Ironically, the rifle-musket that superseded it had but a brief reign as queen of battle before it too was gone. The future belonged to the breechloader.

Chapter 6

REPEATING RIFLES

THE CLIMACTIC MID-WAR STRUGGLE AT GETTYSBURG saw the last stand of the smoothbore musket and the high point of successor small-arms technology, including the rifle-musket and semi-fixed ammunition breechloaders like the Sharps. It also witnessed the beginning of the wave of the future: small arms firing the self-contained metallic cartridge. The first day's fight involved some single-shot Sharps and Hankins metallic cartridge guns in the hands of the Ninth New York Cavalry. The final day of the battle, however, featured the much more significant Spencer repeating rifle, a gun that would ride the crest of military small-arms innovation for the next two years before becoming rapidly obsolete itself in an ever-evolving international arms race.[1]

In the mid- to late 1850s, state-of–the-art repeating rifle technology was symbolized by the Colt New Model 1855 rifle. This revolving-cylinder side-hammer gun was a result of the development work of Samuel Colt and his factory manager Elisha K. Root. The rifle entered production in 1857 in .36 and .44 calibers, and the army purchased over 400 for field testing. Colt subsequently increased the frame size of the Model 1855 to accommodate a five-shot .56 caliber cylinder, which Sam Colt, in his never-ending quest for large government contracts, hoped would be more acceptable for military use. Just before the Civil War, the Colt Company developed a .65 caliber revolving rifle for consideration by the navy. The larger-caliber Colts were designed to use standard .58 and .69 caliber standard rifle-musket ammunition, respectively, in a pinch.[2]

Although they appeared on the frontier shortly after their introduction, Colt Model 1855 repeating rifles seem to have first entered large-scale combat in the Italian *Risorgimento* war of 1860. One account of the Colt in action noted, "It appears that from our correspondent of the London News, that this rifle possesses breech-loading advantages and dis-advantages; and admits of great rapidity of fire at a given moment. The difficulties are first, that the instrument requires care to keep it in order, and may at times clog; a common trouble of all breech-loaders; it offers peculiar temptation to too rapid and careless firing [punctuation original]."[3]

Colt revolving rifles, some in .44 but most in .56 caliber, subsequently came to be the first repeating rifles used in a major conflict, the American Civil War. Although disregarded and demeaned in postwar literature, the Colt Model 1855, especially in the war's first two years, was usually praised for its effectiveness and considered a desirable arm. Not only was the 1855 a repeater, it was judged to be accurate as well. In an 1859 U.S. Navy test, a .56 Caliber Colt was fired 250 times at a target of unspecified size at a range of 500 yards, and only seven shots missed. The officer in charge of the tests reported that the Colt rifles "were not cleaned, and sufficient time only allowed for them to cool when hot. They worked smoothly and easy. None failed to go off, and the cylinders showed less [fouling] deposit than usual.[4]

Despite this, the men of Berdan's Sharpshooters, initially issued Colts, "thought at first that these Colts would not shoot true, but this proved not exactly the case, as they were pretty good line shooters." Charles A. Stevens, the unit historian, recalled that sharpshooter "Andrew J. Pierce . . . while on the way down the Potomac made a trial shot of the five chambers . . . at a buoy bobbing up in the river some 400 yards distant" and hit it twice.[5]

In 1861, if you wanted rapid fire, you wanted a Colt. During the first year of the war, Swiss military observer Ferdinand Lecomte noted that while his country "has always been distinguished by the specialty of the *aim* [emphasis original], he recognized that America had "much contributed heretofore to the improvement of the rifle." Lecomte thought the Colt to be a major, albeit special-purpose, American improvement. He advised his government that he had heard "many favorable remarks about a rifled revolver of five shots" and recommended it for "choice battalions, or for a select company in a battalion," noting that five shots delivered rapidly on the right occasion could be a "great advantage."[6]

In 1861, the Colt embodied the only well-known proven repeating arms technology available. While quick to fire, it was relatively slow to reload, however. The .56 caliber Colt's five cylinder chambers were loaded individually from the front by inserting a paper cartridge in each and then ramming it home with the loading lever attached to the gun's frame and resting under the barrel. The nipples on the rear of the chambers were then primed, in the same manner as a single-shot musket, with percussion caps. The gun could also be loaded with loose powder and ball, but the military usually provided cartridges.

There were other drawbacks. Colt had produced revolving rifles off and on for twenty-five years. Although early models had experienced unintended multiple chamber ignitions, the latest version, along with proper ammunition, seemed to have resolved that problem. Due to the escape of hot gas and occasional lead slivers from the Colt's chamber/barrel junction on firing, however, it was not advisable to shoot it with the left hand supporting the stock in advance of the action, the usual position when firing a rifle.

The historian of the Ninth Illinois Cavalry remembered that "the Colt's revolving rifle was an excellent arm, and had served us well on many an occasion; but there was one serious objection to them: when being discharged they would shoot splinters of lead into the wrist and hand of the man firing. This problem, characteristic of all revolvers, even modern ones, occurs when they "go out of time," creating a slight misalignment between chamber mouth and barrel, causing lead to shave from a bullet making the jump between the two. It is seldom noticed in handguns, however, when with the preferred nineteenth-century one-hand hold, the shooter's left hand and arm were nowhere near the cylinder-barrel gap. Other problems occurred in service as well. A captain in the Second Michigan Cavalry reported that his men's Colts were "liable to get out of order and can't easily be repaired." Some officers complained that the stocks and locks of the Colts were more liable to break than more simply constructed guns. Lastly, Colt

Colt "New Model 1855" sidehammer revolving rifle. These guns were in great demand in the first two years of the war, as the only repeating rifle systems available. By 1863, with the advent of the Spencer and Henry, demand for these guns diminished. Berdan's Sharpshooters were originally equipped with Colts, but turned them in for Sharps rifles. There were no Colt rifles carried on the ordnance reports of Union units engaged at Gettysburg, although some Confederate cavalrymen may have been armed with them. (*John Kuhl*)

paper cartridges were subject to the problems of all paper ammunition: susceptibility to rough handling and moisture.[7]

Some Colt Model 1855s already in government storage or purchased on the open market were in the hands of troops in the field as early as the fall of 1861. Between November 1861 and February 1863, the Federal government purchased another 4,613 Model 1855s directly from Colt. When Colonel Berdan's regiments turned in their Colts for Sharps rifles, the Colts were sent to the west, where they were in demand. There was no such demand in the Army of the Potomac, however, and no Colt rifles were reported as in service by any of that army's units at Gettysburg.[8]

There were also some Colts in Southern hands. Many of the 765 Colt revolving carbines and rifles purchased by the government in the years leading up to the Civil War were stored in Southern arsenals and subsequently issued to Rebel units, along with some Model 1855s captured from Yankee forces. North Carolina began the war with sixty Colt carbines and 120 Colt rifles, which were issued to state troops. Among other Rebel units armed with at least some Colt repeating long arms were the First Virginia, Third Texas, and Thirteenth Tennessee Cavalry, as well as the Eighth Virginia and Eleventh Mississippi Infantry. Since the First Virginia Cavalry and Eighth Virginia Infantry, as well as the Eleventh Mississippi Infantry, fought at Gettysburg, it is quite possible that some Colts found their way to the battle in Confederate hands.[9]

Colt's dominance of the repeating rifle field would be short-lived. By 1860, the relentless advance of nineteenth-century industrialization and technology had led to the development of two practical breechloading repeating magazine rifles: the Henry and the Spencer. These revolutionary arms fired self-contained (bullet, priming compound, and powder all enclosed by a waterproof copper case) rimfire cartridges, the invention of which had made them technically possible. "Rimfire" ammunition featured fulminate priming compound spread around the case rim, in the same manner as a modern .22 long rifle cartridge. As with many advances in nineteenth-century firearms technology, the new ammunition had its beginnings in France, the brainchild of one Gustave Flobert. At the age of sixteen, Flobert was apprenticed to a Paris gun and sword maker named Sattler. During the 1840s, Flobert, aided by his younger brother Ernest, developed a new style of cartridge. Flobert ammunition used a large fulminate percussion cap as both detonating device and, aided by a bit of gunpowder, propulsive charge for a small bullet fitted into its open end. The space between priming compound and bullet was not entirely filled with powder, according to Flobert, to "confine the burning inside the cartridge" rather than in the barrel. The Flobert cartridge, developed in 1846 and patented in 1849, was intended for indoor target shooting and was far too anemic to attract the attention of military men.[10]

Developmental progress by the Americans Horace Smith and Daniel Wesson resulted in an improved version of Flobert's ammunition. Smith and Wesson lengthened the copper case and increased its power, producing the first complete rimfire cartridge, which, however, remained minimal by military standards. By 1860, B. Tyler Henry, in the employ of New Haven arms, had managed to develop a .44 caliber rimfire round with a charge of twenty-six grains of powder loaded behind a 216-grain bullet to shoot in his modification of the previously unspectacular "Volcanic" magazine rifle, originally designed to fire a self-contained but low-powered "rocket ball" with powder held inside the hollow-base bullet and priming compound affixed to its base.[11]

Christopher Spencer's rifle, which appeared on the scene around the same time, used a cartridge developed for him by the cartridge making company of Crittenden and Tibbals of South Coventry, Connecticut, in

1861. In the few years since Smith and Wesson had introduced their .22 rimfire cartridge, companies like Crittenden and Tibbals had expanded rimfire technology so that the manufacture of much larger calibers was feasible. For Spencer, the company developed a large copper-cased rimfire round that they labeled their "No. 56 Army" and that later became popularly known as the .56-.56 Spencer round. Though theoretically a .52 caliber cartridge, it actually fired a bullet in the same nominal .54 caliber diameter as the Sharps rifle.[12]

The outbreak of civil war in America provided the inventors, manufacturers, and promoters of the Spencer and Henry rifles (all New Englanders) with a potential mass market they perceived might make them rich and save the nation at the same time. In the summer of 1861, Oliver Winchester's New Haven Arms Company was tooling up to produce the Henry rifle—his improvement on the "Volcanic"—and brothers Charles and Rush Cheney, who had secured manufacturing rights to Christopher Spencer's invention, were in the first stages of production planning for that gun.

Both rifles used manually operated levers to extract fired cartridge cases and load fresh ammunition from their magazines. The Henry's magazine extended under its barrel from the action (firing mechanism) to the muzzle, moving cartridges under spring pressure onto a carrier that lifted them up to the chamber as the lever was worked. The Spencer's seven-shot spring-powered magazine was housed in its buttstock and fed cartridges into the action from the rear via a lever-actuated rolling breechblock. The Henry's lever also cocked the gun's hammer for firing, while the Spencer required a separate manual hammer cocking motion after a cartridge was chambered.

Winchester and the Cheneys exploited political connections (particularly a friendship with Navy Secretary Gideon Welles) and the uniqueness of their products to arrange a series of government tests in 1861. Both guns received favorable reviews, but with ultimately disappointing results to their promoters. The army ordered no Henrys or Spencers, although the navy contracted for 700 Spencer rifles. General Ripley was, to be kind, not enthusiastic about adopting unproved weapons systems of any type in the midst of a crisis in which arms representing current technology were in short supply.[13]

Tests like those afforded the Henry and Spencer were conducted under controlled conditions on hand-assembled prototype arms, and although they might suggest further consideration, they did not promise ultimate success in the field. The long-term durability of new weapons and ammunition could only be determined through extended field testing under combat conditions. Even should they prove durable, expensive innovative arms that lacked the facilities or machinery to produce both guns and spare parts and using new and unproved ammunition with limited sources of supply presented potentially serious logistical problems. At the time of testing, there were no Henry rifles commercially available, and Spencer and the Cheney brothers did not even have a factory building, much less the tooling necessary to produce their gun. Ripley needed to equip a vast army of raw recruits with standard Springfield-pattern Model 1861 rifle-muskets as rapidly as possible, so contracts for these guns were, correctly, his highest priority, and he paid even less attention to repeaters than to breechloaders in general.

Colt revolving rifle production was limited as well, but when war broke out, the Colt was the only repeating military arm actually in production. Because of this, commanders like Major General William S. Rosecrans, whose military thoughts ran to new tactical models that fast-moving troops equipped with fast-firing small arms would facilitate, relentlessly petitioned his superiors in Washington for Colts. They were, in fact, the only field-proven repeaters available.[14]

Repeating rifles firing self-contained metallic cartridges did not become available to the military and public until June 1862, when several hundred Henrys arrived at civilian gun dealers in Louisville, Kentucky. Although the statement of a Union officer forced to surrender to a force of Rebel horsemen armed with "16 shooters" in August 1862 indicates that Confederate cavalry may actually have first used privately purchased Henrys in combat, increasing personal and some state sales had several thousand of them in the hands of soldiers, mostly Union, by the following year.[15]

While Henry distribution depended on the private sector, the Cheney brothers, through intensive lobbying, finally managed to secure an army contract for 10,000 Spencer rifles to add to their navy

The army ordered 10,000 seven-shot Spencer repeating rifles in 1862, but first deliveries did not take place until December of that year. Although a significant number went to Colonel John T. Wilder's brigade in the west, the Fifth Michigan Cavalry was completely armed with Spencers as was a significant portion of the Sixth. Both regiments fought at Gettysburg in the cavalry fight at Rummell's farm. (*John Kuhl*)

order. According to the terms of the contract, the first delivery of 500 guns was scheduled for March 1862—a goal that proved impossible to fulfill. Although the Spencer company was assessed a 2,500-gun order reduction as a penalty for late delivery, company treasurer Warren Fisher succeeded in deferring deliveries until December 1862, while Christopher Spencer set up a factory in the Chickering Piano Company building in Boston. Deliveries on the initial contract continued through June 1863, and as the Spencer made a name for itself in combat, future contracts would be forthcoming. Most were for the shorter carbine version of the gun, intended for cavalry use. Spencer cavalry carbines were first delivered in October 1863.[16]

It is alleged that the first Spencer used in combat was a prototype rifle carried by Sergeant Francis O. Lombard of the First Massachusetts Cavalry. According to the story, Lombard fired his Spencer at Confederates in October 1862 in a skirmish near Cumberland, Maryland. There is, however, only one unconfirmed anecdotal source for the story.[17]

The first Spencers shipped on the army contract left the factory in December 1862 and were issued to Colonel Joseph Tarr Copeland's newly raised Fifth Michigan Cavalry. Copeland, who envisioned his new regiment as a mounted infantry force, had lobbied for repeating rifles for his men. He had some political pull and used it to secure Spencer rifles. Copeland's troopers were initially assigned to the defenses of Washington, however, and would wait some time to use their innovative arms on the enemy.

Spencers gained their earliest, and perhaps greatest, fame in the hands of the men of Colonel John T. Wilder's brigade. Wilder's foot soldiers had been mounted in accordance with General Rosecrans' desire to have an elite force able to move quickly and seize critical terrain in advance of his main army and hold it until the rest of the army was able to reinforce success. At first, though, they remained armed with muzzleloading rifle-muskets.

The colonel, who fully shared General Rosecrans' tactical concepts, was initially interested in the Henry repeater, which had seen limited combat use in Kentucky since the summer of 1862, to arm his shock troops. On March 20, 1863, Wilder wrote Oliver Winchester from Murfreesboro, "at what price will you furnish me *nine hundred* of your 'Henry's Rifles,' delivered at Cincinnati, Ohio, *without* ammunition, *with* gun slings attached? Two of my regiments, now mounted, have signified their willingness to purchase these arms, *at their own expense* [emphasis original]."[18]

Wilder's contacts with Oliver Winchester failed to pan out, however, due to the painfully slow 200-gun-per-month production rate at New Haven Arms. The eager young colonel did not have time to get on the Henry waiting list, so for him Christopher Spencer's visit to the Army of Tennessee was fortuitous. The inventor, traveling at the behest of his company in the spring of 1863, was demonstrating the Spencer rifle in order to create interest among officers in the field and generate more contracts after the initial 7,500-gun army order was filled.[19]

It made sense that Spencer and Wilder would hit it off, since both were self-made men of the new industrial age. Spencer, although still a young man, had extensive experience in the firearms and other industries and invented a wide range of useful production machinery in addition to his gun. Wilder had learned the trades of draftsman, pattern maker, and millwright on the job and had invented a number of hydraulic machines, a field in which he was a widely acknowledged expert by 1860.[20]

Popular history would have it that after witnessing Spencer's product demonstration, Wilder was so eager to get his hands on a shipment of the inventor's rifles that he proposed that his men purchase the guns directly from the factory, using his personal line of credit as security.

This was the case when the colonel and his men were considering Henrys, but existing evidence suggests that it was an unnecessary step to acquire Spencers and actually not even possible at the time. While Henrys were available (albeit limited by production capability) in the open market to anyone, the entire production of the Spencer Company was committed to filling its government contract in a timely manner. The inventor's trip to Rosecrans' Army of the Cumberland was intended to spur Spencer requests from commanders through the normal conduits of supply, exhausting the current contract and stimulating new ones, not to promote individual sales. Spencer's own account seems to confirm this scenario. He noted that after meeting Wilder, the colonel "asked me to ride over to Headquarters with him and show the rifle to Gen. Rosecrans whom he thought would make a requisition for them for his [Wilder's] troops. The visit was successful."[21]

Wilder's men began to receive their new repeaters on May 15, 1863. Although they never engaged in any training with the guns other than informal familiarization firing, on June 4, they had their first chance to use them in a skirmish with several Confederate cavalry regiments at Liberty, Tennessee. One of Wilder's officers recalled that following the fight the colonel was "highly delighted with the rifles."[22]

Toward the end of June, Rosecrans began to maneuver his army in hopes of driving Confederate General Braxton Bragg out of Tennessee. Wilder's brigade—composed of the Ninety-eighth and 123rd Illinois, the seventeenth and Seventy-second Indiana Mounted Infantry, and Captain Eli Lilly's Eighteenth Indiana Battery—was assigned the task of seizing the key terrain of Hoover's Gap. The brigade did so with aplomb, scattering surprised, outnumbered, and outgunned Rebel defenders. Brigadier General William B. Bate's infantry brigade counterattacked Wilder and ran into a blizzard of Spencer bullets. His frontal assault stopped cold by the volume of Wilder's fire, Bate ordered his Thirty-seventh Georgia to turn the Federal flank. Although initially pinned down by Spencer fire from the Seventeenth Indiana, the Georgians gained ground when the Seventeenth, fulfilling a prediction of repeating-rifle opponents, ran out of ammunition. Colonel Wilder, however, was a hands-on commander and able tactician and ordered up eight companies of the Ninety-eighth Illinois he had held in reserve to restore the line. The Confederates eventually broke off the action, leaving Hoover's Gap in Yankee hands, enabling Rosecrans to successfully outflank Bragg, who abandoned middle Tennessee and fell back into Georgia.[23]

Spencer rifles played a significant part in Rosecrans' relatively bloodless victory, but the men behind the guns as well as the proper tactical use made of repeaters was as important, if not more so, than the actual technology of the weapons. Confederate casualties had not been inordinate, and the Rebels might have driven Wilder's Brigade from its position, had the colonel not skillfully manipulated his reserve force. Colonel Wilder had begun to engage a tactical learning curve—the proper tactical use of repeating rifles.

By June 3, 1863, Robert E. Lee's veteran infantry were sidling west from the Rappahannock line toward the Shenandoah Valley while Lieutenant General Ambrose P. Hill's Corps remained in defensive positions at Fredericksburg, confronting the puzzled General Hooker. Aware the enemy was moving, but not knowing where, the Union commander ordered his VI Corps to conduct a reconnaissance in force across the river; and on June 5, the corps's Second Division secured a bridgehead on the south bank.

General Lee, meanwhile, was on his way to Pennsylvania with the bulk of his army. On June 9, the Federal cavalry clashed with its Confederate counterpart at Brandy Station. The ensuing battle, one of the largest mounted encounters of the war, firmly established the improved quality of the Yankee horse and confirmed the Army of Northern Virginia's shift toward the Shenandoah Valley invasion route. Ironically, the Spencer-armed Fifth and Sixth Michigan Cavalry, with the most potential firepower of any mounted units in either eastern army, remained in garrison in the defenses of Washington as Brandy Station raged.

By June 13, General Ewell was advancing his corps of the Army of Northern Virginia on Winchester, Virginia, then occupied by forces under the command of Union Major General Robert H. Milroy. Although outnumbered, Milroy decided to stand and fight Ewell but made the mistake of limiting his defense to the static forts west of the town. Feinting to the south and east, Ewell countermarched north and overwhelmed a Union outpost, then moved to block the road leading north from Winchester. Outmaneuvered, Milroy retreated to Stephenson's Depot, where he was forced to surrender the bulk of his force. Ewell reported a loss of 269 men, while Federal casualties of over 4,400 included more than 3,300 men captured. Although some Union troops managed to escape, and many of the prisoners were sick and wounded from other commands hospitalized in Winchester, the disaster did not bode well for the developing campaign.

One aspect of the Winchester debacle of 1863 that is often overlooked is that it provided the eastern theater introduction to combat of the Henry rifle. It appears that several of Milroy's regiments were armed in part with Henrys. Colonel J. Warren Keifer of the 110th Ohio, whose command was badly battered defending one of Milroy's outposts, reported that he could not "refrain from calling attention to my sharpshooters. Armed with the Henry rifle, in each engagement they fired almost continuous streams into the enemy's ranks, causing great loss of life. They also, under my own eyes, shot down a number of the enemy's officers." Despite Keifer's praise, there is no evidence that the Henrys of the 110th made any significant impression on Ewell's victorious Confederates.[24]

The Twenty-third Illinois, another regiment deployed in western Virginia in the summer of 1863, mustered at least one Henry rifle during the Winchester fight. The Twenty-third, also known as the "Irish Brigade of the West," had begun the war as a hard-luck outfit. Commanded by Colonel James A. Mulligan of Chicago, the predominantly Irish American unit was mustered in on June 12, 1861, and moved to Missouri shortly afterward. By September, the Twenty-third was in Lexington, where it was part of a 2,700-man force besieged by ten times that number of Confederates. After a nine-day siege, the Lexington garrison surrendered and was paroled. The regiment was first mustered out of service, then exchanged, reorganized, and sent to Harper's Ferry, Virginia. It remained in the eastern theater for the remainder of the war.

The men of the reorganized Twenty-third were determined to have every advantage should they find themselves in a tight situation again. Lieutenant John Brown, a company commander in the Twenty-third, privately purchased a Henry from a gun dealer named Adams in Wheeling, West Virginia, apparently in the spring of 1863. Brown was so enthused with the rifle that on September 26, he wrote New Haven Arms regarding the purchase of "from fifteen to twenty-five—perhaps thirty—for my company."[25]

Although repeating rifles had begun to appear here and there in the Union armies in the east, until the end of June, 1863, they were still absent from the Army of the Potomac. As that month passed, General Hooker's cavalry, under the command of Brigadier General Alfred Pleasonton, continued to probe the shifting Confederate army, engaging in bitter little cavalry fights with Major General J. E. B. Stuart's Rebel horsemen at places like Aldie and Middleburg, Virginia. Hooker and Pleasonton called for reinforcements for their stretched and strained mounted units, lobbying for Major General Julius Stahel's mounted division to be added to the Army of the Potomac.

Stahel, a Hungarian-born immigrant who had served heroically in his country's 1848 revolution against the Hapsburgs, came to America in 1856, where he worked as a journalist in New York and became friendly with German American leaders. Appointed as lieutenant colonel of the predominantly German Eighth New York Infantry in 1861, Stahel rose to brigade command in 1862 and temporarily commanded the XI Army Corps in early 1863. In March, he was personally assigned by President Lincoln to form the three cavalry brigades in the defenses of Washington into a division and aggressively pursue John Singleton Mosby's partisan rangers, who had been penetrating Union lines at will. Stahel never caught Mosby, but he organized the cavalry, including the Spencer-armed Fifth and Sixth Michigan, and got it into the field in Virginia. Hooker's needs assured that the Wolverines would travel much further afield in the high summer of 1863.

While in Washington, the green Fifth and Sixth Michigan Cavalry regiments had been brigaded with the Seventh Michigan Cavalry, another new unit, and all placed under the command of Brigadier General Copeland, whose tactical concepts paralleled those of Rosecrans and who was instrumental in equipping the Fifth and part of the Sixth with Spencer rifles. In late June, the Michigan troopers were attached to the Army of the Potomac and sent north toward

The .44 caliber Henry repeating rifle fired a smaller cartridge than the Spencer, but had a 15 round magazine. Although some privately purchased Henrys were used during the Gettysburg campaign by the 110th Ohio Infantry in the Shenandoah Valley battle of Winchester, there is no evidence that any Henrys were present at Gettysburg. *(John Kuhl)*

Pennsylvania, following the Confederates. On the way, they were placed under entirely new division and brigade leadership. In the wake of General Hooker's resignation and General Meade's elevation to command of the army, General Pleasonton cleaned house. At the end of June, both Stahel and Copeland found themselves out of active-duty cavalry jobs as Pleasonton took the opportunity to jump several of his favorite young officers into positions of authority.

Stahel's replacement was Judson Kilpatrick, and Copeland gave way to young George Armstrong Custer, who had previously unsuccessfully lobbied for a regimental command in the Michigan brigade but now commanded the entire unit, which was stiffened by the addition of the veteran First Michigan Cavalry. Joining Custer in brigade command under Kilpatrick in what became the Third Division of the Army of the Potomac's Cavalry Corps was Elon Farnsworth, another young captain advanced to brigadier general. Pleasonton had little chance to see his favorites perform in their new roles, however, as General Meade, who had assented to the promotions, kept his cavalry commander close to army headquarters, where Pleasonton acted more as a staff officer and advisor than combat commander. The Cavalry Corps's divisions would act as semi-independent entities in the Gettysburg campaign.

Each Federal cavalry division was assigned a screening and reconnaissance mission of its own by Meade and Pleasonton, and the Yankee horsemen rode hard, seeking out the enemy and occasionally skirmishing with Stuart's Rebel riders, who were off on a grand raid through Maryland and into Pennsylvania. On June 29, Kilpatrick led his Third Division out of Frederick, Maryland, toward York, Pennsylvania. By the following morning, the division was approaching Hanover, which had recently been occupied by Confederate cavalry, with Custer and his First and Seventh Michigan in the lead.

After gathering intelligence and passing through the town, the Yankee rear guard engaged a number of Confederates, initiating a fight in which the Eighteenth Pennsylvania Cavalry was pushed back into Hanover. A Federal counterattack drove the Rebels back, battering the Second North Carolina Cavalry and capturing its commander, Lieutenant Colonel William Payne, whom a New York trooper helped climb out of a vat of brown dye into which he had been pitched when his horse was shot.

General Farnsworth's brigade barricaded itself in Hanover, and combat soon broke out across the fields around the town, with regiments from both sides fed into the fight piecemeal. By early afternoon, all elements of the Michigan Brigade had returned to the scene and were deployed outside the town to the northwest. As more of Stuart's horsemen arrived, a desultory stalemate punctuated by artillery fire settled in on the battlefield.

In an attempt to break the impasse, General Custer dismounted Colonel George Gray's Sixth Michigan and ordered the Wolverines, armed with a mix of Spencer rifles and Burnside carbines, to move under cover of some trees against one of Stuart's artillery batteries and a cavalry detachment posted to protect it. The Michigan men surprised the Rebels, opening fire on them at a range of between 200 and 300 yards. As Spencer bullets fell in and around the enemy position, the Confederate cavalry took off for the rear. The Yankees advanced but then retreated as Brigadier General Fitzhugh Lee hastened reinforcements to the danger point. The Federals advanced again unsuccessfully and settled down to positions from which they could keep the Rebel line under fire. After dark, Stuart disengaged and withdrew. Hanover was the first time Spencer rifles were used by a unit in combat in the eastern theater. They would get a more thorough test within days.

On July 1, the Michigan Brigade moved toward East Berlin, Pennsylvania. The troopers could hear the rumble of guns in the distance as the battle of Gettysburg began, opened by General Buford's division with its single-shot breechloaders, but they did not move to the sound of those guns until Kilpatrick was ordered to bring his division to the battlefield on July 2.

The early morning hours of July 3 found the Michigan men camped at Two Taverns. Roused at 7:00 AM by General Kilpatrick after three hours' sleep, the Wolverines prepared to follow their division commander and Farnsworth's brigade to an assigned position on the Union left flank. An hour later, however, as the Michigan men began to leave camp following Kilpatrick and Farnsworth's departure, a staff officer arrived with a message for Custer from Brigadier General Gregg, commander of the Second Division of the Cavalry Corps. The general was concerned about the Yankee right flank, and he needed help.

General Gregg was an 1855 West Point graduate and an experienced, astute, and well-liked leader. Late in the day on July 2, his men had fought Confederate infantry at nearby Brinkerhoff's Ridge, successfully diverting the Stonewall Brigade from the main Rebel infantry attack directed toward East Cemetery ridge. Gregg realized the critical tactical importance of the intersection of the Hanover and Low Dutch roads, key to the Federal right and rear, and asked Custer to temporarily cover the critical crossroads with his brigade.

Gregg left one of his two brigades, under his cousin Colonel John Irvin Gregg, to link up with VI Corps infantrymen in the vicinity of Wolf Hill and led his other brigade, under Colonel John B. McIntosh, to relieve Custer and enable the Michigan brigade to rejoin Kilpatrick. By mid-morning, Gregg's assumption that there might be a Confederate attempt to loop around the Union right flank appeared to be correct. Major General Oliver O. Howard advised Pleasonton that a large Confederate mounted force was heading that way down the York road. Despite this intelligence, the Federal cavalry commander did not countermand Custer's orders to move toward Little Round Top. It was soon abundantly clear to Custer that Confederate cavalry were moving toward the Rummel Farm, to his front.

The mounted force was Major General J. E. B. Stuart's division. The Confederate cavalry commander arrived at the Rummel Farm that morning hoping to take advantage of any opportunity that presented itself to disrupt the Federal right and rear. There is no evidence that there was any coordinated plan for him to attack the Yankee rear in concert with General Longstreet's assault on the Union center, but Stuart was free to do whatever he wished to abet the overall Confederate tactical goal.

Stuart ordered one of his artillery batteries to fire four shells in different directions, most likely in an attempt to discover the Union positions by provoking a reaction. Eric Wittenberg, author of the most recent and detailed study of the July 3 cavalry fight at Gettysburg, believes that he was planning an ambush of Gregg's men. Stuart's subsequent actions appear to confirm this assumption.[26]

The first Confederate units to reach the field were the brigades of Brigadier General Albert G. Jenkins and Colonel John R. Chambliss. Jenkins had been wounded by a shell fragment the day before and was not present. Many of his men had been detailed to guard prisoners, but the rest remained with Stuart. The lead unit of Jenkins' brigade and the whole of Stuart's division was Lieutenant Colonel Vincent Witcher's Thirty-fourth Virginia Cavalry Battalion. The twenty-six-year-old Witcher was a tough man from a tough family. Just prior to the war, his father and other relatives had engaged in a gun and knife fight at a local store over depositions filed in a divorce that they believed sullied the honor of a female extended family member. Old man Witcher and his son and son-in-law shot and stabbed the aggrieved husband, James Clement, and his two brothers to death but were acquitted on grounds of self-defense.

Although attached to the Army of Northern Virginia for the Gettysburg campaign, the Thirty-fourth had previously served in an irregular and raiding role in western Virginia and was more accurately classified as a mounted infantry unit than a traditional cavalry outfit. The battalion evolved from an independent company that Witcher raised in 1861, which eventually grew into a battalion. Witcher's men were initially armed with U.S. Model 1841 "Mississippi" rifles in .54 caliber. By mid-1863, the unit's armament was more diverse, including some Enfield and Richmond rifle-muskets and Richmond Armory short rifle-muskets purpose built for mounted infantry use (all in .577 or .58 caliber) as well as some Austrian Lorenz rifle-muskets (most likely in .54 caliber) in the Thirty-fourth's ranks. In addition, most of the men of the Thirty-fourth carried revolvers.[27]

Stuart ordered Witcher to dismount his battalion and occupy the Rummel Farm, personally posting the Virginians in the barn and along a nearby stone wall. Witcher's men quickly went to work fortifying the barn by cutting loopholes in the walls to poke their muskets through. While they worked, an artillery battery set up and began to fire at Custer's men across the fields to their front. Stuart's other brigades were held in reserve and masked from the Federals by a woodlot, although some of Chambliss' men were apparently in the open.

Custer ordered Lieutenant Alexander C. M. Pennington's Battery M, Second U.S. Artillery, to return fire on the Rebel guns and dismounted cavalry occupying the farm, and effective Yankee counterbattery fire soon silenced the Confederate artillery. As Pennington's gunners opened fire, General Gregg arrived on the field with Colonel John B. McIntosh's Brigade. McIntosh quickly began to deploy his men to replace the Michigan troopers covering the crossroads, but Gregg, concerned about the potential force to his front, asked Custer to stay on in support. Custer replied that if ordered to do so, he would, and Gregg wasted no time issuing the order.

The Michigan brigade waited in reserve while McIntosh advanced the dismounted First New Jersey Cavalry on the Rebels occupying the Rummel Farm. Reaching a covering stone wall, the Jerseyans unslung their Burnside breechloading carbines and began to trade a desultory fire with Witcher's men. The Jersey regiment mustered 199 effectives, but the First's skirmish line was no more than 150 men, due to the need to detach horse holders.[28]

As the enemy fire intensified, McIntosh sent the 335 troopers of the Third Pennsylvania in to support the Jerseymen. Some of the Pennsylvanians remained mounted in reserve while others dismounted, with horse holders detached, and added their Sharps carbine fire to the fight. While the Yankees engaged the Thirty-fourth, Stuart held the rest of his command—the brigades of Colonel John R. Chambliss and Brigadier Generals Fitzhugh Lee and Wade Hampton—behind and in a nearby woodlot. It appears that he might have used the Thirty-fourth as bait to spring an ambush on Gregg's men, whom he hoped would engage and be distracted by the dismounted Rebels, leaving them open to an attack by his mounted brigades. When McIntosh's two regiments ran short of carbine ammunition, they withdrew, to be replaced on the skirmish line by Custer's Fifth Michigan and part of the Sixth Michigan, which had moved up in support positions.[29]

As the Jerseyans and Pennsylvanians exchanged places with the Michigan men, the Virginians also ran low on ammunition and fell back to a second line. Relying on a statement in General Stuart's report, many believe that the men of Jenkins' brigade were carrying only ten rounds of ammunition each. This was, according to Lieutenant Colonel Witcher, "absolutely untrue." Although the members of the brigade detailed to guard prisoners were limited to ten rounds each, those committed to the battle on Rummel's Farm started out with full cartridge boxes. When several enlisted men sent to bring up more ammunition from the rear failed to return, Witcher himself went to investigate and found one of his men had been wounded but had acquired a supply of cartridges, which he brought back to the firing line.[30]

As the men of the Thirty-fourth refilled their cartridge boxes, they were reinforced by elements of the Fourteenth and Sixteenth Virginia Cavalry. Thus bolstered, the line advanced, with, according to Witcher, "all told, 600 men besides officers in line" covering a front of "some 300 or perhaps 400 yards long." It is presumed that this estimate deducts unit horse holders already to the rear. Based on its June 30 strength reports, and deducting losses incurred earlier in the campaign, the Fifth Michigan fielded 646 men, including officers, deploying approximately 484 men in a dismounted skirmish line.[31]

Witcher's men crossed several stone walls, entered a wheat field, and advanced up to a fence line before they engaged the Michigan regiment. A fierce firefight ensued. Spencer slugs filled the air, and the Virginians were hit by a hail of bullets. Captain Edward Bouldin of the Fourteenth remembered that "the fire was very severe. We were lying down on the ground behind the bottom rails. So deadly was the fire that once, when one of my men was wounded, two others were struck as soon as they rose to bear him from the field." Another officer from the Fourteenth recalled that "our opponents poured a rain of bullets and shells on us, but were forced slowly to fall back. We lost heavily."[32]

The fight went on for some time until it proved too much for the Fourteenth and Sixteenth. Riddled by Spencer fire, both units took off for the rear. Witcher recalled that they "left me and the field," and the Thirty-fourth had to face the Spencers alone. The battalion hung on, though, slugging it out. It is unlikely that the Virginians had been fully trained in marksmanship to the military standards of the day, involving range estimation and consequent trajectory compensation. Still, the range of combat on Rummel Farm was relatively short, and Witcher's men, Mountaineers all, knew well how to draw a bead and smoothly squeeze a trigger. They gave the Wolverines as hot a time as they could handle.

One Michigan veteran remembered that "an hour's fighting and we think our line is solid, but 'tis might stubborn work. The rebs are solid also in their position. 'Greek has met Greek.'" Major Noah Ferry, commanding the dismounted men of the Fifth, stood up on a tree stump to survey his firing line, but was pulled down to safety by his men. Ferry, with the fury of the fight upon him, then climbed up on a rock, yelling, "Michigan to the res—" as a bullet hit him in the head, killing him instantly. Eventually the Michigan men began to fall back, as, like the case of the Seventeenth Indiana at Hoover's Gap, they ran out of ammunition.[33]

Seeing the Wolverines move toward the rear, Stuart ordered Colonel Chambliss' brigade to charge. As the Thirty-fourth advanced on foot and Chambliss' horsemen thundered downhill toward the dismounted Yankees, the Seventh Michigan rode to the rescue, clashing with the enemy riders and dismounted riflemen along a fence line. The Seventh's troopers could not get over or through the fence and began to pile up as their horses shied away from the rails and were shot down. The Thirty-fourth poured a stream of bullets into the Michigan men until they fell back in disorder. Under heavy and effective Federal artillery fire from Pennington's battery and Captain Alanson M. Randol's four-gun consolidated Battery E/G, First U.S. Artillery, plus whatever the Seventh could hit them with, Chambliss' brigade fell back as well.

Stuart then launched a second mounted charge, hurling Lee's and Hampton's brigades at the Federals. This time, the First Michigan, along with part of the First New Jersey and Third Pennsylvania, charged headlong into the Rebel advance and stopped it cold in a melee of slashing sabers and barking revolvers. While this desperate mounted fight took place, Witcher's men continued to fire into the mounted Yankees from their flanking position. The Thirty-fourth engaged the Fifth Michigan once more, as some men of that regiment, although out of Spencer cartridges, remounted and joined the fight with their revolvers but were driven back by Virginia musketry.

Stuart's riders retreated beyond the Rummel Farm buildings as the fight abated, and toward the end of the day, the Thirty-fourth fell back as well. The battalion held the farm, however, until the Confederates evacuated the area the following morning. Lieutenant Colonel Witcher's men paid a heavy price for their constancy. Almost twenty-three years later, Witcher painfully recalled that he could "never, no never, forget that eventful night when, accompanied by one courier, my adjutant Edwards & sergeant major, both being wounded. I full of grief and Bitterness, rode to the barns in our rear and saw, with tears in my eyes, my brave fellows, from away over the mountains in West Virginia, laid out in windrows, torn and bleeding. I shall never forget that night, or the next morning's parade when I could muster but 96 enlisted men." The Thirty-fourth, which lost only one man as a prisoner, had an incredible 75 percent casualty rate.[34]

The Fifth Michigan reported fifty-six men killed, wounded, and missing—most of its casualties inflicted by the Thirty-fourth—for an 8.7 percent casualty rate. The Seventh Michigan, which suffered the heaviest losses in the Wolverine brigade, many of them caused by rifles and rifle-muskets as the Thirty-fourth fired into the regiment when it piled up at the fence, lost 100 men, for a rate of 26.1 percent. The entire Michigan Brigade, which entered the fight with 1,925 men, lost 257, or 13.3 percent.[35]

Spencer rifles in the hands of the Michigan men proved very effective in a defensive role and inflicted a large number of casualties in the dismounted fight, pouring out bullets and badly shooting up Witcher's command. Spencer fire totally demoralized the two Virginia units that fought alongside Witcher and drove them from the field, but the Wolverines were unable to capitalize on this by advancing to a position that would determine the outcome of the battle. The Thirty-fourth, indeed, held its ground and, even with terrible casualties, was able to hang on until the Fifth ran out of ammunition and then advance to inflict casualties on the Seventh and First Michigan.

The July 3 cavalry fight at Gettysburg ended in a tactical stalemate. That deadlock prevented Stuart from looping around the Union right, however, and in that sense was favorable to the Federals. Were the Spencer rifles decisive in producing this result, or was the tough horse-to-horse saber and revolver brawl that blunted the attack of Hampton and Fitzhugh Lee following the Fifth Michigan's fight with the Thirty-fourth the decisive act of the Rummel Farm struggle? The evidence suggests the latter.

In the end, however, it was apparent that if the buck-and-ball volleys of the Twelfth New Jersey and Irish brigade represented the past, and the deadly musketry of the Thirty-fourth Virginia the present, the rapid-fire stream of bullets poured out by the Fifth Michigan signaled the ultimate future of small arms in war. In the high summer of 1863, although General Custer determined on the spot that the Spencer rifle was the best weapon that army cavalrymen could be issued, the jury still seemed out to many. Nevertheless, its decision was quickly forth-coming.

Custer was correct. The Michigan Spencers at Gettysburg proved that repeating rifles firing self-contained metallic cartridges could play a significant tactical role in the war. That those repeaters would be used by the Union army in increasing numbers was now a given. How they would be used was still problematic in the aftermath of Gettysburg, as a tactical model was not immediately apparent. The final years of the struggle would, however, begin to provide a glimpse of the modern.

During the 1864 Atlanta campaign, both infantry and cavalry sol-diers armed with Henrys and Spencers were used increasingly on the skirmish line. At the siege of Atlanta, the potential firepower of Spencer-armed cavalrymen resulted in their replacing several times the number of rifle-musket-armed infantry in the trench lines, freeing the foot soldiers to maneuver. In the spring of 1865, Major General James Wilson's cavalrymen advanced in open formations using Spencer car-bines to deliver a "marching fire" on enemy positions. That same spring, General Custer deployed dismounted Spencer-armed cavalry-men to fix an enemy force in position while mounted cavalry maneuvered around their flanks. Infantrymen armed with Spencer carbines and rifles provided covering fire for attacking troops at Fort Fisher and Petersburg in the final months of the conflict.

Following the end of the Civil War, the Spencer, its action unable to chamber the long-range metallic military cartridges then coming into vogue, quickly lost popularity and was succeeded by a single-shot breechloader. The repeating rifle would not return to the army inventory until the adoption of the Krag-Jorgensen bolt action in 1892. The Spencer's markets dried up, and with no ability to generate new sales or adapt to the firearms future, the Spencer Company went out of business shortly afterward. The Henry, although it never shared the official role of the Spencer in the Union army, evolved into the Winchester series of lever-action rifles, which served sporadically in foreign forces—most notably the Turkish army—but, more importantly, became world famous as sporting rifles, down to the day the factory closed in 2006.

Chapter 7

SHARPSHOOTERS

———◆◆◆———

SHARPSHOOTERS HAVE SERVED IN AMERICAN armies since Virginia and Pennsylvania riflemen joined the siege of Boston in 1775. Perhaps the most famous early sharpshooter was Timothy Murphy, who shinnied up a tree at Saratoga, took a careful bead with his flintlock long rifle, and shot British General Simon Fraser out of the saddle from between 200 and 300 yards away. Fraser's death was credited with breaking British morale and turning the tide of battle in favor of Murphy's American comrades.

Revolutionary War riflemen were at their best while skirmishing on their own hook and taking potshots at enemy officers at what were, for the time, long ranges. Since their rifles were not fitted for bayonets and had, at best, one-third the rate of fire of smoothbore muskets, riflemen could not stand the rush of a line of battle. General Washington later reduced the number of riflemen in his army, converting many into rapidly moving musket-armed light infantrymen. In his second Continental army enlistment, Timothy Murphy himself shouldered a smoothbore musket as a light infantryman in the Pennsylvania Line.

Forever after, the role of the sharpshooter in the U.S. army was muddled. The rifle regiments raised during the War of 1812 and the rifle companies within regular infantry regiments were assigned roles as skirmishers, taking a toll on enemy skirmishers or the enemy line of battle until it was engaged by their own smoothbore-armed line of battle. Sniping at officers and artillery crews at extreme long range was, if

considered, largely an afterthought. With rifles firing ballistically inferior round balls, it was also unlikely to be very effective. Despite this, the
occasional very long shot, by a much-practiced rifleman, was possible. In
the spring of 1813, an Indian sharpshooter reportedly climbed a tree and
fired on American water-carrying details from a fort along the Maumee
River in Ohio at a range of 600 yards. Although he wasn't taken seriously initially, over time, he managed to wound two soldiers. In
response, so the story goes, a Kentucky militiaman named Elijah Kirk
carefully observed the sniper's tree, adjusted his aim to compensate for
wind and distance, and dropped the Indian to the ground. In the 1930s,
muzzleloading shooter and writer Walter Cline attempted to duplicate
the feat with a .53 caliber long rifle, a duplex black powder load of fine-
and coarse-grained powder, and a wad between powder charge and
patched round ball. Cline fired ten shots at 600 yards, compensating as
he fired, and hit a man-sized target four times.[1]

In Civil War armies, where every man was, in theory, supposed to be
armed with a rifled weapon firing a conical projectile capable of long-
range accuracy, the rifleman's prior special status as skirmisher became
blurred. According to the manuals, every rifle-musket-armed soldier
was potentially a skirmisher. What, then, would the role of the especially good shot become in the strife between the states, an elite skirmisher
or long-range sniper? It was a conundrum that was never really
resolved during the course of the conflict, with aspects of both roles in
evidence at Gettysburg.

When the word "sharpshooter" is mentioned in the context of the
Civil War, the units that most often come to mind are Colonel Hiram
Berdan's First and Second United States Sharpshooters (U.S.S.S.).
These two regiments of green-uniformed Federals gained an awesome
reputation in the Northern press during the war and have maintained
it ever since.

Berdan, born in New York and raised in Michigan, was a talented
engineer, practical scientist, and inventor responsible for such diverse
devices as a gold-crushing machine and a mechanical bakery. In addition, he was one of the premier American rifle shots of the 1850s.
Berdan's inventive genius, applied to firearms, would secure his place in
history. The Berdan centerfire primer for metallic cartridges, for exam-

A squad from the Second U.S. Sharpshooters photographed in early 1862, when they were still armed with Colt .56 caliber revolving rifles. By Gettysburg, when they supplied a skirmish screen for the Union left flank, the Sharpshooters were carrying Sharps rifles. There were no Colts in service in the Army of the Potomac at Gettysburg, although there may have been some in the ranks of the Army of Northern Virginia's cavalry. The Colt was the only practical repeating rifle available in 1861, but by 1863 it was outclassed by the newer Henry and Spencer rifles firing self-contained cartridges. (*National Archives*)

ple, is still in use worldwide. One thing Hiram was not, however, was a great soldier. He was, in fact, despite his genuine accomplishments, perceived by many (including some of his own men) to be a self-promoting windbag with an aversion to combat.[2]

Berdan's personal failings, including his alleged strong reluctance to personally confront the enemy, led to an unsuccessful attempt to court-martial him for cowardice and was a factor in his resignation from the army at the end of 1863. Much of the reputation his men gained was genuine, however. And were it not for Berdan, they may never have had the opportunity to gain it. At the outbreak of the Civil War, a number of people, including Caspar Trepp, a veteran Swiss officer then living in America (who later became one of Berdan's chief accusers), called for the formation of a special Union army sharpshooter corps. Berdan had the political influence, promotional ability, and pure *chutzpah* to bring such a unit to life—and gain himself a commission as colonel.[3]

In the summer and fall of 1861, sharpshooter companies were raised in a number of states, including Minnesota, Michigan, New Hampshire,

New York, Pennsylvania, Vermont, and Wisconsin. Most, but not all, of these units were consolidated into the First and Second U.S.S.S. regiments, the First commanded by Colonel Berdan and the Second by Colonel Henry A. Post, although Berdan was understood to be in overall command of both regiments. The First mustered ten companies and the Second, eight. Two Massachusetts companies, designated "Andrew's Sharpshooters" after Massachusetts governor John A. Andrew, were originally designated for the Second U.S.S.S. but were, instead, attached as supplementary companies to Massachusetts line outfits, the Fifteenth and Twenty-Second Massachusetts Infantry Regiments.[4]

In order to be accepted as a sharpshooter, a volunteer had to be familiar with rifle shooting and pass a qualifying marksmanship test. A Minnesota newspaper advertised for sharpshooter recruits who were "able bodied men used to the rifle," and prospective sharpshooters were expected to shoot "a string of 50 inches in 10 consecutive shots at 200 yards, with globe [aperture] sights or telescopic sights from a rest." None of the bullet holes were to be more than five inches from the center of the bull's-eye. A candidate shooting offhand was required to achieve a fifty-inch string at a distance of 100 yards.

A "string" score was made by measuring the length of a string that extended from the center of the bull's-eye to each of the bullet holes. The criterion, roughly a ten-inch group by today's shooting standards, was not unusually demanding of a practiced marksman. Needless to say, many future sharpshooters fired groups considerably under the minimum requirement. One, Charles H. Townsend of Wisconsin, "fired five shots at 200 yards with a total measurement of three and three-quarters inches." About fifty percent of sharpshooter aspirants were able to pass the shooting test.[5]

Hiram Berdan's recruits were promised sixty dollars for the use of their own target rifles, should they desire to bring them to war. Recruiting officers promised those who reported unarmed, however, that they would be issued Sharps breechloading rifles. This pledge led to problems for Berdan, as he had originally ordered Springfield Model 1861 rifle-muskets for his men. Needless to say, Ordnance chief James W. Ripley, who had a dim view of breechloaders for infantry use and didn't want to divert the Sharps factory from making much-needed carbines, readily concurred with the new colonel's request. When Berdan changed his weapons preference to agree with that of his men, however, General Ripley "stonewalled" him.[6]

Most of the men of the First and Second U.S.S.S. arrived in camp at Washington unarmed, and they remained so while Berdan, Ripley, and assorted politicians wrangled over their eventual armament. One recruit, fifty-two-year-old Truman Head, also known as "California Joe," purchased his own Sharps Model 1859 rifle. When Joe brought his new Sharps to camp for inspection, sharpshooter enthusiasm for the gun increased, putting Berdan in an even tighter spot vis-à-vis General Ripley.

The sharpshooters spent the winter of 1861–1862 muttering over the small-arms difficulties but still training for the coming fight. Their exercises appear to have been based on French *Chasseur* and Zouave tactical concepts, with extensive open-order skirmish drill-and-bugle commands. Drill was not the only example of European military thinking manifested in the sharpshooter

Colonel Hiram Berdan, inventor and crack shot, raised two regiments of sharpshooters in 1861. At Gettysburg he commanded a reconaissance which engaged in a firefight with General Cadmus Wilcox's Confederate brigade, later claiming, erroneously, that he had uncovered General Longstreet's move on the Federal left flank. (*Library of Congress*)

regiments; their green uniforms, calfskin knapsacks with the hair left on, and leather leggings set them apart from run-of-the mill Union volunteers.[7]

Interestingly, target practice was not formally on the sharpshooters' training schedule. The men who brought their own rifles into service engaged in informal shooting matches, however, usually at a range of 220 yards. They were good. On one occasion, Vermonter Ai Brown shot a string of four and a quarter inches. Colonel Berdan could shoot with the best of his men, and once turned in an offhand string of five and nine-sixteenths inches.[8]

Although the winds of war began to stir strongly in the spring of 1862, Berdan's sharpshooters remained virtually without weapons until March of that year, when they received Colt's revolving rifles, which they accepted reluctantly until the promised Sharps guns could be provided. Berdan personally expressed enthusiasm for the Colts, and one historian has implied a possible financial arrangement between him and Colt (which, considering his postwar connections with the company, is possible). Despite this, the sharpshooters eventually got to trade in their Colts for Sharps. The First Regiment, which accompanied General George B. McClellan's army to the Virginia Peninsula, was issued the breechloaders in May, 1862, and the men of the Second received theirs a month later. As accurately predicted by General Ripley, however, the run of rifles had brought carbine production at the Sharps factory to a standstill for several months.[9]

The "Berdan Sharps" model, of which 2,000 were produced, was the basic Model 1859 rifle with a thirty-inch barrel and nominal weight of eight pounds twelve ounces. Unlike the standard Sharps infantry model, it was fitted with a double-set trigger and a "fly" in the lock to provide a smoother trigger pull. One trigger would "set" the other, which then required very little finger pressure to drop the gun's hammer. The Berdan guns were designed to take a socket-style bayonet that slipped over the gun's muzzle, rather than the large sword bayonet that most Model 1859 rifles were designed to use. These guns were accurate at long range in the hands of practiced shots who could estimate distance, could be loaded and fired rapidly, and were light enough for use on the skirmish line. As an added benefit, they used the same cartridges as the Sharps carbine, which were readily available throughout the army.[10]

Together, the two sharpshooter regiments never mustered 2,000 men, and after active campaigning began, there were never more (and most of the time considerably less) than 1,000 sharpshooters on duty with both outfits together at any one time. Excess Sharps rifles from Colonel Berdan's order were stored in Washington. Much to Berdan's dismay, a number of these rifles were hijacked by other units, most notably the "Bucktails" of the Forty-second Pennsylvania Infantry (also known as the Thirteenth Pennsylvania Reserves), who carried some of them at Gettysburg. The Sharpshooter colonel spent considerable time and effort, which coincidentally kept him away from the battlefield, trying to get his guns back, and the Pennsylvanians did return some. Despite these unauthorized issues, there were more than enough rifles in Washington to fill Berdan's requirements.[11]

In March 1863, both sharpshooter regiments turned in their weapons and were completely rearmed with new and reconditioned Sharps rifles from the supply remaining in storage. There were still enough left over for periodic issue to recruits, men returning from sick leave, and as replacements for worn-out or combat-damaged arms. Sharps rifles were also replaced or repaired within the units. Outfits like Berdan's, which were not armed with the standard rifle-musket, were authorized a regimental armorer; and first echelon maintenance, which included replacement of springs and hammers, was conducted at sharpshooter regimental level.[12]

During the 1862 siege of Yorktown, Berdan's men discovered that the Rebels had some sharpshooters of their own, even if not formally organized into units. In April 1862, Private S. M. Ide lost his life in a duel with a Confederate sniper. The green-coated Yankees gave as good, if not better, than they got, however. Private George M. Chase of the First's Company E single-handedly kept a Rebel cannon crew away from their piece with his thirty-two-pound 'scoped target rifle.[13]

The First's fast-firing Sharps rifles were put to good use during the Seven Days Battles, silencing a Confederate battery at Garnett's Farm and contributing to the defense of Malvern Hill. In all, the regiment lost twenty men killed and mortally wounded in the Peninsula Campaign.

While the First was bloodied on the Peninsula, Colonel Post's Second U.S.S.S., assigned to Major General Irvin McDowell's Washington covering force, skirmished with enemy pickets in northern Virginia. The first real fight for the Second was Antietam, where, assigned to an infantry brigade and inappropriately fighting in line of battle, the outfit lost twenty-one men killed.[14]

The First U.S.S.S. distinguished itself at Chancellorsville, where it captured a large number of men from the Twenty-third Georgia regiment. In most battles, however, the sharpshooter regiments were broken up into company or battalion-sized detachments and deployed as skirmishers across a broad front or as adjuncts to other units' less professional skirmishers. It was difficult and dangerous work, but Berdan's men had trained for it, and they excelled.

As the war progressed, the sharpshooters seldom engaged in extreme long-range shooting, and the telescope-sighted heavy target rifles several companies brought to the Peninsula and used at the siege of Yorktown were found to be a hindrance in more mobile warfare. Some of these guns, apparently one per company, were still carried in the regimental supply wagons, however. Weighing as much as thirty pounds, the target rifles were brought forward and exchanged for the Sharps rifles of "the most trusted and best" shots whenever a static tactical situation warranted their use. When the unit moved, the sharpshooter who had a target rifle assigned, one man per company, "had to take the rifle to the case at the wagon train and put the rifle in it, for transportation." Although not as accurate at extreme range as the telescope-sighted heavy rifles, the Sharps was not a bad long-range rifle in its own right. Unfortunately, it was only sighted to 800 yards. On one occasion, sharpshooters whittled wooden extensions for their rear sights and successfully drove Rebel signalmen off a signal tower some 1,500 yards distant, by their estimate. In skirmishing, however, ranges were often relatively short, and the rapidity of fire from the sharpshooters' Sharps rifles meant more than their accuracy. In a pinch, the sharpshooters could fire around ten rounds a minute from their breechloaders.[15]

Although the First and Second U.S.S.S. began their careers in separate army corps, both were later reunited in Major General David B. Birney's division of the Army of the Potomac's III Corps, the unit they fought with at Gettysburg. Both regiments were nominally attached to General Ward's brigade but were deployed by Birney as a sort of separate divisional task force under Colonel Berdan's command.

In addition to Berdan's men, the two companies of "Andrew's Sharpshooters" attached to the Fifteenth and Twentieth Massachusetts Infantry regiments also fought at Gettysburg. Although Berdan offered the Bay State marksmen Sharps rifles from his original allocation in mid-1862, they chose to keep their heavy target guns. At

An accurate and fast shooting breech loading single shot rifle using combustible linen or paper cartridges, the Sharps Model 1859 was a near perfect skirmishing weapon. The Sharps rifle was in service with Colonel Hiram Berdan's Sharpshooter regiments and other smaller Union units at Gettysburg. At least one Rebel, Confederate sharpshooter commander Major Eugene Blackford, brought his personally owned Sharps to the battle. (*John Kuhl*)

Antietam, the company serving with the Fifteenth was credited with silencing an artillery battery, but "for ten minutes fought the enemy in large numbers at a range of from 15 to 20 yards, each party sheltering themselves behind fences, large rocks, and strawstacks [sic]." The result of this short-range firefight was that the company was "badly cut up . . . in a close engagement where rapid loading and quick shooting with them was out of the question, their guns being little better than clubs . . . ." Asa Fletcher, a middle-aged recruit, joined the Fifteenth's company as it prepared to go into battle at Antietam. Although "an expert gunner, and "crack rifle shot," Fletcher was hastily issued a .54 caliber Model 1841 rifle and twenty rounds of ammunition. He managed to shoot five Rebels before his rifle fouled, but his war ended abruptly when he was severely wounded while trying to ram a ball down its muzzle.[16]

A breechloading Sharps rifle would have increased Asa Fletcher's chances of survival considerably. Following the debacle at Antietam, the Massachusetts companies accepted Berdan's Sharps offer, although the First Company kept some of their target rifles for special service. Unlike Berdan's men, the Andrew's Sharpshooters did not bring their own guns into service in exchange for monetary compensation. In 1861, the state of Massachusetts bought 112 target rifles with telescopic sights from a Boston gun maker named W. C. Langdon for $7,940 and then paid Langdon another $1,081 for "Sundries to Sharpshooters." These guns and accessories were no doubt for issue to the two Massachusetts sharpshooter companies. On December 31, 1863, the state armory reported forty-nine "target rifles, unserviceable, various" in storage. They might have been guns turned in after an issue of new Sharps rifles.[17]

The Massachusetts men also acquired some Merrill breechloaders, the thirty-three-inch-barrel rifle version of the carbines carried by the Seventeenth Pennsylvania Cavalry, which, although they had a reputation for being quite accurate, used the same delicate paper cartridge as the carbines. The Federal government purchased 566 Merrill rifles during the war, with most of them going to the Twenty-first Indiana Infantry and other units serving in the western theater. The only Merrill rifles known to be at Gettysburg were those in the hands of the First Company of Andrew's Sharpshooters, although there might have been another one—a gun issued to an unknown selected marksman in Colonel Samuel S. Carroll's II Corps brigade at Chancellorsville. Carroll was impressed and requested that "two companies of his brigade be armed with the Merrill," although there is no evidence that his wish was granted.[18]

Another separate Federal sharpshooter unit at Gettysburg was the company of Minnesotans that originally served with the Second U.S.S.S. but was transferred to the First Minnesota Infantry as an additional company in the summer of 1862 and never returned to the Second. The Minnesota boys took their Sharps rifles with them to their home state regiment, adding to that unit's eclectic mix of Springfield .58 rifle-muskets, .69 caliber rifled muskets, and .69 caliber smoothbores.[19]

Much less is known about Confederate sharpshooters than their Union counterparts. Limited, for the most part, to muzzleloading weapons (although Alabama's Major Blackford carried a personally owned Sharps), Confederate sharpshooter guns were usually standard infantry patterns, but sharp-shooting Rebels easily matched their Yankee opponents in courage and shooting skill. While they might have been at a firepower disadvantage against breechloader-armed Federals, Confederate sharpshooters were quite effective. Southern sharpshooters increased in numbers, organization, and tactical skill during the course of the war. This was in marked contrast with the Union policy of allowing Berdan's regiments, which made their reputations in the first two years of the conflict, to decline in numbers and eventually cease to exist as distinctive organizations.

Initially, however, the Rebels had to play catch-up. In the spring of 1862, the Confederate army "reorganized" its regiments, which had initially enlisted for one year's service, by essentially conscripting their men for the duration of the war. As might be expected, there was more than a little grumbling, and some mini-mutinies occurred as a result of this action. To stifle some of this opposition, Southern soldiers were given the authority to select new officers and, in some cases, form new outfits.

One new unit was the "Palmetto Sharpshooters," formed by men from the Second, Fourth, Fifth, Sixth, and Ninth South Carolina Infantry. Marksmanship requirements for joining the regiment, if any, are unknown. It appears the Palmetto Sharpshooters believed they would, like Berdan's men, serve as elite skirmishers and flank guards and, when the occasion demanded, snipers. Like the First Michigan Sharpshooters, a unit that went to the front in early 1864, the men of the Palmetto Sharpshooters spent most of their war fighting as line infantry.

Although the Confederate Congress authorized the raising of sharp-shooter battalions for each brigade in the army in April, as we have previously seen, implementation of the legislation was erratic. Major Blackford's battalion of General Rodes' brigade appears to be one of the first units organized. Even when these battalions were actually established, with certain exceptions, they do not appear as distinct units on any Confederate army's table of organization. Unlike the Union marksmanship standard of a ten-inch group at 200 yards from a rest, Confederate sharpshooter qualifications criteria were never officially specified; ad hoc competitions were established to find the best shots in any given unit, who were then detailed as sharpshooters, providing they met other soldierly criteria. Although later in the war, it appears that Confederate sharpshooters preferred the two-band Enfield rifle (the same gun issued to rifle regiments in the British army), in 1863, they carried whatever weapons they had before joining the newly created sharpshooter battalions.

Gun choices other than varieties of rifle-musket were relatively rare in Confederate service in 1863. Samuel C. Robinson, a Connecticut manufacturer who had moved south before the war, founded the S. C. Robinson Arms Manufactory in Richmond to make knockoff versions of the Sharps carbine for the Confederate cavalry. There is evidence he made at least one, and perhaps two or more, Model 1859 rifle clones as well. The engraved surviving example, which has a twenty-five-inch barrel rifled with sixteen grooves rather than the regulation six, was at one point claimed to be a "prize won by a Confederate sniper" that had been captured by a New Hampshire soldier.[20]

The rifle usually associated with Confederate sharpshooters is the very costly English-made Whitworth. Confederate agent Major Anderson bought two sample English Whitworth long-range target rifles as early as July 2, 1861, noting that Sir Joseph Whitworth, designer of the gun's unique hexagonal rifling system "asks enormously of them." The first mention of Whitworths with telescopic sights in actual service dates to Charleston in the summer of 1863, but it appears some were issued in the Army of Tennessee in the spring of that year. There is no irrefutable evidence, however, that any made it to the Army of Northern Virginia by the time of Gettysburg.[21]

The only mention of possible Whitworth rifle presence at Gettysburg is the 1907 account of Benjamin M. Powell, a South Carolina sharpshooter from Perrin's brigade and one of the claimants to the shooting of Major General John Sedgwick at Spotsylvania in May 1864. Many years later, Powell wrote that "a few days before the battle of Gettysburg . . . I was presented with a long-range Whitworth rifle with a telescope and globe sights and with a roving commission as an independent sharpshooter and scout." It should be noted that Blackwood Benson, whose account of Perrin's sharpshooters at Gettysburg is fairly comprehensive and included in Berry Benson's book, does not mention Powell as having a Whitworth as of that date, although his brother Berry does credit Powell with using a Whitworth at the time of the Sedgwick shooting.[22]

It seems a few Confederate sharpshooters at Gettysburg were armed with target rifles, perhaps those converted from sporting guns at Macon Arsenal and mounted with English telescopic sights run through the blockade. The vast majority, however, were simply good shots armed with rifle-muskets and trained in marksmanship basics and distance estimation to the best abilities of their unit commanders.

"Entrance to Gettysburg, sharpshooters firing from the houses." Confederate sharp-shooter positions in the outskirts of Gettysburg. Rebel sharpshooters holed up in hous-es and on rooftops engaged in deadly duels with Union skirmishers and sharpshooters on July 2 and 3. (*Library of Congress*)

They did what they could to improve their odds, however. Bill Adams, a keen student of Confederate army material culture, has examined hun-dreds of examples of arms and equipment from the era with proven provenances, including a number with individualized modifications. He posits that it appears likely that "a few CS sharpshooters had military rifles with 'tuned' actions, and a few carried standard infantry arms with an added sear adjusting screw." The latter would be similar to Mickey Sullivan of the Sixth Wisconsin's alteration of his rifle musket.[23]

Until the war's final year, Confederate sharpshooter units were often disbanded at the close of a campaign. In the spring of 1863, a number of brigade sharpshooter battalions were organized in addition to Blackford's. Applicants accepted from the line regiments of Brigadier General Samuel McGowan's South Carolina Brigade (Colonel Abner M. Perrin's Brigade at Gettysburg) that year were expected to be young men who demonstrated "courage and other good soldierly qualities." McGowan's 120 sharpshooters were divided into three companies assigned to skirmish and picket duty and could be deployed at the brigade commander's discretion in a general engagement.[24]

Another sharpshooter unit organized in the spring of 1863 was the Third Battalion Georgia Sharpshooters, composed of fifty men selected from each of the five Georgia regiments in Brigadier General William T. Wofford's brigade. One of the battalion's lieutenants, William Rhadamanthus Montgomery, wrote home after Chancellorsville that "we are always in front of the Brigade, about 300 to 400 yds., to clear out the way & and I tell you we done it too, to perfection." Unlike other such battalions, the Third Battalion was carried on a table of organization as an official subunit of Wofford's Brigade.[25]

The most significant references to the effectiveness of Confederate sharpshooters at Gettysburg arise out of the death of I Corps Commander Major General Reynolds on July 1. Reynolds met the corps's leading infantry unit, Cutler's brigade, ordered it into position to protect Hall's Battery, and then personally led the Iron Brigade regiments into Herbst's woods. The Iron Brigade's Second Wisconsin, the first regiment into action, almost immediately began its bloody firefight with the Fourteenth Tennessee. As the men of the Second wavered under heavy fire from the Tennesseans, Reynolds rode forward to urge the Badgers to advance, which they did.[26]

Although one account has Reynolds "leading the charge" of the Second, it seems more likely he was riding behind the right wing of the regiment. As the general swerved in his saddle to see if the rest of the Iron Brigade was coming up to support the Wisconsin men, he was hit by a projectile in the back of the neck and—the accounts seem to agree—swayed in the saddle and fell off his horse, dead. The same blast of fire that killed Reynolds dropped a horse and felled several of his orderlies. The general's body was quickly moved into Gettysburg under the supervision of a sergeant on his staff. Despite Reynolds' reputation as a competent commander and leader, his positioning himself in the front line on July 1 was foolhardy, as his invaluable leadership was lost to the Union army for the rest of the battle and the war.

Reynolds' death gave rise to a number of explanations and claimants as to its exact cause. Some posited that he was killed by Confederate artillery fire, perhaps a ball from a spherical case shot or shell fragment, and several unlikely claimants to having fired that cannon shot presented themselves following the war. More common, however, was the story that Reynolds had been killed by a "Confederate sharpshooter." To the uninitiated, this would no doubt suggest a soldier some distance away sniping with a heavy barreled rifle mounted with a telescopic sight. As noted, however, the average Confederate "sharpshooter" at Gettysburg was simply a good soldier with, if he was lucky, training such as that provided by Major Blackford and armed with a Springfield or Enfield rifle-musket.

One candidate as the Reynolds shooter, according to a 1947 newspaper story, was Frank Wood of Surry County, North Carolina. Although Wood is described as using his issue rifle-musket at a range of about 200 yards, which is believable, the rest of his story, when examined, does not seem likely. As David Martin points out in his assessment of Reynolds' death, "there was no Frank Wood listed as a member of the 55th North Carolina, the only North Carolina unit engaged at this time . . . ." Martin also dissects the rest of the account, noting that Wood's claim that he heard Reynolds yelling, "Give them hell boys" at a range of 200 yards is unlikely, to say the least, considering the distance and battle noise.[27]

Another claimant, Benjamin C. Thorp, did indeed serve as a sergeant in compa-

General John F. Reynolds commanded the left wing of the Army of the Potomac on July 1, 1863. While in the front line positioning troops from the Iron Brigade in Herbst's woods, he was killed in action. Although it has been claimed that Reyolds was sniped by a "sharpshooter," and several Rebels later claimed the honor, his death was most likely the result of the blizzard of bullets in the air during the infantry firefight. (*Library of Congress*)

ny K of the Fifty-fifth North Carolina. Thorp claimed to be "first sharpshooter" of his company, which was, inferentially, a sharpshooter company and, in accordance with Confederate sharpshooter tactical employment, assigned skirmish duty on July 1. Thorp claimed that he had climbed a tree to fire at a Federal battery (Hall's), and his company commander, looking though field glasses, saw a mounted officer by the battery and said to Thorp, "There's a general, try him." According to Thorp, the captain told him the range was 1,100 yards, and he raised his sight to that range and missed, then lowered it to 900, then 800, firing each time, until he hit on the third shot. Although the extreme sight settings are impossible for an Enfield or Springfield (normal Southern sharpshooter issue), Thorp claimed as "first sharpshooter" to have a heavy barreled target rifle, and it is possible, from what we know of the Macon production of such guns. The most telling arguments against Thorp's story are that Reynolds was not shot while near an artillery battery and that he could not have been seen from the position that Thorp describes himself as being in at the time of Reynolds' death. In 1903, Thorp himself cast doubt on his initial allegation that he shot Reynolds. He still maintained that he shot "some officer" off his horse at a range of 900 yards, although it is unlikely he could have distinguished an individual officer at a range of 900 yards or more, even had his rifle been mounted with one of the low-power telescopic sights of the era.[28]

Captain Joseph G. Rosengarten, an officer on the general's staff, supported the argument that a "sharpshooter" was responsible for Reynolds' death. According to Rosengarten, Reynolds "was struck by a minnie [sic] ball, fired by a sharpshooter hidden in the branches of a tree almost overhead . . . ." As David Martin points out, this claim is dubious, since the Confederate line of battle and skirmishers were to the front, advancing into the area, and Reynolds was behind the Second Wisconsin's line, making it unlikely that a Confederate would have been able to climb a tree "almost overhead." Another more likely account by Rosengarten describes "a sharp fire from the Rebels" that "was drawn upon Reynolds when they saw his mounted escort."[29]

After sifting through the various versions of Reynold's death, Martin concludes that Reynolds "was not killed by a sharpshooter or a stray shot" but was felled by fire from Archer's line, either attracted by the general's mounted staff or simply the fire directed at the Second Wisconsin. It is, of course, distinctly possible that he and other members of his party were indeed shot by sharpshooters—not snipers firing at officers from a great distance, but elite skirmishers taking on targets of opportunity in advance of Archer's main line of battle.[30]

Although documented accounts of Confederate sharpshooter battalions in action at Gettysburg are as scarce as organizational information on the units, we have a few hints as to how they were deployed.

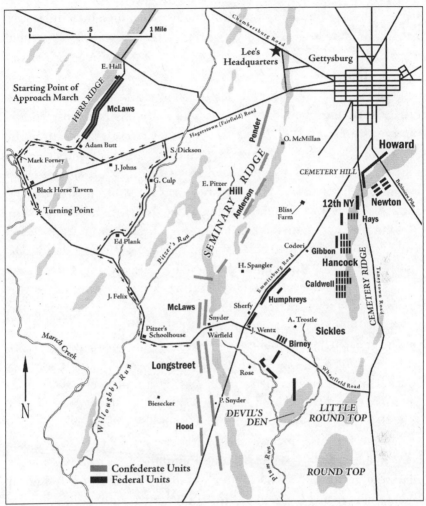

Map 4. The Union Cemetery Ridge line, showing the Bliss Barn, which was occupied by Confederate sharpshooters until it was finally burned to the ground.

Blackwood Benson of the First South Carolina Infantry and Perrin's brigade of Major General William D. Pender's Division related his battalion's actions in a letter to his brother Berry at home on convalescent leave. According to Benson, his battalion, in accordance with the sharpshooter tactical concept, "always marches in front of the Brigade."[31]

Following the initial contact of July 1, Pender's division fell into line to the right of Heth's men. Perrin's sharpshooter battalion was, according to Benson, "flanked to the right and marched forward a mile and a half, leaving the brigade to take care of itself." This sort of detachment would later prove fatal to Iverson's brigade, but Perrin's brigade was more fortunate.[32]

On July 2, the South Carolina sharpshooters deployed as skirmishers between the lines. Benson noted that that his company, held in reserve, "threw up little Gibraltars" as cover against small-arms fire and artillery, opposite Cemetery Ridge. Benson's company ended up to the left of the Bliss barn, and when the Twelfth New Jersey and Fourteenth Connecticut took it in turns on the morning of July 3, it suffered losses from Yankees firing down on them from the barn. Benson mistakenly attributed the burning of the barn to Confederate artillery, rather than the Fourteenth, stating that both sides disengaged and fell back after the building caught fire. During the retreat after Gettysburg, the sharpshooters of Perrin's brigade, who had led the advance to the town, performed their other primary duty as rear guard, fighting off Union cavalry on the retreat south.[33]

The most detailed account of a Confederate sharpshooter unit's work at Gettysburg is Fred Ray's account of Major Blackford's Alabamans. Following their hard fight north of town on July 1, Blackford's men were withheld from combat until the evening of July 2. At that time, General Rodes instructed the sharpshooter commander "to draw a skirmish line as closely across the enemy's works as I possibly could, and when daylight came annoy them with all my power." Blackford deployed his soldiers in Gettysburg houses facing Cemetery Ridge and prepared for action by dispatching men with a baker's cart to go through the town and pick up discarded cartridge boxes littering the streets for ammunition resupply. Some of his sharpshooters climbed atop roofs, putting them on a level with the Yankees on the hill, and took shelter behind brick chimneys.[34]

The sharpshooters' constant fire during the morning of July 3 told heavily on the Federal troops on Cemetery Ridge, driving artillerymen from their guns. In response, the Federals assigned skirmishers, including a detachment of ten men from the Forty-fifth New York under Sergeant Charles Link, to counter-snipe the Rebels. Unlike the careful selection and training of his Confederate counterparts, Link was instructed to subjectively pick "good shots" for the mission. Some may have been indeed pretty good, because one Yankee bullet grazed Blackford's knees.[35]

The fight waxed hot. During the morning and afternoon of July 3, Major Blackford estimated that he fired eighty shots from his personal Sharps and that his men put around 200 rounds each through their Springfields and Enfields by midday. They fired even more in a vain attempt to assist in Longstreet's assault on the Federal center later in the day. It was a bloody day for sharpshooters. Blackford's battalion's casualties were not reported separately from those of the regiments to which his men were originally assigned, but he admitted "a good many casualties." Many of the Rebel killed and wounded no doubt resulted from the eventual assignment of a portion of Captain William Plumer's First Company Massachusetts Sharpshooters on July 2 to counter Blackford's intense and destructive fire. The Massachusetts men were professionals, but Sergeant Link's amateur Yankee counter-snipers exposed themselves too much and suffered heavily. The historian of the Forty-fifth New York recalled that all of Link's men were "killed or wounded."[36]

Most Yankee skirmishers were assigned by the luck of the draw in their parent outfit, but the few units in the Army of the Potomac actually designated as sharpshooters were deployed as such in their entirety. Assignments, however, were haphazard, and rather than being positioned at critical points from army headquarters, which their skills would seem to indicate should have been the case, both of Hiram Berdan's regiments were under the command of General Birney, to whose III Corps division they were assigned.

Neither sharpshooter regiment had seen action on July 1, but by mid-morning of the following day, the sharpshooters were deployed in a wide semicircle well in advance of General Sickle's line on Cemetery Ridge. A detachment of the First U.S.S.S. was stationed along the Emmitsburg Road near Spangler's Woods, exchanging sporadic fire with Confederate skirmishers, no doubt sharpshooters themselves. As the morning progressed, the picket firing got pretty hot, alarming General Birney, who was unsure of the enemy's main positions and concerned that a considerable number of Rebels might be massing to his front.

There was no quick way to find out. On the morning of July 2, General Pleasonton ordered Buford's cavalrymen, who had screened the left flank of the III Corps, the left of the whole Army of the Potomac, to withdraw. Although another mounted unit was supposed to replace Buford, it did not, and an apparent confusion of orders led to an absence of cavalry available for a mounted reconnaissance to Birney's front and left.[37]

In late morning, the nervous Birney secured permission from General Sickles to order an infantry reconnaissance. He assigned Colonel Moses B. Lakeman's Third Maine infantry, along with companies D, E, F, and I of the First U.S.S.S. under Lieutenant Colonel Trepp, to cross the Emmitsburg Road and push into the woods beyond. Birney assigned overall command of the small force, which totaled 314 officers and men, to the sharpshooters' Colonel Berdan. Berdan set out around noon, marching the column, with his own men in the lead, down the Emmitsburg Road past the Peach Orchard, then moved west until he struck a small road leading to Pitzer's Woods. A local boy pointed to the woods and advised the colonel that there were "lots of rebels in there." Berdan shook out his sharpshooters into a skirmish line and pushed into the woods, followed by the Maine men.[38]

The "lots of Rebels" were Brigadier General Cadmus Wilcox's Alabama brigade of Major General Richard H. Anderson's Division of General Hill's Third Corps of the Army of Northern Virginia. The brigade was composed of the Eighth, Ninth, Tenth, Eleventh, and Fourteenth Alabama Infantry regiments, which totaled 1,726 officers and men. When he encountered Berdan, Wilcox was deploying his brigade to secure what was then the Confederate right flank.[39]

The ensuing fight was what is called a "meeting engagement," with both sides on the move at the time of contact. Berdan, riding ahead of the column, spotted the Alabama skirmishers slipping through the woods around 150 yards away and ordered his sharpshooters to advance on them firing. Ironically, Wilcox, a prewar champion of marksmanship training and the employment of sharpshooters, had apparently not established a brigade sharpshooter battalion like other Confederate commanders. The skirmishers who engaged Berdan's men were from the line companies of the Tenth Alabama, supported by the rest of the Tenth and the Eleventh Alabama Infantry, with a total strength of 622 officers and men.[40]

Firing broke out almost immediately, and the advancing sharpshooters, spying the Eleventh Alabama enter an open field in line formation, opened up on that regiment's line of battle, dropping a major from the saddle. The Eleventh fell back in confusion before the rapid fire of breechloading rifles, pursued by enthusiastic sharpshooters, who were abruptly checked and driven back by the musketry of the Eighth Alabama, which mustered 477 fighting men that day. The Third Maine, armed with Springfield rifle-muskets, double-quicked to the aid of the sharpshooters, deployed, one presumes, in line of battle, although possibly as skirmishers, as Colonel Lakeman later maintained that "the Sharpshooters, who had been advancing as skirmishers, had secured nearly all the trees [for cover]." In an exchange of fire that lasted between fifteen and twenty minutes, the Alabamans, with most of the fighting apparently done by the Tenth regiment, exacted a heavy toll from the Yankees. The Rebels killed and wounded forty-eight Maine men and eighteen sharpshooters before an advance on the part of the Tenth Alabama caused Berdan to order a withdrawal from the woodlot. As the Alabamans abandoned the pursuit to complete their initial assignment of protecting the Confederate right flank, Berdan fell back across the Emmitsburg Road, where he reported his findings, that there were indeed Confederates in the woods, to General Birney.[41]

Interestingly, despite the reputation of the sharpshooters as deadeye rapid-fire shots, the Alabamans only suffered a total of fifty-six casualties, all in the Tenth and Eleventh Alabama, even though Berdan's men apparently fired around ninety-five rounds each before they withdrew from the woods. In later years, the unit's historian claimed the sharpshooters had done "great execution with their reliable breechloaders." As is often the case, time enhanced memory. By 1892, one Sharpshooter "remembered" that Berdan's detachment had "stopped 30,000 foes." Another, captured during the engagement, recalled that on his way to the Rebel rear it was "impossible . . . to describe the slaughter we had made" and that he saw "hundreds of wounded" Confederates at an enemy field hospital.[42]

By the twenty-fifth anniversary of the battle, retrospect, self-interest, and a raging argument on General Sickles' conduct in advancing his corps, as well as General Longstreet's role on the Confederate side, had established Gettysburg in the minds of many as the "turning point" of the war. Berdan, the Maine men, and Sickles claimed that their reconnaissance had uncovered Longstreet's troops forming for his assault on the Union left and that the intelligence saved the day for the Union army. This assertion conveniently ignored the fact that Wilcox's brigade was part of Hill's Corps and, on its march south toward Pitzer's Woods, had actually passed Longstreet's men awaiting orders. Berdan's men claimed the credit of having "saved the day for the Army of the Potomac" and characterized their skirmish as the most critical action of the most critical battle of the war. This argument neatly dovetailed with General Sickles' claim that the advance of his III Corps from Cemetery Ridge to a new line along the Emmitsburg Road, across the Wheatfield and to Devil's Den, predicated upon the "discovery" of Confederates on the move to the Union left, was justified, even though that line proved too extensive to be defended by his available manpower.[43]

The most significant tactical lesson learned from the Pitzer's Woods fight is that by all accounts, the rapid fire of the breechloaders, delivered from men who were combat veterans and excellent shots, did not necessarily lead to the result one might expect. The odds were not that lopsided. At the height of the fight, Berdan's veteran force of slightly more than 300, a third of them armed with breechloaders, faced Wilcox's Eighth and Tenth Alabama. The two Confederate regiments fielded a combined force of around 800 men, many of them recent draftees. Although Berdan was outnumbered more than two to one, the rapid-fire capability of the 100 Sharps rifles in the hands of expert shots should have been sufficient to counter those odds. In the end, casualties were about even, and the expenditure of Sharps ammunition—ninety-five rounds in less than twenty minutes—seemed to fulfill the predictions of ammunition wastage by conservative ordnance men like General Ripley.[44]

Following the Pitzer's Woods engagement, both regiments of sharpshooters established a skirmish screen across the III Corps front. Sickles' advance had forced Longstreet to modify his original plan, as he found the III Corps further forward (and more vulnerable) than he had anticipated. As Longstreet's two divisions moved into place in the late afternoon, skirmishing began all along the line.[45]

While the First U.S.S.S. covered the corps front in the vicinity of the Peach Orchard, Major Homer Stoughton's eight-company Second U.S.S.S. screened the left of the III Corps and, as it turned out, the entire army. Stoughton kept two companies in reserve and deployed one atop Big Round Top, another in the adjacent ravine, and the remaining four stretched out to and beyond the Slyder farm. As the afternoon waned, Stoughton pushed his men forward as far as he dared and posted some actually "onto the Emmitsburg Pike." As the Rebels appeared, the sharpshooters abandoned their position in the road and fell back to the farm where, positioned five yards apart, they fired until the enemy was within 100 yards, then fell back to new positions. One sharpshooter believed he and his comrades "made it interesting for some of the Johnnies" in Longstreet's advance, until they were in as great a danger from Union musketry and artillery from their own lines.[46]

It became "interesting" for the sharpshooters as well, as the Confederates came "yelling and firing and struggling over fences and through the timber." Brigadier General Evander M. Law, commanding a brigade of Alabamans in General Hood's Division at the far right of the advance, deployed ten percent (five companies) of his entire force as skirmishers. Available evidence, however, seems to indicate that the sharpshooters encountered his main force with no skirmishers in its front. Although they gradually fell back, the sharpshooters peppered the Alabama battle line; one Sharps slug hit Lieutenant Colonel Isaac B. Feagin of the Fifteenth Alabama in the knee.[47]

There is reason to believe that Law's skirmishers might have been organized prior to the battle as one or even two separate battalions, in accordance with the brigade sharpshooter battalion tactical concept. Harry W. Pfanz, foremost chronicler of the second day at Gettysburg, notes that Law's skirmishers "operating as two separate battalions . . . passed to the right around Round Top and ended their movement on its northern slope." They were, perhaps, intended to operate as a separate tactical strike force, and such procedure was previously evident in the separation of the sharpshooter battalions of Perrin's and Iverson's brigades from their parent units on July 1, with, in Iverson's case, disastrous results. Law's battalions, however, simply drifted out of the area where they could significantly support the Confederate attack.[48]

Sharpshooter Wyman White of the Second U.S.S.S. recalled that the advancing mass of the enemy "was at least ninety men to our one. Still they noticed that there was some opposition to their charge for we were armed with breech loaders and, as we took the matter very cooly, many a brave Southron threw up his arms and fell." How many casualties the Second actually inflicted on the Rebels during their initial advance is unknowable, however, as the units they opposed were later involved in heavy fighting and suffered severe losses near Little Round Top. As they reached the Union line, the sharpshooters integrated themselves into its defense. Around a dozen of them teamed up with Company B of the Twentieth Maine and helped that company in its assault on the Confederate right flank that ended the attack on the Federal left on the afternoon of July 2.[49]

On the evening of July 2, portions of the two sharpshooter regiments rejoined the remnants of Ward's brigade and on the following day, were able to get in some shots at the Confederate attack on the Federal center. Men from the Second U.S.S.S. supported the 150th Pennsylvania Infantry on July 3, and one Pennsylvanian clearly recalled Major Stoughton advising his men, "keep cool boys, alter your sights to suit your distance, and make sure of your man before you fire" twenty years after the battle.[50]

During the course of the battle, the First U.S.S.S., with 312 men engaged, lost forty-nine, including six killed, thirty-seven wounded, and six missing; while the Second U.S.S.S., which entered the battle with 169 officers and men available, suffered forty-three casualties, with five killed, twenty-three wounded, and fifteen missing, for percentage losses of 15.7 percent and 25.4 percent, respectively.[51]

There were other Union sharpshooter units on the field at Gettysburg, most of them the separate companies originally intended for Berdan's regiments that had been held back or transferred out of the U.S.S.S. regiments by state governors fearful of losing enlistment credits. The regiments the First and Second Andrew's Sharpshooters were attached to—the Fifteenth and Twenty-second Massachusetts—were in the II and V Corps, respectively.

Although the First Company had, after its hard knocks at Antietam, accepted Hiram Berdan's offer of Sharps rifles, the company's ordnance

One of the most famous Gettysburg photos credited to Alexander Gardner, but apparently taken by Timothy Sullivan on July 6, 1863, is one of an alleged sharpshooter killed in Devil's Den. The Devil's Den "sharpshooter," however, according to photography scholar William Frassanito, was the body of a dead infantryman moved to the location to intensify the drama of the image. The Springfield 1861 rifle-musket in the photo plays a part in several Gardner Gettysburg photos. The distance from this position to Little Round Top, seen peripherally in the distance is 580 yards. (*Library of Congress*)

report in the first quarter of 1863 indicated that the unit fielded eighteen Sharps rifles and eleven target rifles. By Gettysburg, the company was no longer part of the Fifteenth Massachusetts but classified as "unattached" and assigned to the Second Division of the II Corps. The unit's monument on Cemetery Ridge, opposite the site of the Bliss barn, features a soldier with a heavy barreled rifle, and these guns were apparently used to counter long-range fire from the barn. A captain from the 111th New York recalled that on July 2, he had a conversation on Cemetery Ridge with a sharpshooter armed with a telescope-sighted rifle who demonstrated his ability by sniping a mounted Confederate officer off his horse at long distance.[52]

Captain Richard S. Thompson of the Twelfth New Jersey's smoothbore-armed infantrymen watched some sharpshooters, either from the First Company or the sharpshooter company of the First Minnesota, armed with telescope-sighted heavy target rifles, shooting at

Confederate sharpshooters in the Bliss barn. According to Thompson, the sharpshooters worked in three-man teams, calculating the slow speed of a bullet over the more than 600-yard distance in their sniping technique. The captain recalled that one sharpshooter would fire a shot at a Rebel firing from an opening in the barn, and the Rebel would duck when he saw the smoke from the gun's discharge. After a momentary delay, and before the Confederate popped back up, the other two sharpshooters would fire, hoping the arrival of their bullets would coincide with his reappearance. Most of the Massachusetts men later ended up deployed in Ziegler's Grove and over toward the cemetery, dueling with Major Blackford's and other Rebel sharpshooters holed up in the houses at the edge of Gettysburg.[53]

While dueling with the Alabamans, thirty-five-year-old Sergeant Edward Hutchins of the First Company, described as "having a thorough practical and theoretical knowledge of the telescopic rifle," which "in his hands became an instrument of terrible efficiency . . ., was shot through the head, by the side of his captain . . . ." A Confederate sharpshooter in the town fired that fatal shot, and the captain was William Plumer, who recalled his shock and sadness at Hutchins' death more than twenty years later, describing Hutchins as "one of the coolest and bravest men I ever knew, and a splendid rifle shot."[54]

On July 3, Lieutenant Bicknell of the First Company led some of his sharpshooters to the Union center, apparently where the unit's monument now stands, to assist in repelling Pickett's Charge. Bicknell recalled that "when the pressure upon our lines was at its height, [his men] picked off two or three mounted officers who were pressing their men against our line just to the left of my position." As the Confederates fell back, Bicknell joined the Eighth Ohio Infantry in moving down the Bryan farm lane, firing into the enemy's flank and rounding up several hundred prisoners.[55]

At Gettysburg, the men of the Second Company apparently functioned as skirmishers for their brigade, the First of the First Division of the V Corps, led by Colonel William S. Tilton. The company fought with the brigade near Stony Hill on the edge of the Wheatfield, and the unit's monument, a sculpted soldier armed with what appears to be a standard rifle-musket, stands there today.

In mid-1862, Company L, the Minnesota company of Berdan's First U.S.S.S., was transferred to the First Minnesota Infantry, to serve as "a company of sharpshooters and skirmishers" and spent the rest of its term of service with that regiment. At Gettysburg, Company L was detached from the regiment and assigned to Cemetery Hill, where it may well have participated in the long-range duel with the Rebels in the Bliss barn along with the First Company of the Andrew's Sharpshooters and also may have engaged some of Major Blackford's Alabamans. Due to this duty, the sharpshooters were fortunate enough not to participate in the almost suicidal charge made by eight companies of the First Minnesota that staggered the Confederate advance in the evening of on July 2.[56]

Another Union sharpshooter outfit in action at Gettysburg, but often overlooked, was "Brady's Sharpshooters." This company was raised in Detroit in February, 1862, by Captain Kiniston S. Dygert and named by him after General Hugh Brady, a militia general Dygert had served under in the 1840s, although the Michigan Adjutant General's office formally designated the unit the First Independent Company of Sharpshooters. Dygert's men were attached as an eleventh company to the Sixteenth Michigan Infantry, which had been in the field since the fall of 1861. The leadership of the Sixteenth apparently appreciated marksmen and knew good guns and, in 1862, had appropriated 300 Sharps rifles belonging to Colonel Berdan, returning them reluctantly when the sharpshooter commander discovered the Michigan men had absconded with them.[57]

Dygert used the same marksmanship standards as Berdan in selecting his men and, like Berdan in his early recruiting, encouraged them to bring their own target rifles to the army, for which they would be compensated. He was specific, however, in limiting the weight of the privately owned guns to sixteen pounds. Those who did not come into service with target rifles were issued standard Springfield rifle-muskets. Brady's Sharpshooters served, along with two line companies of the Sixteenth, as skirmishers in the area near Little Round Top, in which duty it appears they were armed with a mix of target rifles and rifle-muskets, although by the spring of 1864 they exchanged them for Sharps rifles.[58]

Other units, although not specifically designated as sharpshooters, brought Sharps rifles to the battlefield at Gettysburg. Among these regiments were the Forty-second Pennsylvania in the V Corps, the II Corps's Fourteenth Connecticut, and the Second New Hampshire in the III Corps. None of these regiments was exclusively armed with the Sharps, however. The Bucktails, like the Sixteenth Michigan, had appropriated Sharps rifles from the trove Colonel Berdan left in Washington when his units took the field. Berdan accused the Pennsylvanians who had been issued his surplus rifles as misrepresenting to arsenal representatives in Washington that the whole regiment was supposed to be issued breechloaders. Berdan claimed that the Bucktails lied their way into a total of 650 of his rifles, but that seems excessive. The Forty-second's ordnance report for the fourth quarter of 1862 revealed 140 Sharps rifles in service in the regiment at that time. By Gettysburg, the Bucktails were armed with a mix of Sharps rifles, as well as Enfield and Springfield rifle-muskets and .69 caliber smoothbore muskets. The number of Sharps in the regiment remained steady, with 153 reported in the ranks as of September 1863. Unlike some other regiments, the Forty-second did not issue breechloaders to selected companies intended to function as skirmishers. A survey of the small-arms distribution of the regiment as of January 1863 suggests an issue of "14–25 in every company."[59]

The Connecticut guns were part of a state purchase of Sharps rifles, some of them initially intended for the Egyptian government, in 1861. The Fourteenth Connecticut, which burned the Bliss barn after the Twelfth New Jersey's raid and Massachusetts Sharpshooters' bullets had failed to silence the Rebel sharpshooters using it as a shelter, had two companies, A and B, armed with Sharps rifles. The regiment's ordnance report for the second quarter of 1863 lists twenty-seven Sharps rifles in Company A and twenty-three in Company B. These companies were not trained for any special duty, although they were most likely on the skirmish line more often than their comrades armed with Springfield rifle-muskets. At the end of the day on July 3, when Pickett's Charge had ebbed, the regimental adjutant recalled that "hardly a man in the regiment had over two or three cartridges left. Dead and wounded rebels were piled up in heaps in front of us, espe-

Confederates overrun Devil's Den. The Federals beginning to withdraw are most likely the men of the Fourth Maine. (*Library of Congress*)

cially in front of Companies A and B, where Sharpe's [sic] rifles had done effective work."[60]

During the attack of July 3, Sergeant William B. Hincks of the Fourteenth's Company A blazed away at Rebels crossing the Emmitsburg Road with two Sharps rifles that another man kept reloading for him. At one point, Hincks jumped over the stone wall and ran forward to capture a Confederate flag, dashing though the buck-and-ball crossfire being put out by the smoothbores of the Twelfth New Jersey. A Marine Corps test of the Sharps rifle versus the rifle-musket prior to the war revealed "the difference in rapidity of loading and firing was vastly in favor of Sharps' rifle, being as 4 or 6 to 1," so it was not surprising that the Connecticut men ran out of ammunition at the height of the fight. As a field expedient, they stuffed oversized .58 caliber Springfield paper cartridges in their Sharps and fired them without damage in the sturdy breechloaders.[61]

The men of the Second New Hampshire fought in the maelstrom of the Peach Orchard but left no record of Sharps rifle usage differing from that of their rifle-muskets. One private, however, recalled firing his rifle at a range of 400 yards at a Confederate artillery battery that had displaced forward to give direct support to attacking Rebel infantry. The number of Sharps in the ranks of the Second is unclear. Two companies, B and C, failed to report their arms for the second quarter of 1863, and all other companies reported Springfield rifle-muskets. At the close of the third quarter, Company B reported forty-one Sharps rifles, and Company C reported forty-two Springfield rifle-muskets. Available evidence, then, suggests that one company of the Second New Hampshire was armed with Sharps rifles at Gettysburg.[62]

Devil's Den, a jumble of glacier-tumbled boulders across Plum Run from Little Round Top, also known in the nineteenth century as "Devil's Trap," has gained a reputation in modern times as the ultimate Gettysburg sniper position. As much as the death of Reynolds, the mention of Devil's Den elicits thoughts of sharpshooters. This characterization is largely the result of tourist interest in geological oddity, a famous photograph (which proved under analysis to be staged), and an extremely heavy rifle of dubious provenance allegedly pilfered from Devil's Den by John H. Rosensteel, which eventually found a home in the National Military Park museum. No doubt the unique topography, which held decomposing bodies in nooks and crannies out of reach of burial details, added to the horror and mystery of Devil's Den. In later years, sharpshooter historian Charles A. Stevens characterized Devil's Den a "fitting resort for witches, freebooters—and rebel sharpshooters." Since the position was within Union lines during most of July 1 and the epicenter of battle from late afternoon until dusk on July 2, any significant Confederate sharpshooter or sniping activity had to occur on July 3.[63]

Considering the ricochet factor presented by the boulders, exacerbated by exposure to intense Union artillery fire at relatively close range, it would seem that Devil's Den itself was, in fact, an unlikely spot to set up a sniping shop or, for that matter, a defensive line. Colonel Elijah Walker of the Fourth Maine thought it a terrible place to fight from and said that he "would not go into that den unless I was obliged to." When his regiment was ordered in, he "remonstrated with all the power of speech I could command, and only (as I then stated) obeyed because it was a military order—the enemy were near, there was no further time for argument." In another account, Walker explained that even when ordered to Devil's Den, he positioned his regiment to the left of the rock jumble, extending his line across the rocky terrain and Plum Run into the woods at the foot of Big Round Top, placing a single company deployed as skirmishers in the Den. Flanked left and right as the battle heated up, he withdrew, but described no fighting of note in and among the rocks.[64]

There is no denying that considerable skirmishing did occur on the southern end of the lines on the morning of July 3. According to Stevens, Rebel skirmishers around Devil's Den spent part of the morning "exchanging shots" with "Michigan men," most likely from the Sixteenth Michigan and probably including Brady's Sharpshooters "scattered behind the bowlders at the foot of Little Round Top." The likely scene of the Confederate positions, the rocky terrain stretching across Plum Run in the vicinity of the current National Park restroom, is a measured average of 434 yards from the crest of Little Round Top, and 340 yards from the Union positions slightly down the hill on the "military crest" of its southern face as indicated by regimental monuments. Sergeant Richard W. Tyler of the Second U.S.S.S. led a sortie on the morning of July 3 "across the marsh" (wetlands around Plum Run) that captured twenty Rebel skirmishers "caught in a cave" who had, they said, been pinned down by Federal fire. These men were apparently from the Third Arkansas Infantry.[65]

The Arkansans, a number of them wounded, may have just been seeking shelter in a storm of fire. Thomas Scott, who served in Battery D, Fifth U.S. Artillery on Little Round Top, noted that "the rebel sharpshooters were posted in the valley west of Houck's Ridge and between the ridge and the Emmitsburg road," not in Devil's Den. Battery D was greeted with sharpshooter fire at dawn on July 3, but Scott recalled that Berdan's Sharpshooters solved the problem. His recollection is worth quoting in full for the insight into sharpshooter tactics it provides, which appear to be directly adopted from those of the French *Chasseurs* described by Brent Nosworthy in his detailed tactical study *The Bloody Crucible of Courage*.[66]

> About 6 o'clock two companies of Berdan's Sharpshooters came up
> the hill in rear of our battery and said: "Boys, do the reb sharpshoot-
> ers trouble you any this morning?" We told them they had wounded
> one of our men already. The Berdans deployed from their center to

the right and left, and every second and fourth man dropped on his hands and knees, and crawled between our guns and to the very brow of the hill and found good shelter behind the rocks. They now lay flat on their stomachs and kept a good watch, while numbers one and three did the same thing, except that when they got to the brow of the hill they worked down the west face of the mountain. When they got down into the Devil's Den they crawled from one rock to another until they got across the Den and took possession of Houck's Ridge, when they covered the ground for numbers two and four, who did the same thing. That was the last we saw of them, though we could hear the sharp crack of their guns now and then. We could now walk around on top of the hill or sit on guns, as the rebel sharpshooters bothered us no more.[67]

Scott's account of the sharpshooters' progress suggests that although Confederate skirmishers were active in the area, none were occupying the actual Devil's Den on the morning of July 3, though they apparently returned later in the day to both the Den and Houck's Ridge. Overall, however, there is no evidence that Devil's Den itself saw any more, and perhaps witnessed less, sharpshooter activity than the intense small-arms duels that occurred in other areas, including the Bliss barn and Major Blackford's fight with the Massachusetts sharpshooters from the streets and houses of Gettysburg. Postwar legend, spread by self-appointed "guides" to the battlefield, was apparently responsible for many of the Devil's Den sharpshooter stories.[68]

Since Houck's Ridge was essentially treeless, any Confederate sharpshooter positions would have been in the fringe of the Rose woods. Modern measurements to the tree line behind the ridge from the crest of Little Round top average 550 yards. The distance from the site of the Alexander Gardner "sharpshooter's last sleep" photograph to the crest is even further—a long 580 yards. Individuals can be seen moving at that distance, but the barleycorn front sight of an Enfield or Springfield rifle-musket, or for that matter, a Sharps rifle, would entirely cover several people at that range, at which a slight error in distance estimation would result in a complete miss. These facts, coupled with the chaos and powder smoke of battle, make it more likely that the officers killed atop

Little Round Top were killed by shots directed at the general area, to which they were more exposed due to their up-front leadership style, than by specific aimed sharpshooter fire.[69]

Most of the Rebel bodies littering Devil's Den may well have been victims of the original fight of July 2, when fast-moving Confederates swept over the area in several waves. One soldier who visited Devil's Den the week after the battle, when bodies were still plainly evident, thought "in charging across the piles of rocks at Plum Run many dead and wounded fell in the chasms between." Stevens recalled that the Confederates the sharpshooters captured, a number of them wounded, had been pinned down in a cave, so much so that they could not return fire on the Yankees who rushed their position. He also stated that Colonel Van H. Manning of the Third Arkansas told him after the war that he had withdrawn the bulk of his men behind Houck's Ridge at the end of the July 2 fight. Geology and popular culture will win out, however, and Devil's Den will probably remain the classic sharpshooter position of the war to the general public.[70]

Gettysburg witnessed the full extent of sharpshooter activity on both sides, from the classic heavy rifle sniping of the First Company, Andrew's Sharpshooters, and a few Confederates like Benjamin C. Thorp, to the primary sharpshooter role of the era, skirmisher extraordinaire. Practitioners of the latter skill were represented on the skirmish line by the organized sharpshooter battalions of the Army of Northern Virginia, armed with rifle-muskets, and designated Union sharpshooter units like Berdan's regiments and Captain Dygert's company, carrying Sharps rifles and light target arms.

As in many other tactical and small-arms areas, Gettysburg proved, in retrospect, a mid-war watershed. In the spring of 1864, the Army of Northern Virginia's brigade sharpshooter battalions were formalized on an armywide basis. By the end of that year, divisions and brigades in the Army of the Potomac were forming their own integral sharpshooter units, arming them with some target rifles and a larger number of Spencer repeating rifles and carbines and assigning them the same missions as their Confederate counterparts.[71]

Chapter 8

SIXGUNS AND SABERS

———◆———

THE CONCEPT OF A REPEATING FIREARM USING a revolving breech with individually loaded chambers is an old one. As early as 1662, Samuel Pepys recorded in his diary that he witnessed "a gun to discharge seven times, the best of all devices I ever saw." Two years later, he recorded that "there were several people by, trying a new fashion gun to shoot often, one after another, without trouble or danger, very pretty." These repeaters could have been either revolvers or some sort of magazine gun, but the former types were more common.[1]

In 1698, the British Gunmakers Company reported "a gun with four chambers" made by one James Gorgo. Other early revolving flintlock repeater makers included gunsmiths John Shaw and John Dafte, who produced revolving handguns and muskets in the early eighteenth century. James Puckle is probably the best known of the early repeating-arms inventors, for his proto–machine gun, a hand-cranked revolving breech cannon mounted on a tripod and designed to fire "round bullets against Christians and square bullets against Turks." A 1722 test of the Puckle gun left British military authorities unimpressed, although two of them were apparently purchased for a 1727 expedition to the islands of St. Lucia and St. Vincent.[2]

Most early revolving breech guns were limited to prototype models and were too heavy to be considered for practical use. A more sophisticated and lighter early repeating arm—a flintlock using the principle of a cylinder bored to accept several charges revolving around a central arbor to provide successive shots—was patented by American Elisha H. Collier in the United States in 1816 and in Britain in 1818. The Collier gun's cylinder rotated each chamber into firing position by use of a spring, while another spring moved the cylinder forward to provide a gas seal at the breech, and a small powder magazine automatically refilled the gun's priming pan each time it was cocked.[3]

Although everyone agreed that the Collier was an ingenious design, when the inventor demonstrated it before a British military board in 1819, the board members decided it was "too complicated and expensive." Collier subsequently redesigned his gun for the new percussion cap ignition and simplified it further by eliminating the complex cylinder rotation method, returning to Britain for another field trial in 1824. Manually rotating the cylinder and reloading the gun, Collier managed only 100 shots in twenty-nine minutes, hitting a target of unspecified size at 100 yards seventy-nine times. The Collier gun's rate of fire, as one authority points out, was "little better than the performance of a musket" for a comparable length of firing time."[4]

Despite the percussion Collier turning out to be an ingenious failure, it inspired less complex and more effective revolving arms. The first significant one would be the invention of Samuel Colt. Born in 1814, Colt, who some historians believe got a good look at a Collier revolving rifle on a trip to London as a young man, had gunsmiths making prototypes of his own improvements as early as 1832 and patented a revolving cylinder repeating firearm in February 1836. In that year, he founded, with family financial support, the Patent Arms Manufacturing Company in Paterson, New Jersey.

Though rifles were part of Samuel Colt's product line from the beginning, he is historically better known for his handguns, which, in the end, were destined to succeed, while revolving cylinder rifles eventually proved a technological dead end, superseded by magazine guns like the Spencer and Henry. Despite later triumphs, Colt's early efforts in the gun business were not successful. Attempts to sell his revolving carbines to the military foundered following field tests in the Florida Seminole War that resulted in occasional multiple chamber ignition and cylinder explosions. These safety problems, coupled with a failure of parts interchangeability, halted government procurement of Colt carbines and hastened the end of the Patent Firearms Company of Paterson, which went bankrupt in 1842. Sam Colt was out of the gun business, perhaps, he may have thought, forever.[5]

In Texas, meanwhile, Colt's "revolving pistols" were sowing the seeds of a legend. The Texas navy ordered 180 Paterson pistols and a like number of revolving rifles in 1839. Despite mixed results from the Florida tests, the U.S. Army and navy continued to occasionally purchase Paterson handguns and carbines from Colt, and then from the company that bought out his assets, between 1838 and 1845. Some of the Texas navy guns ended up in the hands of the Texas Rangers, who wrote the most notable combat chapter in the early history of the revolver. Five convenient rapid-fire shots of adequate power in a portable firearm turned out to be a valuable asset on the frontier. In 1844, an outnumbered company of Rangers shot up a band of Comanche Indians with their .36 caliber Paterson "five shooters," giving birth to the saga of the Colt revolver.[6]

The outbreak of war with Mexico in 1846 led a suddenly revolver-hungry U.S. military to scour gun shops for remaining Colt handguns. Colonel Samuel Walker of the U.S. Mounted Rifles, a former Texas Ranger who had witnessed the effectiveness of the Paterson in the 1844 Comanche fight, traveled east to look up Sam Colt and offer some ideas for an improved version of the gun. The result was the massive six-shot .44 caliber "Walker" Colt revolver.[7]

Despite a disturbing tendency to occasionally blow up in a shooter's hand (attributable to poor quality control in the Eli Whitney factory where it was built), the "Walker" put Sam Colt back in the gun business for good. For the next twelve years, the terms "revolver" and Colt" were synonymous to most Americans. Except for the momentary aberration of introducing a .58 caliber single-shot rifled pistol with a shoulder stock designed to fill a dual role as cavalry handgun and carbine in the 1855 series of arms, after 1848, the army was committed to the revolver.

The born-again Colt firm churned out a number of handgun models for civilian consumption as well, from .31 caliber pocket guns to big .44 caliber army-pattern Dragoon revolvers, from its new Hartford, Connecticut, location. Perhaps the most popular Colt model among civilians in the pre–Civil War era was the Model 1851 .36 caliber Navy revolver. Despite its name, the navy revolver was also popular with the army. Following the 1857 expiration of Colt's patents, a number of new revolvers began to appear on the market, just in time for the Civil War. In the end, however, the Colt, although challenged by Remington later in the conflict, was the most common handgun of the war.

The Colt 1860 Army, a streamlined gun that retained the effective .44 caliber of the Dragoon while reducing weight considerably, became the predominant handgun in Union service. One scholar has commented that Sam Colt "redefined the architecture of handguns." Indeed he did. His 1860 model, with its flowing lines, outstanding balance, beautiful finish, and smooth rack-and-pinion loading lever, ranks among the best looking handguns ever made. Although Colt had more than a bit of the huckster in him, there is no doubt that he had an artistic sense as great as his mechanical and advertising genius, verified by the 1860 model revolver. The Art Deco design of the New Model series, which was initiated by the 1860 Army, has been characterized as being "favorably compared to some of the best custom automobile coach work produced in the 1930s."[8]

The Federal government also purchased large numbers of Remington, Starr, and Whitney revolvers, as well as the guns of other makers, including the bizarre-looking and clumsy Savage, with its second "ring trigger" cocking device, and the sidehammer Joslyn. Most of the Joslyns were turned in by 1862 "due to their utterly worthless field service."[9]

A survey of handguns in Union cavalry service at Gettysburg revealed 8,608 Colt .44 caliber revolvers. Although ordnance reports did not differentiate between the 1860 model and the earlier Dragoons, it is likely that virtually all of these guns were the Model 1860, making it beyond question the predominant handgun used in the battle. The next most common handgun was another Colt, the .36 caliber Navy, in either the 1851 or 1861 configuration, with 569 examples noted. Remington revolver numbers would dramatically increase in the final two years of the war. This fact was long believed to be a result of that gun's lower price and the fact that Colt production was crippled following an 1864 factory fire. Recent research by Donald L. Ware, however, indicates that the cause was more complex. Complaints regarding a particular problem that developed with the Colt in service—damage to the "creeping" loading lever ratchet and its corresponding holes in the barrel, rendering both parts useless—coupled with the cost of replacement parts added to the dissatisfaction with Colt. By the end of 1863, Ordnance Captain George T. Balch was recommending that the War Department consider "cutting loose from this [Colt] monopoly." It did. At Gettysburg, however, the Remington was not yet strongly represented in Union ranks, with only 555 guns in .44 and 503 in .36 calibers. In addition to the Colts and Remingtons, there were a few other handgun models in cavalry service at Gettysburg. The Eighth Pennsylvania Cavalry's Company A was armed with thirty-three Allen .44 caliber revolvers and Company A of Maryland's Purnell Legion Cavalry carried 110 Lefaucheux revolvers in twelve-millimeter caliber.[10]

The Allen, also known as the Allen & Wheelock, produced by Ethan Allen and his brother-in-law Thomas P. Wheelock of Grafton, Massachusetts, was the improved design of a series of revolvers first manufactured in the late 1850s following the expiration of Colt's patents. Although initially made with a sidehammer like the hapless Joslyn, by 1861, the Allen used a central hammer system. The chief difference between the Allen and other cap-and-ball revolvers was its unique combination trigger guard and loading lever. Less than 1,000 Allen .44 revolvers were purchased directly or on the open market by the Federal government. The First Massachusetts Battery, Light Artillery, which served at Gettysburg in the VI Army Corps, was issued a number of the company's older-style .36 caliber side hammer revolvers.[11]

Unique among Union handguns, the imported French Lefaucheux fired a self-contained metallic "pinfire" round, with powder, bullet, and priming all in one neat package. Unlike the rimfire rounds used in the Henry and Spencer repeating rifles, in which priming compound was detonated by a hammer blow to the cartridge case rim, the pinfire fired when the gun's hammer hit a pin protruding from the cartridge base and drove it into an internal fulminate primer. When the Lefaucheux was loaded, the cartridge pins projected slightly from the cylinder.

Although there may have been some privately purchased small-caliber rimfire handguns—most notably the Smith and Wesson in .22 or .32 caliber—in Federal holsters at Gettysburg, most revolvers in Union service at the battle were of the cap-and-ball variety. These guns could be loaded by pouring a charge of powder from a flask into each chamber, followed by a round or conical ball rammed home with the loading lever permanently affixed under the gun's barrel. In military service, however, revolvers were usually loaded in a more convenient manner by inserting cartridges made of paper or other material containing powder and bullet (the latter usually, but not always, conical in shape) in the front of the chamber and ramming them home. After the chambers were loaded, the revolver was primed by affixing a percussion cap on the nipple screwed into the rear of each chamber.

Private E. L. Dye of the Seventh Kansas Cavalry displays a Lefaucheux revolver. Most of these guns, chambered for a twelve millimeter self contained metallic "pinfire" cartridge, were issued to western soldiers like Dye, bur company A of Maryland's Purnell Legion Cavalry carried 110 of these handguns at Gettysburg. (*USAMHI*)

There were some "double action" revolvers, in which the gun could be fired by simply pulling the trigger, available at the time of the Civil War, most notably the early Starrs. Most handguns, however, were "single action," requiring the shooter to manually cock the hammer before pulling the trigger. With either type, when the falling hammer hit the percussion cap at the rear of a chamber, the gun fired, as long as the cap exploded—occasionally they did not.

Confederate soldiers were initially armed with an assortment of privately owned handguns, most of them Colts (because Colts were the most common revolvers in civilian hands in the late 1850s) as well as sixguns from state arsenals or confiscated Federal stores. In the first months of the war, former Texas Ranger Ben McCulloch required each recruit for his First Regiment, Texas Mounted Riflemen, to "provide his own horse, saddle, blankets, canteen, 'six shooting pistol' and, if possible, a shotgun or rifle." Some Rebels brought the smaller .31 caliber Colt five-shot revolver to the war. The Eighth Texas cavalry reported 584 "Colt Navy 6 shooters," ninety-two "Colt Army 6 shooters," and sixty-four "Colt 5-shooters" in service in October 1861. Revolvers also imparted an air of belligerent masculinity to infantry volunteers. In June 1861, rakish Rebel foot soldiers from South Carolina postured in "Havelock and Garibaldi shirt, and the invariable revolver in a belt around the waist . . . a brigandish look which is quite captivating."[12]

Personal and confiscated revolvers were supplemented by arms purchased from Northern manufacturers prior to the actual outbreak of hostilities. Virginia bought large numbers of Whitney .36 caliber revolvers before the war and issued them in 1861. Some of the Adams revolvers in Confederate service were the American-made version from the Massachusetts Arms company. Virginia bought 900 of these guns, and Georgia acquired an undetermined number. The Rebel revolver supply was also bolstered by captured weapons and imported handguns like the French-made Le Mat and Lefaucheux, the British Adams and Kerr, and a small number of domestically produced handguns. Revolvers manufactured in the Confederacy were mostly more or less copies of older model Colts, predominantly of the 1851 Navy model.[13]

Even in Texas, "six-shooting pistols" were not always readily available in 1861, however, and some cavalrymen set off for war with old-fashioned single-shot "horse pistols." The soldiers of the Third Texas Cavalry left for the front armed with, in addition to an eclectic assortment of shotguns, "common rifles," and Sharps rifles, a supply of "brass-mounted pistols." Although the terms "pistol" and "revolver" were often used interchangeably during the Civil War, these handguns were, no doubt, part of the "consignment of 1,550 brass mounted [single shot] pistols" delivered to the regiment in July 1861. South Carolina and Virginia also issued old .54 caliber smoothbore single-shot pistols, some converted to percussion and some in their original flintlock configurations, to cavalrymen in 1861.[14]

As noted, the Confederacy attempted to initiate domestic production of handguns, but making revolvers was a more complex task for the South than producing long arms. The Federal gun-making machinery captured by the Rebels at Harper's Ferry Armory was designed for producing muskets and rifles, since handgun manufacture in the North was a private enterprise. Following the example of the Union, the Confederate government farmed out pistol production to arms entrepreneurs. The most effective Southern handgun maker was, ironically, born a Connecticut Yankee. Samuel Griswold moved to Georgia before the war and, in partnership with another Northern émigré, Daniel Pratt of New Hampshire, established several mills and factories to make soap, candles, and cotton gins at a town that came to bear his name. Griswoldville, also known as Griswold Station, grew up along the Central Railroad of Georgia near Macon.[15]

In 1862, Griswold converted his cotton gin factory to the production of pikes (long-obsolete weapons promoted by Georgia governor Joseph Brown, perhaps emulating the late but unsurprisingly unrelated John Brown) as home guard arms. Later that year, Griswold partnered with a Mr. A. W. Gunnison, who had fled the Yankee occupation of New Orleans with some rudimentary revolver making machinery, to produce more realistic armament, copies of the Model 1851 Colt Navy. Short of steel, Griswold used bronze for his revolver frames and iron for other parts and managed, with a workforce of twenty-four (twenty-two of whom were slaves) to turn out an average of five handguns a day until November 22, 1864. On that day, Union cavalry raiders destroyed his factory during Major General William Tecumseh Sherman's march from Atlanta to the sea.[16]

There were few Confederate handgun makers of any significance other than to modern collectors beyond Griswold and Gunnison, who produced approximately 3,700 guns between 1862 and 1864. Leech and Rigdon made 1,500 revolvers in Columbus, Mississippi, and Greensboro, Georgia; and Rigdon and Ansley produced 1,000 guns in Augusta, Georgia. All were .36 caliber copies of the Colt 1851 Navy. Spiller and Burr turned out 1,450 guns based on the .36 caliber Whitney Navy revolver in Atlanta and Macon, Georgia.[17]

The Confederates imported more handguns than the Union did. The famed Le Mat "grapeshot revolver" was invented and patented by

Doctor Jean Alexandre Francois Le Mat of New Orleans prior to the war. A native of France, Le Mat returned to Paris following the outbreak of the conflict, where, in partnership with a man named Girard, he produced his unique handgun for sale to the Confederacy. The Le Mat revolver featured a nine-shot .42 caliber cylinder revolving around a central arbor that also served as a .63 caliber smoothbore barrel loaded with buckshot. The shooter could manually shift the nose of the hammer to hit a percussion cap firing either the revolver chambers or the "grapeshot" barrel.[18]

The Confederate navy acquired some 400 Le Mats in the summer of 1862, but it appears that 360 of them remained in storage in Richmond as late as November. At that time, Colonel Gorgas, stating that these guns were "very much wanted to arm Cavalry," requested they be issued to Southern horsemen, which they apparently were. Le Mat serial number 115 became the personal property of J. E. B. Stuart, and it appears that General P. G. T. Beauregard, a business partner of Le Mat, presented an engraved gun to General "Stonewall" Jackson in October 1862. Although the number is hard to determine from available sources, it is very likely that Le Mat revolvers from the original navy order were in the ranks of Stuart's cavalry at Gettysburg.[19]

The second most notable imported handgun in Confederate service was the Kerr, produced by the London Armoury and favored over the Le Mat by Rebel arms broker Caleb Huse, who was based in England and appears to have had business ties with London Armoury. Le Mats shipped from France had to be inspected By Huse, and he held up shipments in favor of the Kerr—unjustifiably, according to Doctor Le Mat.[20]

The five-shot Kerr percussion ignition revolver was patented by Englishman James Kerr, who assigned manufacturing rights to the London Armory, in 1857. Made in both .44 and .384 bore diameters, the Kerr was described as a "well made and excellently finished" handgun that "was looked upon with great favor by Confederate soldiers." It had a sidehammer, like the Joslyn and the earlier Allen revolvers, rather than the centrally hung hammer of the Colt and Remington and a smaller grip than the usual American revolver. The first 500 Kerrs left Britain for the South aboard the steamer *Fingal* in November 1861, and 380 more arrived in Wilmington, North Carolina, in April 1862. Kerrs were imported in fairly large but undetermined quantities throughout the war, but the number in service with the army of Northern Virginia in July 1863 is unknown. There were definitely some, probably more than a few, including the one carried by Captain John D. Smith of Colonel E. Porter Alexander's Artillery Battalion.[21]

Like their Confederate counterparts, some volunteers who flocked to the Union colors in 1861 brought their own handguns with them, differing in that they were not asked to do so by their government and were more likely infantrymen than cavalry soldiers. An account of the Seventh New York Militia leaving for Washington in April 1861 noted that "A Mr. Murphy had sent two sons and two employees with the Seventh, and armed them with fine revolvers. Other soldiers had been presented with revolvers also, and a general display of five or six shooters ensured." More than a few of these Yankee recruits were ignorant of the basics of gun safety and often mixed gunpowder with alcohol. A Jersey City soldier from the Second New Jersey Militia accidentally shot a fellow soldier while "skylarking" with his revolver on his way to the front in April 1861. Two months later, an officer from the Second chased a private through the regiment's crowded camp, taking potshots at him with his sixgun.[22]

In the Fifteenth New Jersey Infantry (and, by implication, a number of other units), an 1862 regimental order banned handgun possession by enlisted men after an accidentally discharged ball bounced into a major's tent and caromed off his boot. Although such prohibitions were widely disregarded, some infantrymen sold or discarded their personal pistols, along with much other excess gear, after their first forced march.[23]

Some foot soldiers did, however, keep their handguns for at least a while. Private Alfred Bellard of the Fifth New Jersey Infantry lost his when it was stolen, along with the rest of the contents of his knapsack, while he was tending wounded men following the battle of Williamsburg in May 1862. Sergeant John Crater of the Fifteenth New Jersey, a champion forager who disregarded the regimental order, was still using his revolver to dispatch ducks, chickens, pigs, rabbits, and other edible enemies of the Union as late as December 1862. Violating regimental orders, Private George Henderson of the Fifteenth hung on to his sixgun until May 3, 1863, when, at the battle of Salem Church, it saved his life by stopping a Minié ball. Hard marching eventually made most infantrymen minimalists regarding weight, however, and by the time of Gettysburg, few still carried privately owned handguns. For the same reason, revolvers became scarce in Confederate infantry ranks by mid-war as well. British Lieutenant Colonel Fremantle observed in June 1863 that "the six-shooters and Bowie knives gradually disappeared, and now none are to be seen among the infantry" of the Army of Northern Virginia.[24]

Some infantry color bearers, including those of the Fourteenth and Fifteenth New Jersey, were issued or requested handguns; and in 1861, the Third Maine Infantry was actually issued "ninety-one revolvers and appendages," presumably for noncommissioned offices, but this was the exception rather than the rule. During the Atlanta campaign, Confederate infantrymen received revolvers for use in a successful trench raid. Generally, however, infantry enlisted men on either side seldom carried revolvers after 1861. Although revolvers were supplied to light artillery batteries, their actual issue was usually limited to noncommissioned officers and drivers, who used them primarily to shoot wounded and out-of-control horses. For example, New Jersey's Light Artillery Batteries A and B, with 98 and 131 men in the ranks at Gettysburg, reported fifteen and sixteen Colt Army revolvers, respectively, in their inventories at the time of the battle.[25]

Both infantry and artillery officers often carried privately purchased handguns, as well as swords, but, since an officer's job was to direct his men and not become directly engaged in the vulgar brawl of combat, these guns were seldom fired except in dire circumstances. There was no formal revolver marksmanship training or range qualification requirement for officers, and any shooting practice was purely voluntary. Captain John W. DeForest of the Twelfth Connecticut Infantry amused himself while on shipboard bound for New Orleans thusly: "I load my revolver and shoot at gulls or floating tufts of seaweed ." Lieutenant Colonel Elisha Hunt Rhodes of the Second Rhode Island Infantry was more gunwise than the average officer. During the 1864 siege of Petersburg, Rhodes recorded that he and his fellow officers "practice fencing every day, and a little pistol firing."[26]

Most of the revolvers purchased by the Federal government, as well as those captured, bought, or produced by the Confederacy during the course of the war, wound up in the hands of cavalrymen. The story of the handgun in the Civil War is, therefore, largely a cavalry story. There was general military agreement that the revolver was an ideal weapon for mounted men. One Texas horse soldier thought equines and sixguns "just run together like molasses." For most cavalrymen, revolver meant Colt, a presumption validated by arms historian John D. McAulay's analysis that "eighty-four percent of all the [Union] revolvers on hand [at Gettysburg] were the Colt M1860 Army."[27]

Although the Colt factory was a large and competently run operation, it took a while to adjust to the increased demand brought about by the war. While it is a given that the Confederacy had handgun production problems, even the industrially superior North did not have enough modern revolvers to arm all the Yankee horsemen flocking to the colors in 1861. The U.S. government dug several thousand old single-shot horse pistols out of storage and bought more from private arms dealers, and the state of Massachusetts purchased 200 of these obsolete handguns in August 1861. Colonel Charles W. Carr of the Third Illinois Cavalry, raised in August 1861, reported at the end of February 1862 that his men had "never been furnished with revolvers of any kind." By the end of that year, the regiment's 249 "U.S. pistols, m/1822-1840" outnumbered the 135 Colt revolvers the Third reported in service. As late as the second quarter of 1863, the Illinois men still carried 156 horse pistols. The Third served in the western theater, where the supply of more modern weapons for all branches of the service was always a step or more behind the situation in the east.[28]

In the eyes of some theorists, most notably Colonel Philip St. George Cooke, author of the prewar United States Army cavalry manual, sabers were equal to handguns in importance, and the two were the only weapons a cavalryman needed. Among Southern horsemen, Confederate *beau sabreur* Major General J. E. B. Stuart was a devotee of the saber as well; one of his subordinates recalled that "to come to the saber best suited his [Stuart's] fiery organization, and he did come to it, personally, on many occasions." Despite a common popular belief, neither side abandoned the saber during the course of the war. Even

Jefferson Davis, who introduced the rifle-musket to the United States army during his tenure as Secretary of War, remained an advocate of cold steel for cavalrymen. In an August 14, 1864, conversation with his ordnance chief Josiah Gorgas, Davis "spoke again of a long Sabre that Gen. [Wade] Hampton wanted made for his cavalry, and remembered that on a previous occasion he spoke of the armament of cavalry and said that if they had sabres they should not have guns, but be made to depend on the sabre." The Confederate chief executive firmly believed "that if our cavalry were to depend on the sabre alone that they would then come to close quarters, & run off their antagonists who depend on their long-range guns."[29]

The sabers most Yankees depended on were the Model 1840 heavy cavalry, or Dragoon model, and the 1860 light cavalry saber. Both were slashing weapons with single-edged, curved blades and leather-covered wooden grips. The 1840 model—with a blade at thirty-five and three-quarter inches, a copy of the French model 1822—was nicknamed "Old Wristbreaker" due to its heft. The 1860, although superficially similar to its predecessor, was reduced in weight, and its blade of thirty-four and five-eighths inches was not as wide.[30]

The Model 1840 was by far the most commonly issued saber during the first half of the war, and at Gettysburg, a considerable number were still in service. An examination of the First New Jersey Cavalry's ordnance report for the second quarter of 1863 reveals, for example, that about half the regiment was armed with Model 1840 and half with 1860 sabers. For the same quarter, the Eighth Illinois Cavalry reported 307 Dragoon sabers and 14 light cavalry sabers, and the Twelfth Illinois, nothing but the heavier arms. Confederates were armed with a variety of sabers, including older models from state armories, captured Yankee cutlery, some imports, and a fairly healthy domestic production that at one point in 1862, totaled 3,500 per month.[31]

Jefferson Davis was not alone in his assessment of the importance of cold steel to cavalry operations. In his postwar tactical assessment of the Federal and Confederate mounted arms, Lieutenant Frederick Whittaker, later a sympathetic biographer of General George Custer, opined that even though "armament and training of our volunteer cavalry on both sides were more practical and efficient than those of any

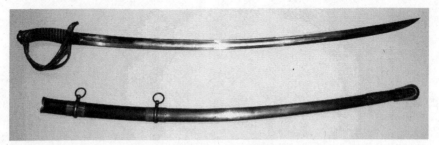

The Model 1840 heavy cavalry saber, nicknamed "Old Wristbreaker" was a copy of the French Model 1822 cavalry saber. Although technically superseded in 1860 by the new light cavalry saber, large numbers of Model 1840 sabers were used in the Civil War, with many in service at Gettysburg. (*National Park Service*)

regular cavalry in Europe," he believed that American cavalry armed with sabers, had they fought a saber-armed European mounted force, would have been "routed," because "our men had little or no confidence with the sabre." Whittaker faulted the training American cavalrymen received, claiming that that they "were never taught to use it [the saber] properly."[32]

Foreign officers, perhaps unsurprisingly, agreed with Whittaker. Although saber drills, first dismounted and then mounted, were part of every Union and many Confederate unit training schedules, a Prussian observer "declared it 'apparent that the American does not understand how to use the saber properly.'" This lack of proper training is reflected in Whittaker's critique that "our system of sabre exercise, as laid down in the tactics, is radically bad, and our men never fenced together." Properly or not, sabers were actually used fairly extensively. A perusal of Stephen Z. Starr's definitive three-volume study, *The Union Cavalry in the Civil War*, reveals forty-six saber charges. The vast majority of these were, however, on the squadron, battalion, or regimental level, not the massive operations across level fields common in Europe.[33]

Due to organization, training, and terrain, saber-armed cavalry was seldom given the opportunity to perform in the large formations that had established its reputation as a shock arm in Europe. When the opportunity arose, however, even during the last year of the war, the saber—or the threat of it—was put to good use. The mere possibility of a saber charge by Gamble's Brigade at the flank of the advancing Southern infantry at Gettysburg on July 1 caused the Rebel foot soldiers to halt and deploy. The subsequent delay in the Confederate advance assisted the survivors of the badly battered I Corps in their retreat to Cemetery Ridge and safety. It is hard to say what would have happened if Gamble's men had actually charged, considering Elon Farnsworth's disastrous ride on July 3. When infantry was already in a disorganized retreat, however, as in several 1864 battles in the Shenandoah Valley, massed Federal saber charges did prove quite effective. Even small mounted assaults succeeded against infantry on occasion. Colonel John Hunt Morgan's "Kentucky Squadron of Cavalry" charged a disorganized Yankee skirmish line at Shiloh with good effect, although one participant recalled that "real execution" was only accomplished with "[shot]gun and pistol," while some of the men's attempts "trying to cut them down the saber" resulted in "ridiculous failures."[34]

The true saber charge was usually reserved for cavalry-to-cavalry combat. On June 27, 1863, a hell-for-leather rush by Brigadier General Robert H. G. Minty's brigade of Yankee horsemen thoroughly trounced Confederate Brigadier General Joseph Wheeler's Rebel cavalrymen near Shelbyville, Tennessee. "Of the 256 Rebels killed and 549 wounded, most fell beneath the stroke of the saber." Minty, an Irish veteran of the British army, was such a cold-steel enthusiast that his command was nicknamed the "Saber Brigade."[35]

The saber was successfully employed at Brandy Station, Toms Brook, and the battle of Opequon, among other fights. One of General Stuart's staff officers noted after Brandy Station that "most of the dead bore wounds from the saber, either by cut or thrust." On September 19, 1864, at Opequon, twenty regiments of Federal horse soldiers advanced across a field "open and free from obstructions" against the Confederate left flank. According to one participant, the Federal "horses rapidly increased from the walk to the trot and from the trot to the gallop . . . . The scene as we rode into the rebel ranks baffles description." The Rebels, infantry and cavalry, cracking already from an overwhelming infantry assault on their front, took to their heels.[36]

Despite successes like Opequon, however, one prominent Confederate horse soldier openly scoffed at sabers. Countering the

opinions of officers who argued
that a saber was "always loaded,"
John Singleton Mosby believed
edged weapons "were of no use
against gunpowder." Mosby's
Partisan Rangers, who favored
the .44 Colt Model 1860 Army
above all other handguns, found
rapid-fire revolvers ideal for
close-range surprise charges on
supply wagons or Federal patrols.
James J. Williamson, of Mosby's
men, remembered that "With us
the fighting was mostly at close
quarters and the revolver was
then used with deadly effect."[37]

Union soldiers armed with Colt Model
1860 revolvers and either Model 1840 or
Model 1860 sabers. (*Library of Congress*)

Some Yanks agreed with
Mosby, especially when they
viewed the handgun as a special circumstance weapon. Even Whittaker,
who believed the saber to be the horseman's primary arm, noted that
"the true use of the revolver lies in irregular warfare where single com-
bats and sudden encounters of small parties take place, on horseback, in
narrow lanes among woods and fences, where the saber cannot be used.
In such places, and wherever regular order is broken up, the revolver is
invaluable." Others, like Mosby, were dismissive altogether of saber
tactics. One Federal officer wrote that his regiment "had never yet
drawn the saber in a charge, and never would charge with anything but
pistols," and General James Wilson wrote that "the saber is just as
much out of date for cavalry in a country like ours as the short sword
of the Roman soldier is for infantry. It is in the way and is of no value
whatever in a fight." Unlike Mosby, however, Wilson placed his greatest faith not in the revolver, but in the repeating Spencer carbine.[38]
Many of the complaints lodged against the saber by Civil War cavalrymen contended that it was simply not as deadly a weapon as the handgun. There were some decidedly differing opinions, however. Francis J.
Lippet stated at the close of the war that "in any compact formation, it

[cavalry] must rely on the sabre." In contrast to Mosby, Lippet posited that a moving horse was a poor platform for delivering effective fire from either a carbine or revolver, noting that "when it [cavalry] closes with the enemy at full speed and with uplifted saber, it has acquired the most important element of its efficiency."[39]

Lieutenant Whittaker believed that although poor training was a factor framing the conventional wisdom regarding the ineffectiveness of the saber, the fact that it was rarely sharpened was a more significant factor in creating that perception. He declared that "sabres are issued blunt enough to ride on to San Francisco. The steel is hard. Grindstones are not to be found. The soldiers lose confidence in the weapon, and prefer the revolver." He maintained that "if the War Department would simply require in all future contracts for sabres that they should be delivered, each sharp enough to cut a sheet of paper, by striking the paper on the sword lightly, the American cavalry of the future would be revolutionized." Citing the well-honed weapons of Arab tribesmen, "in whose fights men are frequently cut in half at the waist," Whittaker rhapsodized at the thought of future American horse soldiers riding into battle armed with "three foot razors."[40]

The dream of razor-sharp steel aside, there were, of course, situations in which, as we have seen, even Whittaker conceded that handguns fit the tactical model better and in which he would not have disagreed fundamentally with Mosby. Some of the most significant devotees of the sixgun during the Civil War were the irregular warriors of the Border States. In contrast to Mosby, whose men were enlisted in a recognized unit and whose partisan operations had a clear military purpose and value, Kentucky, Missouri, and Arkansas guerillas, whether they professed loyalty to the Union or Confederacy, were often little better than bandits—a trade many adopted as a postwar career. Like Mosby, however, the guerillas found sixguns ideal for ambushes, where a blizzard of bullets rapidly delivered at close range was superior to either an impressive array of massed drawn sabers glinting in the sunlight or the longer-range accuracy advantages of rifle-muskets or breechloading carbines.

Men who depended on the revolver as a primary weapon often carried a number of them. Many of Mosby's troopers holstered two handguns on their belts and another two in their saddles. Private Joseph Edwards of Mosby's Forth-third Battalion, Virginia cavalry declined to surrender his weapons at the end of the war and rode home with four .44 caliber Model 1860 Colt Armies, a Colt shoulder stock, and a Sharps carbine. Rebel guerillas in Missouri outdid the Virginia partisans and often carried as many as six sixguns. On one occasion, Cole Younger, who fought with William C. Quantrill's guerilla command, was described as having "four dragoon pistols belted about him." As early as 1861, the infamous Quantrill was "armed with a Sharpe's [sic] carbine and four navy revolvers."[41]

James C. Dodd, Private, Company C, Fourth South Carolina Cavalry. The Fourth, formed in January, 1863, did not serve at Gettysburg, but this trooper is a typical Confederate horse solder at mid-war. (*Library of Congress*)

In September of 1864, Federal troopers in Missouri "killed 6 of ["Bloody Bill"] Anderson's gang, taking from their bodies 30 revolvers." Bloody Bill himself met his end shortly afterward, and the Yankees removed "four revolvers, two watches, and about $500 in gold and greenbacks" from his body. When another Missouri bushwhacker, Bill Stewart, was killed by cattleman W. H. Busford, who he was attempting to rob, "four revolvers were taken off his [Stewart's] person."[42]

It has been asserted that guerillas, as well as regular cavalrymen on both sides during the Civil War, carried spare loaded cylinders to speed revolver reloading. The provenance for this, however, seems sketchy. An 1861 report concerning the issue and use of revolver cartridges maintained that "it [is] almost an impossibility to load [a revolver] on Horse back," but does not suggest extra cylinders as a remedy or option. Revolvers were not issued with extra cylinders, and there is no evidence that spare cylinders were readily available. An early twentieth-century analysis of Civil War cavalry tactics by Captain Alonzo

Gray of the Fourteenth U.S. Cavalry makes reference to Mosby's men as "armed with the revolver only, except that most men had two, besides carrying extra cylinders to slip loaded into the weapon when all loads were exhausted." Unlike his other tactical examples, however, Gray does not offer a source for the claim. In contrast, John W. Munson, one of Mosby's men, described the guerilla armament as "two muzzle-loading Colt's army revolvers of forty-four caliber. They were worn in belt holsters. Some few who could afford it, or had succeeded in capturing extra pistols or who wanted to gratify a sort of vanity, wore an extra pair in their saddle-holsters or stuck into their boot legs." Munson made no mention of extra cylinders and noted that guerilla fights were "fast and furious and quickly over, one or the other side withdrawing at a dead run when the pistols were empty."[43]

Although cylinder switching, which was an option with early Colt revolvers, may have occurred on occasion as some writers suggest, available evidence by Munson and others indicates that when procurable, cavalrymen preferred multiple handguns to boost firepower and that this option was more readily available to guerillas than men in line cavalry outfits. Anyone who considers the probability of switching cylinders should disassemble a Civil War–era Colt and imagine himself doing so on the back of a bucking, or even trotting, horse. In addition, the "timing" of a spare cylinder may or may not have been synchronized with the spring, bolt, and hand turning mechanism of a given revolver. Lastly, a capped and loaded cylinder was much like a hand grenade if dropped any distance—a distinct possibility on horseback.[44]

Since the usual Federal issue was one handgun per cavalry soldier, Union troops operating in guerilla-infested areas or on the frontier often increased their personal armament by private purchase. Those who did not occasionally paid the supreme penalty. Lieutenant Stephen Watson of the First Oregon cavalry was killed in a fight with hostile Indians on May 18, 1864. According to an observer, Watson's men "discharged their pistols and . . . had no reserve fire" by the time they reached the Indian position.[45]

Given the chance, any sensible horseman in hostile territory carried more than one handgun. William M. Hilleary of the First Oregon Infantry, who cautiously rode up Willow Creek Canyon in October of

1865 admitted, "my thoughts would *sometimes* wander to the ambush that might be here, while at the same time two navy revolvers hung at my sides." Fortunately for Hilleary, the only thing he got to use his navies for was potshooting grouse. A sergeant in the Twelfth Kansas cavalry purchased ten Remington .44-caliber Army revolvers, one Colt .44 caliber Army, and two Remington .44 caliber Navies in a Leavenworth gun store in the summer of 1864. A lieutenant in the Second Colorado Cavalry, a unit operating against Missouri guerillas, bought seven Remington Armies in the same store. These officers were no doubt making group purchases for their commands in an effort to boost firepower.[46]

George Maddox, a scout with Quantrill's raiders, holding a pair of Remingtons. (*Dr. Thomas Sweeney*)

According to John N. Edwards, author of *Noted Guerillas*, the Missouri irregulars opposing these Yankee officers' outfits had an intense, almost erotic, personal relationship with their own handguns. Edwards, who also innocently recorded several cases of guerilla transvestitism, portrayed one bushwhacker disassembling his sixgun who "touches each piece as a man might touch the thing that he loves."[47]

Edwards, whose fondness for bourbon was legendary, spent his postwar years as a newspaper editor and apologist for Jesse James, Cole Younger, and other former guerillas turned bandit. Much of his work, especially concerning Federal casualties and guerilla shooting skills, does not stand up to a perusal of other sources, including the *Official Records* or the known technical capabilities of the cap-and-ball revolver. Despite this, Edwards seems to have captured the imagination of the post–Civil War public and was no doubt instrumental in propagating the belief that excellence in the use of a handgun was an innate American characteristic. This myth grew out of the Civil War and was widespread by the turn of the twentieth century, when another veteran would, with slight caveats, write, "It is stated that the Texas Ranger could knock out an eye from on or under his horse. Quantrill's men, they say, could cut a ribbon or strike a keyhole on a dead run. They used to entertain themselves shooting at doorknobs on entering a hamlet or town."[48]

While such claims may be taken with perhaps more than the usual grain of salt, the guerillas did have the opportunity to tailor their ammunition to their guns. Without access to regular supply channels, Missouri guerillas had to provide themselves with ammunition, capturing some and buying some on the civilian market. Most Federal and Confederate soldiers in formally organized units were supplied with revolver cartridges through their supply chain, but guerillas often had to cast their own bullets and roll their own paper ammunition.

The first Colt revolvers on the market in the 1830s and 1840s were loaded by using powder flasks and loose balls. In the case of the first Paterson models, the cylinder had to be removed for loading with a separate tool. In the later Patersons and all successive Colt models, the cylinder remained in the gun during the loading process, and the ball was rammed home with the gun's loading lever. The "Walker" Model Colt .44 of 1847 and its successor Dragoon model were also loaded with flask and ball. By 1850, however, the erratic measurement problems inherent in such powder flasks, still evident today, led to a call from ordnance lieutenant James G. Benton for "the making of a few cartridges for these pistols for trial, as a substitute." Officers in the field quickly expressed their preference for cartridges made at the San Antonio Ordnance Depot to the flask method of loading.[49]

By 1855, the Saint Louis Arsenal was producing large quantities of paper cartridges for the Dragoon .44 and the .36 caliber Colt Model 1851 "Belt," or Navy, revolver, both then in army service. Making these cartridges was a tedious process, and an increasing number of rounds were loaded with a pointed bullet rather than a round ball. The conical projectile was preferable in the .36 caliber to provide more penetration power, although these cartridges proved more fragile than their round-ball-loaded counterparts. To resolve this problem, the bullet was reversed in the cartridge, with its point projecting down into the powder. In loading, paper revolver cartridges were torn open, and powder was poured in a chamber, bullet placed on the chamber mouth, and then rammed home, with the paper discarded. Once the chambers were loaded, the nipples were primed with the percussion caps included in each packet of six cartridges.[50]

By the mid-1850s, Sam Colt was selling a tinfoil cartridge he claimed was combustible; and in 1858, Secretary of War John B. Floyd dictated that Colt cartridges should be used in the Colt arms in service, although they were considerably more expensive than arsenal-made army rounds. The Colt cartridge was inserted in a chamber in its entirety and then rammed home. Capping completed the loading process. By the time of the Civil War, Colt had abandoned the foil cartridge in favor of a nitrate-treated paper combustible round, protected by a stiffer paper outer case that was removed before loading.

Most soldiers seem to have preferred the loading convenience of Colt ammunition, despite its cost, although there were some dissenters. One, Lieutenant Boggs of the Baton Rouge Arsenal, complained that the round balls in some Colt cartridges were so small that they had to be rammed home with extra force to make sure they did not roll out of the chambers. Loose bullets were one cause of multiple ignitions, also called "chainfires," in which more than one chamber fired at one pull of the trigger, a startling experience, to say the least, although usually not harmful to the shooter.[51] Chainfires result from the fire created by shooting one chamber leaping to the powder charges in one or more other chambers and discharging them in rapid succession. Fire can ignite a powder charge from the front of a chamber if it is not sealed by a tight-fitting ball, or the rear of the chamber if the percussion cap does not fit the nipple correctly or falls off. Multiple ignitions can also occur in Colt percussion revolvers when a loose barrel wedge permits excessive front-to-rear cylinder play, allowing caps not fully seated on the nipples to slam back against the gun's recoil shield on firing.

The best way to prevent multiple chamber ignitions is to load well-seated bullets of slightly larger-than-chamber dimension that prevent fire from bypassing them and use proper-size caps that fit the nipples snugly. In April 1860, Major John Symington insisted that "the [revolver] ball or bullet should be so large as to need considerable pressure in the receiver [cylinder], so as to fix it there beyond the chance of being loosened by the motion of riding." Symington noted that when they were loose, "instances have occurred when in firing, the whole six charges have gone off at once." A board of officers testing the New Model .44 caliber Colt in 1860 specifically tested it for potential chain-fires: "The arms were loaded and capped, and then loose powder was scattered around the percussion caps, and also around the balls, when they were so fired without producing any premature discharge, or communication of fire from one chamber to the other."[52]

During the Civil War, most handgun cartridges, whether issued by government arsenals or purchased from private contractors like Colt and others, featured a paper-enclosed powder charge attached to the base of a conical bullet and were loaded by ramming them whole into a revolver's chambers with the gun's integral loading lever. Some of this ammunition was claimed to be combustible, some not, but both types often left paper residue in the chambers after firing. The standard .36 and .44 caliber rounds fit almost all revolvers purchased by the government, although bullet styles varied somewhat by maker or contractor.

A notable design exception to the above was the Bartholow cartridge, an invention of army Assistant Surgeon Roberts Bartholow, which was composed of compressed powder coated with collodion. Bartholow claimed his ammunition was waterproof and totally combustible, but units field testing it in General Buford's Army of the Potomac cavalry division reported that it was "of very inferior quality." According to the cavalry, firing tests revealed that the Bartholow ammunition was erratic in power, failing to penetrate a one-inch board at twenty-five yards and on occasion not even exiting the barrel, breaking up in cartridge boxes, and, despite manufacturer claims, absorbing moisture. In April 1863, General Pleasonton declared the Bartholow cartridge "not a proper one for Cavalry service." Despite this judgment, some of these rounds were still in service at Gettysburg. Dean Thomas notes that bullets from Bartholow cartridges have been found in the area occupied by the Second Pennsylvania Cavalry of General Marsena Patrick's Provost Marshal Headquarters.[53]

The Federal government purchased other "patent" revolver cartridges as well, including the Johnston and Dow linen-wrapped and Hotchkiss patent "skin" (actually formed from pig and sheep intestine) ammunition in both .36 and .44 caliber. Remington supplied both the army and navy with Johnston and Dow ammunition with its revolvers. All of these received varying degrees of complaint and praise for their durability and combustibility, often depending on conditions at the time they were used or tested. The navy was particularly unhappy with Johnston and Dow, noting that the cartridges received with Remington ship-

Colt 1860 Army, the premier handgun of the war. Although some problems apparently occurred with the loading lever in rough service, the Colt's streamlined appearance, balance, and power made it one of the most popular handguns the company ever produced. (*Colorado Historical Society*)

ments in the summer of 1863 were "too large" to be inserted in revolver chambers. The navy eventually refused delivery on Johnston and Dow ammunition, substituting Colt cartridges, although there are no similar complaints from the army. Like separately primed carbine cartridges, however, handgun ammunition of any type inserted in the front of the gun's cylinder was all on the verge of becoming obsolete due to the introduction of the self-contained metallic cartridge. In the event, since handguns were rarely reloaded in combat, the true criteria of a good cartridge was whether or not it would go off when the gun was fired.[54]

Target practice with handguns seems to have been even rarer than that with muskets or rifle-muskets, although officers, as noted previously, sometimes instituted an informal practice program. The Fourth Ohio Cavalry, and presumably other mounted regiments, however, did practice horseback marksmanship in 1861, and officers advised that "men should be practiced at firing at a target while passing at speed." This comports with Cooke's manual, which specified that mounted troopers practice firing their handguns at a target "8 feet high and 3 feet broad; at six feet of its height it is marked with a black band 3 inches wide, with a square at its centre—white." Cooke's program began with cavalrymen sitting their horses at a halt and shooting at ten paces and was steadily expanded so they ended up firing at ranges up to "50 paces." From a halt, practice speed advanced to a walk, a trot, and then a gallop, with the target changing to an eight-foot-high cylindrical post twelve inches in diameter. Although it appears some units, like the Fourth Ohio, attempted to put Cooke's methods into practice, at least in spirit, there is no evidence of any armywide revolver target practice regimen. As with the rifle-musket, such training depended on individual regimental commanders.[55]

Guerilla leader William C. Quantrill allegedly trained his riders in the mounted use of the revolver as well. John Edwards' claim that "A revolver in each hand, the bridle rein in the teeth, the horses at a full run, the individual rider firing right and left—this is the way the Guerillas charged" may well be at least partially true, as some guerillas were noted horsemen. Edwards' assertions of 200-yard revolver shots by guerillas were no doubt witnessed retrospectively through an alcohol haze, however, and it should be noted that Lieutenant Whittaker cautioned that "one thing should be impressed on every man—never to try long shots while on horseback." One aspect of the American handgun mystique not emphasized by any cavalry manuals, a generation of television series and western films notwithstanding, was the "quick draw," although Charley "Ki" Harrison, one of Quantrill's men, allegedly "practiced that kind of revolver shooting which consisted of drawing and the act of firing. Harrison believed his time of two seconds was faster than almost anyone's . . . ."[56]

The Civil War–era percussion revolver was indeed a state-of-the-art handgun for the period. As a short-range point-and-shoot weapon, its effective use did not depend on extensive marksmanship training, and it was as accurate as a modern handgun with similar sights. The revolver was probably the only weapon used in the Civil War that fully lived up to its potential and intended combat role in the hands of troops. At Gettysburg, revolver use, compared to that of the rifle-musket, was of course minimal, especially outside the ranks of the cavalry. Despite the belief expressed by General Ripley's successor, Brigadier General George D. Ramsey, that "the artillery has little or no use for revolvers—and no instance can be cited that I am aware of where the artillery has been called upon to use them," on occasion, artillerymen used handguns in a last-ditch defense of their guns, and

Gettysburg provided several examples of such use. Captain R. Bruce Ricketts, commanding consolidated Batteries F and G, First Pennsylvania Light Artillery, reported that on July 2, "about 8 p.m. a heavy column of the enemy charged on my battery, and succeeded in capturing and spiking my left piece. The cannoneers fought them hand to hand with handspikes, rammers, and pistols, and succeeded in checking them for a moment, when a part of the Second Army Corps [Colonel John Coons' Fourteenth Indiana Infantry] charged in and drove them back."[57]

Infantry officers had opportunities to use their personally owned revolvers at Gettysburg as well. Major St. Clair Mulholland of the 116th Pennsylvania Infantry remembered that when the Irish Brigade clashed with the South Carolinians on Stony Hill during the struggle for the Wheatfield, "Captain Nowlen drew his revolver and opened fire; nearly all the other officers followed his example," an occasion that was such an exception it was noted in the regiment's postwar history. The close fighting in the vicinity of the Wheatfield on July 2 led to handgun use by Rebel officers as well, and Lieutenant Colonel Franklin Gaillard of the Second South Carolina Infantry recalled, "I never saw such stubbornness. It was so desperate I took two shots with my pistol at men scarcely thirty steps from me."[58]

As noted, however, the handgun was not the primary arm of the infantry or artillery, so most handgun fighting those July days occurred during cavalry encounters. The cavalry/infantry fighting of July 1 was never at close enough range for the effective use of handguns, but the July 3 cavalry engagement in the Federal rear witnessed, in addition to the debut of the repeating rifle in the east, a severe revolver and saber fight. The tactical aspects of this engagement are comprehensively covered in a chapter of Brent Nosworthy's forthcoming work, *Roll Call to Destiny: A Soldier's View of Civil War Battle.*[59]

As the Fifth Michigan cavalry ran out of Spencer cartridges and began to withdraw from the front of the redoubtable Lieutenant Colonel Witcher's Thirty-fourth Virginia Battalion, General Stuart, sensing an opportunity to decisively defeat his Federal opponents, advanced Colonel Chambliss' brigade of Virginia and North Carolina regiments. In his study of the Rummel Farm fight, Eric F. Wittenberg posits convincingly that Stuart had originally planned to ambush the Union cavalry and, as the dismounted fight began to break up, saw an opportunity to turn the Yankee right and accomplish what he had intended.[60]

Chambliss, however, soon called for reinforcements, which came in the form of the 310 officers and men of the First Virginia Cavalry of Brigadier General Fitzhugh Lee's brigade. As General Gregg saw the Virginians begin to move toward his position, he ordered the 382-strong Seventh Michigan Cavalry to countercharge them. Newly minted Brigadier General Custer joined the advance of the Seventh, brandishing his saber, turning in the saddle, and crying out, "come on you Wolverines." Some stragglers of the Fifth Michigan with a few rounds to spare fired into the First Virginia and were joined by the dismounted fire of some men from the Third Pennsylvania Cavalry armed with Sharps carbines.[61]

The Rebel horsemen advanced undaunted, however, until they collided with the Seventh Michigan. Both sides came up short of a fence, piling one upon another accordion-style, blocking actual hand-to-hand combat, except for a few men who apparently crossed sabers across the fence line. The men of the Seventh's first ranks drew their .44 caliber Colts and blazed away at point-blank range at the Virginians, who responded in kind. Although some carbines were apparently unslung for this close-range encounter, one Federal account stresses that revolvers were "discharged . . . in the very face of the foe," while a Confederate recollection was that "for many minutes the fight with saber and pistol raged most furiously." As it fought along the fence, the Seventh was also raked by rifle-musket fire from the flank by Witcher's Virginians.[62]

Stuart fed the First North Carolina Cavalry, mustering 407 troopers, and the 246 Mississippians of the Jeff Davis Legion into the fight, led by their charismatic brigade commander Brigadier General Wade Hampton. Hampton's advance finally overlapped the Michigan men, and the Yankees lost a flag amid slashing sabers and a blizzard of revolver bullets. Virtually all of the regiment's casualties were caused by handgun fire and saber slashes, including Major James Carpenter of the Seventh, who was shot out of the saddle. The regiment's Captain

James G. Birney had his clothes ventilated with bullets as he emptied his own revolver, downing two Rebels before being knocked from his horse by a saber cut to the head. Birney survived the gash and was captured but later escaped. Had his assailant subscribed to Captain Whittaker's school of saber sharpening, he would most certainly have been killed.

As the Seventh broke for the rear, Stuart sensed a chance to rout the entire Yankee force and threw the remainder of Hampton's and Lee's brigades forward in a mounted charge that drove toward the junction of the Lower Dutch and Hanover Roads, key to the Union position. The Rebels advanced with drawn sabers, determined to fight it out on horseback, and the awesome sight of glistening steel remained fixed in the minds of their Yankee opponents a generation later. General Gregg, in a last-ditch attempt to stop the advance, ordered Colonel Charles H. Town's First Michigan Cavalry to charge directly at the Confederates. The tubercular Town, barely able to keep to the saddle, ordered his men to draw sabers and advance. The Michigan attack, led by the ubiquitous Custer, closed rapidly on the Rebel force, from which Southern officers were heard shouting to their men to "keep to your sabers."[63]

The Rebels came under heavy fire from Federal horse artillery, and then the carbines of dismounted troopers on their flanks before the First Michigan crashed into them. Although the Wolverines rode through the enemy formations, slashing left and right, handguns were also drawn on both sides. One Confederate recalled that "sabre met sabre and pistol shots followed in quick succession." Despite the injunction to initially "keep to your sabers," Stephen Calhoun Smith of the Fifth Virginia cavalry remembered that he "discharged every barrel [sic] of my pistol and then went to work with my saber." Bullets flew everywhere in the churning mass of men and horses, not always hitting where intended. A First Michigan officer spent much of his time attempting to manage the fight by keeping the men in the regiment's rear squadron from "using their pistols, shooting themselves."[64]

Federal troopers from the Fifth and Seventh Michigan and other outfits, including the Third Pennsylvania and First New Jersey, rallied, mounted, and joined the melee. The Jerseymen made for Wade Hampton, and, although he shot one and fended off others with his saber, one Yankee managed to slash Hampton's head, and another shot him with a handgun. Attempting to disengage, Hampton took yet another saber cut to the head. No doubt, the fact that he was cut with unsharpened blades saved the general's life. As his men led the bloodied Hampton from the field, their charge began to ebb, and then it flowed rearward as fast as it had to the front. The end of the Rummell Farm handgun and saber fight signaled the close of major cavalry action at Gettysburg.[65]

There was one more skirmish, however, that proved the fruitlessness of using cavalry against infantry in small numbers in uncertain tactical scenarios. Late in the afternoon of July 3, Brigadier General Kilpatrick launched a series of mounted and dismounted attacks with hopes of unhinging the Confederate right flank, refused and in a defensive mode over and beyond Big Round Top and on the Slyder farm, site of the massive infantry attack of the previous day.

Kilpatrick initially launched his Reserve Brigade in a combined mounted and dismounted assault, which foundered against Rebel infantry musketry. Another, more fragmented, attack, in which he directed elements of the First West Virginia and First Vermont cavalry to charge through woodlots and down country lanes against Confederate infantrymen in the vicinity of Big Round Top, failed as well and resulted in the death of General Farnsworth. Both attacks were tactically pointless. There was a history, in the muzzleloading era, of cavalry saber charges consistently routing infantry unless that infantry was firmly deployed in a "square" formation. The Rebel foot soldiers who repulsed Kilpatrick's tentative attacks, however, were arrayed in skirmish lines or hasty lines of battle but were deployed in significant numbers on broken terrain with unbroken morale.[66]

Most of the shooting in Kilpatrick's fiasco was at very close range, and the type of weapons used played no significant role in the outcome, which was technologically inconclusive. The fight did not reveal any superiority of the rifle-musket over the smoothbore as a weapon against cavalry or suggest that the rifle-musket had put an end to mounted cavalry action against infantry or that handguns, carbines, or sabers were ineffective arms. In the following year, however, the significant cavalry actions at Opequon and Cedar Creek proved massed saber charges against infantry could still be effective, given the proper tactical scenario. At Opequon, the largest mounted attack of the war, Yankee horsemen caught Rebel infantry in the act of withdrawing and totally routed them.[67]

Sabers continued to be issued in the U.S. cavalry into the early twentieth century, although they were rarely used in U.S. cavalry operations after 1865. In 1913, the army adopted a new model based on the British design of 1908 with an assist from Olympic fencer Lieutenant George S. Patton, whose great-uncle, Colonel Walter T. Patton, was killed commanding the Seventh Virginia Infantry during Pickett's Charge on July 3. Ironically, Patton's grandfather, Colonel George S. Patton, was mortally wounded trying to rally his brigade against the massive Union cavalry charge at Opequon. The "Patton" Model 1913 was actually a sword rather than a saber. It was a double-edged thrusting weapon, not a single-edged slashing one like the 1840 and 1860 Model sabers carried by most cavalrymen at Gettysburg, and it became obsolete within a few years as a result of World War I's four-year-long firepower demonstration.[68]

The collapse of the Confederacy effectively brought the brief military career of the rifle-musket to a close and signaled the advent of the twilight years of the saber, but the end of the Civil War did not toll the death knell for the revolver. Although challenged by rim-fire cartridge conversions, the cap-and-ball revolver remained a premier fighting handgun in military and civilian circles for almost a decade, when it was overtaken by the Smith and Wesson First Model American and the classic Colt Single Action Army, chambered for modern-style center-fire metallic cartridges but with much the same characteristics otherwise. The reputations of many famous and infamous characters of the postwar "Wild West," including Civil War veteran Wild Bill Hickock, were established with percussion revolvers. Their metallic cartridge–firing descendents inherited that legacy. American cavalrymen were still conducting mounted charges, armed with .45 caliber automatic pistols, in training on the eve of World War II. The handgun's iconic status in American history and culture can be directly traced to its coming of age as a personal weapon in the American Civil War.

CONCLUSION

ON THE MORNING OF JULY 4, 1863, GETTYSBURG was indisputably an open-air charnel house. Dead and dying men, army horses, farm animals, and local wildlife were strewn, in whole and in part, haphazardly, in ones and twos and clumps of three and four and larger groups stretched out in line or tumbled one upon another across fields, woodlots, and up and down the streets of the town, surrounded by swarms of flies and rapidly putrefying in the summer sun. Add to that the waste of more than 165,000 men and their animal transportation and decaying rations, and the stench must have been overpowering. As the Army of Northern Virginia disengaged to retreat south, Union burial parties spread out across the battlefield—the first held after the fight by the Army of the Potomac since Antietam—in an attempt to partially remedy the horror.[1]

That evening, details from the Fifteenth New Jersey Infantry and other regiments began burying the dead in the area of the Wheatfield. The blackened corpses, ripened to bursting in midsummer's heat, lay shoeless and with their pockets turned out amid a scattering of paper and debris—letters from home, here and there an image of a loved one. Sergeant Dayton Flint of the Fifteenth picked up an ambrotype lying next to a dead Confederate and mailed it home to his sisters, saving it, if not the grief of those it portrayed.[2]

At their previous battles of Fredericksburg and Salem Church, the men of the Fifteenth had not held the field at the end of the day, and so the Jerseyans had been spared the sights and smells and the ultimate results of the work of war. Their shock was profound. Sergeant Paul Kuhl could not find words to describe the field but hoped he might "never witness another such a sight." Others were not so reticent. Lieutenant Ellis Hamilton was sickened by "dead men lying there all bloated up and with faces black as ink, and pools of blood all around the ground." Sergeant Flint was shocked by bodies "so disfigured that it was impossible for their comrades to recognize them." Sergeant Lucian Voorhees, whose detail interred two Yankees and eight Rebels, prayed that "such a stench as hovered over that battlefield may God never again give occasion for."[3]

. As the bodies were buried, the Army of the Potomac turned its attention to the other detritus of war: torn and broken clothing, shoes, blankets, cartridge boxes, saddles, and guns—thousands upon thousands of guns—that covered the field. One soldier recalled that "in every direction among the bodies was the debris of battle—haversacks, canteens, hats, caps, sombreros, blankets of every shade and hue, bayonets, cartridge boxes—every conceivable part of the equipment of a soldier . . . ." The army had to compete with civilian scavengers traveling from far and wide in search of souvenirs, but the majority of the firearms appear to have been recovered and stacked awaiting transportation to Washington. Many were still loaded, and many of those were cocked and ready to go off. Anyone trying to pull one out of a stack was liable to fire it or an adjacent one by catching the trigger on any protuberance. This happened on several occasions, most notably in the fatal wounding of a local civilian employed by the army to help in the cleanup. In another incident on July 5, a three-year-old child was accidentally shot by his brother, who was playing with a loaded musket. Civilians would die for months after the battle, including both adults and children playing with artillery shells that exploded on them.[4]

Colonel William Penrose of the Fifteenth New Jersey, whose request for replacement arms for his men's Enfields in the wake of Salem Church had gone unanswered, saw an opportunity to address his complaints outside the normal supply channels at Gettysburg. The colonel marched his men down to the Wheatfield, which was littered with the weapons of the fallen of both sides, and where some of his men were on burial detail. The Jerseymen stacked their Enfields and replaced them with Springfield-style guns, including a few Richmond rifle-muskets. Sergeant Lucien Voorhees of the Fifteenth assured the home folks that the Richmond-made guns would be used against their former owners "as chance proffers." Not all of the men in the Fifteenth were glad to exchange their Enfields for Springfields, and the regimental historian remembered that "numbers of our soldiers had learned to love the old Enfields, to which they had grown accustomed, and with which they fancied they could shoot farther, and with more certainty of aim."[5]

Like Penrose, Major Robert L. Bodine of the Twenty-sixth Pennsylvania Infantry rearmed his regiment on the field. Bodine wrote that his soldiers came to the battle armed "with the Austrian rifle of an inferior quality, and I desired to exchange them for Springfield rifles; which was done without the red tape processes. Quite a number of them were taken from the Rebels." Like the Jerseyans, Bodine's men picked up several Southern-made rifle-muskets along with Springfields. Apparently unaware of the Confederacy's production facilities at Richmond, Bodine reported that these guns "had been through the renovating process, and bore the Richmond C.S. stamp." Likewise, Colonel Chamberlain of the Twentieth Maine reported that his men used "intervals in the struggle" for Little Round Top to secure better muskets than their Enfields.[6]

Although Chamberlain's men had to be content with what was on their immediate front, Penrose and Bodine and other postbattle scroungers had much to choose from. One estimate is that "firearms dropped, lost or abandoned by the opposing armies" at Gettysburg may have totaled "30,000 to 50,000," although the latter figure seems somewhat high. This total, of course, would include the Enfield and Lorenz rifle-muskets left behind by the Jerseymen, Pennsylvanians, and other troops when they made their exchanges. They were not the only Yankees to walk away with Confederate made arms, either. Corporal Moses Pugh of the Fifty-fifth Ohio swapped his old gun for a "new bright" Richmond rifle-musket. Like many guns littering the battlefield, this one was still loaded and killed his colonel's horse when it fired after he dropped it.[7]

In the end, the army's ordnance officer, Lieutenant Edie, reported that he forwarded 24,864 usable muskets, along with assorted other arms and accoutrements policed up off the battlefield, to Washington in the aftermath of the battle. While this figure included Union arms abandoned by regiments like the Fifteenth New Jersey, Twentieth Maine, and Twenty-sixth Pennsylvania, as well as individuals like Pugh, Colonel Gorgas estimated that the Army of Northern Virginia had 25,000 small arms lost, destroyed, or captured at Gettysburg. An article in a local Gettysburg newspaper early the following year reported that 24,000 loaded guns were recovered on the field, "12,000 containing two loads, and 6,000 from three to ten loads."[8]

Edie's report not only counted "muskets," a category that presumably included both rifled and smoothbore long arms, but also bayonets (interestingly, a mere 10,589), sabers, revolvers, and carbines. Considering the considerable cavalry action at Gettysburg, both on July 1 and July 3, the total of 114 carbines and a mere five revolvers seems suspect. Although of course there would have been a far smaller number of such arms in use, and hence lost, perhaps it was also easier and more tempting for a civilian or military scavenger to make off with a light (and valuable) carbine or handgun than a bulky rifle-musket.

Gettysburg proved a watershed of Civil War small-arms use, with the obsolete smoothbore musket, obsolescent rifle-musket, and soon-to-be obsolescent externally primed breechloader in action alongside the modern metallic cartridge Sharps and Hankins single-shot and Spencer repeater on the same field. Gettysburg was not the future, but it gave a glimpse of that future to those who cared to think about it, including General George Custer, a man who, though deficient in many ways, knew a good new thing when he saw it—the Spencer rifle.

General Custer would miss it all, but down through the years after the battle, the soldiers came back to Gettysburg, most notably on anniversaries, to celebrate themselves and the fact that they had survived, and poke around for souvenirs. Veterans came to Gettysburg in large numbers in 1888–1889, when many unit monuments were dedicated. They came back again in 1913, both blue and gray, for a formal state-sponsored reunion, with prepaid transportation for "all honorably discharged Veterans of the Civil War." And, then, for one last time, in 1938, when, as in 1913, most of the 10,687 Civil War veterans who showed up, ranging in age from eighty-six to 112, were there by simple virtue of having worn the blue or gray and not because they had actually fought at Gettysburg.[9]

Gettysburg had become more than a battle. It had become a symbol of the war and what came after it. Politicians, including Presidents Woodrow Wilson and Franklin D. Roosevelt, who spoke at the Gettysburg reunions, praised the aged veterans as exemplars of a reunified United States, although final settlement of the basic issues raised by the Civil War and set aside in the interest of reconciliation in the early twentieth century would await another generation for resolution. Before that final step on the long national journey the war had begun, however, the veterans were gone. Many of the guns they carried on those three days still endure, but they, like their former owners, now keep their tales of endurance, heroism, and horror to themselves.

APPENDIX

The following is the official report of ordnance stores found on the battle-field by the Army of the Potomac's Ordnance Officer Lieutenant Jonathan Edie.*

REPORT OF ORDNANCE AND ORDNANCE STORES COLLECTED ON THE BATTLE-FIELD OF GETTYSBURG, AND SHIPPED TO THE WASHINGTON ARSENAL

Collected by Lieut. Morris Schaff, Ordnance Department:

Muskets	19,664
Bayonets	9,250
Small-arms ammunition (rounds)	14,000
Cartridge-boxes	1,200
Sabers	300
Artillery wheels	26

Lieut. William J. Augustine, First Division, Twelfth Army Corps:

Muskets	804
Cartridge-boxes	390
Cartridge-box belts	250
Cartridge-box plates	400
Waist-belts	187
Waist-belt plates	100
Cap-pouches	136
Bayonet-scabbards	100

Lieut. Edward H. Newcomb, Third Division, Eleventh Army Corps:

Muskets	1,142
Bayonets	581
Accouterments	441

Capt. George A. Batchelder, First Division, Fifth Army Corps:

Muskets	800

*O.R., ser. I, vol. XXVII, pt. 1, p. 226.

Capt. James G. Derrickson, First Division, Second Army Corps:

Muskets	425
Cartridge-boxes	50
Sabers	2
Cartridge-box belts	50

Lieut. W. E. Potter, Third Division, Second Army Corps:

Muskets	889
Bayonets	110
Cartridge-boxes	110
Cap-pouches	110
Bayonet-scabbards	110

Capt. G. M. Elliott, Second Division, Twelfth Army Corps:

Muskets	1,680
Bayonets	639
Accouterments	200
Sabers	18

Capt. W. E. Graves, Tenth New York Cavalry:

Cartridge-boxes	84
Carbines	114
Revolvers	5
Swivels	82
Sabers	51
Saber-belts	10
Gun-slings	76

Notes

Preface

1. Amy J. Kinsel's article "From the Turning Point to Peace Memorial: A Cultural Legacy" in Gabor Boritt, ed. *The Gettysburg Nobody Knows* (New York: Oxford Press, 1997) discusses the evolution of thought on the relevance of Gettysburg.

Chapter 1: Breechloading Carbines

1. David G. Martin, *Gettysburg, July 1* (Conshohocken, PA: Combined Books, 1995), pp. 63–64.
2. Joseph G. Bilby, *A Revolution in Arms: A History of the First Repeating Rifles* (Yardley, PA: Westholme, 2005), pp. 25–30.
3. Ibid., pp. 34–35.
4. Louis A. Garavaglia & Charles G. Worman, *Firearms of the American West: 1803–1865* (Albuquerque, NM: U. of New Mexico Press), p. 188.
5. Davis, Carl L. *Arming the Union: Small Arms in the Union Army* (Port Washington, NY: Kennikat Press, 1973), pp. 83–84.
6. Steven Z. Starr, *The Union Cavalry in the Civil War, Vol. I, From Fort Sumter to Gettysburg* (Baton Rouge: LSU Press, 1979), pp. 126–128.
7. Brannen Sanders, "The Georgia Armory Rifle," unpublished research paper, 2007.
8. Bill Adams, an advanced student of Confederate uniforms, arms, and accoutrements, who has actually fired an original Robinson Sharps, disputes the traditional view of the gun. According to Adams, the Confederate Sharps' sling-swivel bar is actually a stronger design than that of the original Sharps, the gun has a faster hammer fall than the original, and its simple fixed sight is more durable and provides faster target acquisition at normal carbine ranges than the more complex Sharps design. He notes that the exploding forearm, caused when loose powder migrates under the gun's forearm and is detonated by a cap, is caused by shooter carelessness and poor training and is possible with either the original Sharps or the Confederate clone, given the same conditions. E-mail from Bill Adams to author, March 9, 2007.
9. Dean Thomas, *Ready, Aim, Fire: Small Arms Ammunition at the Battle of Gettysburg* (Gettysburg: Thomas Publications, 1993 ed.), p. 59.
10. Martin, *Gettysburg, July 1*, pp. 44–45.
11. E-mail correspondence with David Powell regarding ordnance reports of Buford's division; John W. Busey and David Martin, *Regimental Strengths and Losses at Gettysburg*, 4th Ed. (Hightstown, NJ: 2005), 106. Officers were deducted using the Busey and Martin figure of 93% ratio of engaged to June 30 strength in computing enlisted strength.

12. Thomas, *Ready, Aim, Fire*, p. 58.
13. Martin, *Gettysburg, July 1*, p. 45; Eric J. Wittenberg, "John Buford's Defense in Depth at Gettysburg," at http://www.bufordsboys.com/WittenbergBufordDefense.html.
14. Thomas, *Ready, Aim, Fire*, pp. 58–59.
15. For a complete breakdown of Federal cavalry arms at Gettysburg, including revolvers and sabers, see Earl J. Coates and John D. McAulay, *Sharps Carbines & Rifles* (Gettysburg: Thomas Publications, 1996), p. 21.
16. Dean S. Thomas, *Round Ball to Rimfire, Part Two, Federal Breechloading Carbines & Rifles* (Gettysburg: Thomas Publications, 2002), pp. 188–189.
17. Ibid., p. 190.
18. Ibid., pp. 193–196.
19. U.S. Government, *The War of the Rebellion: A Compilation of the Official Records of the Union and Confederate Armies* (Washington, D.C.: Government Printing Office, 1880–1901), ser. I, vol. XL, pt. III, p. 250.
20. White, Russell C. (ed.), *The Civil War Diary of Wyman S. White, First Sergeant, Company F, 2nd United States Sharpshooters* (Baltimore: Butternut and Blue, 1993), pp. 236, 241; Thomas, *Round Ball to Rimfire, Part Two*, p. 188.
21. Thomas, *Round Ball to Rimfire, Part Two*, p. 28.
22. Ibid, pp. 28–29.
23. Coates and McAulay, *Sharps Carbines & Rifles*, p. 34.
24. Newel Cheney, *History of the Ninth Regiment, New York Volunteer Cavalry, War of 1861 to 1865* (Jamestown, NY: Martin Merz & Son, 1901), p. 59; Coates & McAulay, *Sharps Carbines & Rifles*, p. 34.
25. Thomas, *Round Ball to Rimfire, Part Two*, p. 319; Joseph G. Bilby and William C. Goble, *Remember You Are Jerseymen: A Military History of New Jersey's Troops in the Civil War* (Hightstown, NJ: Longstreet House, 1998), pp. 463–465.
26. Martin, *Gettysburg, July 1*, p. 65.
27. Eugene F. Ware, *The Indian War of 1864* (Lincoln, NE: U. of Nebraska, 1994 reprint), p. 6; John D. McAulay, *Carbines of the Civil War, 1861–1865* (Union City, TN: Pioneer Press), p. 42.
28. *O.R.*, ser. I, vol. XVI, pt. 1, p. 750; Ibid., pt. II, p. 301.
29. Thomas, *Round Ball to Rimfire, Part Two*, p. 61.
30. Ibid. It appears the issue was never resolved. The author observed a shooter armed with a reproduction Gallager carbine fire in a North-South Skirmish Association team match in the spring of 2006. The shooter kept a pair of pliers on his belt to extract cartridges, and he needed to use it most of the time.
31. McAulay, *Carbines of the Civil War*, p. 25.
32. Ken Baumann, *Arming the Suckers, 1861–1865: A Compilation of Illinois Civil War Weapons* (Dayton, Ohio: Morningside Press, 1989), p. 60.
33. Colonel Berkeley R. Lewis, *Notes on Cavalry Weapons of the American Civil War* (Washington, D.C.: The American Ordnance Association, 1961), p. 20.
34. Bauman, *Arming the Suckers*, p. 60. A surviving Third Model Burnside whose provenance has been proven is in a private collection.
35. McAulay, *Carbines of the Civil War*, p. 29.
36. Ibid., p. 32.
37. Ibid., p. 35.
38. *O.R.*, ser. I, vol. XXXVI, pt. I, p. 134; Ibid., vol. XXXIII, p. 891; McAulay, *Carbines of the Civil War*, p. 38.

39. Thomas, *Round Ball to Rimfire, Part Two*, pp. 235–237; Lewis, *Notes on Cavalry Weapons*, p. 20.

40. Thomas, *Round Ball to Rimfire, Part Two*, pp. 240–241.

41. Garagavlia and Worman, *Firearms of the American West, 1803–1865*, pp. 183, 194.

42. McAulay, *Carbines of the Civil War*, p. 67.

43. *O.R.*, ser. I, vol. XL, pt. III, p. 250; Ibid., vol. XLVIII, pt I, p. 601.

44. Thomas, *Round Ball to Rimfire, Part Two*, pp. 177–179.

45. Douglas C. McChristian, *An Army of Marksmen* (Ft. Collins, CO: The Old Army Press, 1981), p. 13.

46. Baumann, *Arming the Suckers*, p. 60; Pennsylvania Gettysburg Battlefield Commission, *Pennsylvania at Gettysburg* (1914), p. 885.

47. Busey and Martin, *Regimental Strengths*, pp. 106–107. Busey and Martin cite initial "engaged" strength by using other sources to complement and interpret the actual muster roll strength of a unit on July 1–3, 1863, in comparison to its strength as reported on the June 30 Army of the Potomac muster roll reported strength.

48. Martin, *Gettysburg, July 1*, pp. 63, 66.

49. Ibid., pp. 66–67.

50. Martin, *Gettysburg July 1*, p. 67; Cited in Brent Nosworthy, *The Bloody Crucible of Courage: Fighting Methods and Combat Experience of the Civil War* (New York: Carroll & Graf, 2003), p. 214.

51. Martin, *Gettysburg, July 1*, p. 67; Wittenberg, "Defense in Depth."

52. William T. Ivy, "The Battle of Gettysburg," in Richard A. Sauers (ed.), *Fighting Them Over: How the Veterans Remembered Gettysburg in the Pages of the National Tribune* (Baltimore: Butternut and Blue, 1998), p. 457.

53. Martin, *Gettysburg, July 1*, p. 69.

54. Ibid., pp. 80–82, 155.

55. Ibid., p. 73.

56. Ibid., pp. 85–86; Nosworthy, *The Bloody Crucible of Courage*, pp. 269–275.

57. Thomas G. Day, "Opening the Battle: A Cavalryman's Recollections of the First Day's Fight at Gettysburg," in Sauers (ed.), *Fighting Them Over*, p. 448.

58. Edward G. Longacre, *The Cavalry at Gettysburg* (Lincoln, NE: U. of Nebraska Press), pp. 186–187.

59. Frederick Whittaker, *Volunteer Cavalry: The Lessons of the Decade* (New York: Author, 1871), p. 5.

60. Longacre, *Cavalry at Gettysburg*, p. 60.

CHAPTER 2: THE RIFLE-MUSKET, PART I

1. According to its June 30 Quarterly Ordnance Report, the Eighty-eighth had seventy-eight smoothbore muskets in its ranks. E-mail correspondence on ordnance reports with David Powell, February 2, 2007.

2. T. F. Fremantle, *The Book of the Rifle* (London: Longmans, Green and Co., 1901), pp. 4–5.

3. Lt. Col. Viscount Bury M. P., *Manual of Rifling and Rifle Sights for the National Rifle Association, 1864* (London: Longman & Co., 1864), p. 2; Charles Chenevix Trench, *A History of Marksmanship* (Chicago: Follett, 1972), p. 199; Jaroslav Lugs, *Firearms Past and Present: A Complete Review of Firearm Systems and their Histories, Vol. I* (London: Greenville, 1975), pp. 35–36; W. Y. Carman, *A History of*

Firearms from Earliest Times to 1914 (London: Routledge & Kegan Paul Ltd., 1955), pp. 105–106; De Witt Bailey, *British Military Flintlock Rifles, 1740–1840* (Lincoln, RI: Andrew Mobray, 2002), p. 7.

4. Mark M. Boatner, *Encyclopedia of the American Revolution,* (New York: David McKay Company, 1966), p. 935.

5. Bailey, *British Military Flintlock Rifles,* p. 21.

6. Ibid.; Paddy Griffith, *Forward into Battle: Fighting Tactics from Waterloo to the Near Future, 2nd Ed.* (San Francisco: Presidio, 1990), pp. 44–49.

7. Ibid., p. 15.

8. Ibid., p. 22.

9. John C. Fredrickson, *Green Coats and Glory: The United States Regiment of Riflemen, 1808–1821* (Youngstown, NY: Old Fort Niagara Assoc., 2000), pp. 43–44, 71.

10. Quoted in Philip Haythornthwaite, *Weapons & Equipment of the Napoleonic Wars* (London: Arms and Armour, 1996), p. 27; Henry B. Carrington, "Familiar Hints to Indiana Soldiers Taking to the Field." Undated newspaper clipping from the Greencastle Indiana *Putnam Republican Banner.*

11. Frederick Myatt, *The Illustrated Encyclopedia of 19th Century Firearms* (New York: Crescent Books, 1994), pp. 18–19.

12. Ibid., p. 41.

13. Ibid., p. 42.

14. Ibid.; Alfred Mordecai, *Military Commission to Europe in 1855 and 1856: Report of Major Albert Mordecai of the Ordnance Department* (Washington, D.C.: U.S. Government, 1860), pp. 172–173.

15. C. H. Roads, *The British Soldier's Firearm From Smoothbore to Smallbore, 1850–1864.* (Livonia, NY: R&R Books, 1994), p. 24.

16. Fremantle, *The Book of the Rifle,* p. 45.

17. *New Jersey Adjutant General Report for 1856* (Trenton: State of New Jersey, 1857), p. 10.

18. "The How and Why of Long Shots and Straight Shots," *The Cornhill Magazine* (April 1860); John Norton, *A List of Captain Norton's Projectiles* (Gravesend: Caddel and Son, 1860), pp. 11–12.

19. Myatt, *19th Century Firearms,* pp. 44–45.

20. Carman, *A History of Firearms,* p. 112.

21. Myatt, *19th Century Firearms,* p. 52; Nosworthy, *Bloody Crucible,* p. 214.

22. Roads, *The British Soldier's Firearm,* p. 142.

23. Ibid., p. 69.

24. Thomas K. Tate, *From Under Iron Eyelids: The Biography of James Henry Burton, Armorer to Three Nations* (Bloomington, Indiana: Author House, 2005), pp. 43–51.

25. Ibid., p. 48.

26. Ibid., pp. 88–94.

27. McChristian, *An Army of Marksmen,* p. 9.

28. Philip H. Smith to uncle [Frederick Canfield], July 20, 1862, Canfield/Pickerson Family Papers, New Jersey Historical Society.

29. Garavaglia and Worman, *Firearms of the American West, 1803–1865,* p. 160.

30. *New Jersey Quartermaster General's Annual Report for 1857.* (Trenton: State of New Jersey, 1858).

31. Claud E. Fuller, *The Rifled Musket* (New York: Bonanza Books, 1958), p. 5.

32. *Richmond Daily Dispatch,* 5 January 1861; *New Jersey Quartermaster General's*

Annual Report for 1860 (Trenton: State of New Jersey, 1861), p. 7.

33. Ripley, *Annual Report;* John W. Mallet, "Work of the Ordnance Bureau, *Southern Historical Society Papers* 37 (January–December 1909).

34. *New Jersey Quartermaster General Report for 1861* (Trenton: State of New Jersey, 1862), p. 7; Henry O. Ryerson to sister, August 20, 1861, Ryerson papers, New Jersey Historical Society.

35. John Gross, "A War Fought and Won with 'Inferior' Firearms," *The Gun Report* 47, no. 10 (March 2002).

36. Paul J. Davies, *C. S. Armory Richmond* (Carlisle, PA: Author, 2000), pp. 349–351; Mallet, "Work of the Ordnance Bureau," p. 13; e-mail correspondence with Bill Adams, March 22, 2007.

37. Warren (NJ) *Journal,* 3 May 1861; *NJQM Report for 1861,* p. 7; Alfred Bellard (ed. David Herbert Donald), *Gone for a Soldier: The Civil War Memoirs of Private Alfred Bellard* (New York: Little, Brown, 1975), p. 7.

38. Frank E. Vandiver, *Ploughshares into Swords: Josiah Gorgas and Confederate Ordnance* (College Station Texas: Texas A&M, 1952), p. 115.

39. *Richmond Daily Dispatch,* 19 November 1860; Tate, *Iron Eyelids,* pp. 247–257. Burton contracted for a sample model to be made at Springfield Armory and for machine tools from several New England manufacturers, the latter undelivered due to the outbreak of the war. The subsequent Colt 1861 Special Model rifle-musket supplied to Union forces bears a striking similarity to the description of Burton's design.

40. Wiley Sword, *Firepower from Abroad: The Confederate Enfield and the LeMat Revolver.* (Lincoln, RI: Andrew Mobray, 1986), p. 11.

41. Sword, *Firepower from Abroad,* pp. 9, 67; *O.R.,* ser. IV, vol. 2, pp. 630–631.

42. W. Stanley Hoole, *Confederate Foreign Agent: The European Diary of Major Edward C. Anderson* (University, AL: Confederate Publishing, 1976), p. 5.

43. Sword, *Firepower from Abroad,* p. 13; Leslie S. Bright, *The Blockade Runner Modern Greece and Her Cargo* (Raleigh, NC: NC Dept. of Cultural Resources), pp. 50, 51, 54, 55, 109, 110. The number of imports by mid-1863 was interpolated from Confederate import figures for 1861, 1862 and 1863 provided by Sword, p. 67. A Confederate report of imported arms through the end of 1862 indicates over 80,000 Enfields.

44. Charles E. Davis, *Three Years in the Army: The Story of the Thirteenth Massachusetts Volunteers* (Boston, Estes & Lauriat, 1894), p. xxix; Joseph Keith Newell, *"Ours." Annals of 10th Regiment, Massachusetts Volunteers, in the Rebellion* (Springfield, MA: C. A. Nichols, 1875) p. 30; quoted in Paddy Griffith, *Battle Tactics of the Civil War* (New Haven, CT: Yale University Press, 1987), p. 78; Baumann, *Arming the Suckers,* p. 35.

45. Colonel William Penrose to Major General John Sedgwick, June 24, 1863, Regimental Correspondence Book, Fifteenth New Jersey Infantry, National Archives.

46. Ibid. Enfields were marked "25" or "24" on their barrels to differentiate gauge.

47. *O.R.,* ser. 1, vol. XXX, pt. 2, p. 277.

48. Henry O. Ryerson to sister, April 20, 1864, Ryerson papers, NJHS.

49. Baumann, *Arming the Suckers,* p. 127.

50. Neff, "The Enfield Rifle," *Muzzle Blasts* (July 1979); Dee Brown, *Morgan's Raiders,* (Portland, OR: Smithmark Publishers; reprint ed., 1995), p. 69.

51. Earl J. Coates and Dean S. Thomas, *An Introduction to Civil War Small Arms* (Gettysburg, PA: Thomas Publications, 1990), p. 21; e-mail correspondence with Bill

Adams, March 27, 1999; Mordecai, *Military Commission Report*, p. 170.

52. E-mail correspondence with Bill Adams, March 27, 1999; Howard L. Blackmore, *British Military Firearms, 1650–1850* (London: Herbert Jenkins, 1961), p. 232.

53. Adams e-mail, March 27, 1999; Mordecai, *Military Commission Report*, p. 161.

54. Edwards, *Civil War Guns*, p. 262.

55. Sword, *Firepower from Abroad*, p. 64; O.R., ser. IV, vol. 2, pp. 630–631; Vandiver, *Ploughshares into Swords*, p. 93.

56. Larry J. Daniel, *Soldiering in the Army of Tennessee: A Portrait of Life in a Confederate Army* (Chapel Hill, NC: U. of North Carolina Press, 1991), pp. 46–47.

57. Bellard, *Gone for a Soldier*, p. 38; William H. Davis, *History of the One Hundred and Fourth Pennsylvania Regiment from August 22, 1861 to September 30, 1864* (Philadelphia: J. B. Rodgers, 1866), p. 36; William J. Wray, *History of the Twenty-third Pennsylvania Volunteer Infantry, Birney's Zouaves,* (Philadelphia: Survivor's Assn., 1904), p. 127; Leander Stillwell, *The Story of a Common Soldier of Army Life in the Civil War 1861–1865* (Chicago: Franklin Hudson, 1920 2nd ed.), p. 28.

58. Baumann, *Arming the Suckers*, pp. 181, 189, 197, 211.

59. Ibid., pp. 216, 221; George Norton Galloway, *The Ninety-fifth Pennsylvania Volunteers (Gosline's Pennsylvania Zouaves) in the Sixth Corps* (Philadelphia: 1884), p. 9; O.R., ser. I, vol. XV, p. 649.

60. Edwin B. Coddington, *The Gettysburg Campaign: A Study in Command* (New York: Charles Scribner's Sons, 1968), p. 257.

61. Mordecai, *Military Commission Report*, p. 160.

62. Ibid.

63. William B. Edwards, *Civil War Guns*, (Harrisburg, PA: Stackpole, 1962), pp. 260–266.

64. Mallett, "Work of the Ordnance Bureau," pp. 7–8.

65. Edward Porter Alexander, *Military Memoirs of a Confederate* (New York: 1907), p. 370; Lt. Col. Arthur J. L. Fremantle, *Three Months in the Southern States* (Lincoln, NE: Bison Books edition, 1991), p. 225.

66. O.R., ser. 1, vol. XXV, pp. 811–819.

67. Coddington, *Gettysburg*, p. 253.

CHAPTER 3: THE RIFLE-MUSKET, PART II

1. Coddington, *The Gettysburg Campaign*, p. 252; Grady McWhiney and Perry D. Jamieson, *Attack and Die: Civil War Military Tactics and the Southern Heritage* (Montgomery, AL: U. of Alabama Press, 1982), pp. 6, 49; Bruce Catton, *Mr. Lincoln's Army* (New York: Doubleday, 1951), pp. 187–188; Richard E. Berringer, Herman Hattaway, Archer Jones, and William N. Still, Jr., *Why the South Lost the Civil War* (Athens, GA: U. of Georgia Press, 1986), pp. 14–15; Robert L. O'Connell, *Of Arms and Men: A History of War, Weapons, and Aggression* (New York: Oxford University Press, 1989), pp. 197–198; Michael A. Bellesisles, *Arming America: the Origins of a National Gun Culture* (New York: Alfred A. Knopf, 2000), p. 427.
Ironically, McWhiney and Jamieson, who O'Connell and Bellesisles cite to buttress their arguments, base their own opening argument on casualties incurred at Malvern Hill, a battle fought largely with smoothbore muskets on both sides, where even those troops armed with rifle-muskets had little to no training in their proper use. O'Connell uncritically accepts McWhiney and Jamieson's premise that the rifle-musket created a revolution in warfare. In addition, McWhiney and Jamieson base

their idea on the dubious premise that high Confederate casualties were a result of a
Scots-Irish "Celtic" racial or ethnic preference for the unrestrained offensive in the
face of effective rifle-musket fire. Although accepting the argument that the extended
range of the rifle-musket increased casualties, Beringer, et al., effectively deconstruct
the McWhiney and Jamieson contentions that the offensive spirit or racial tendencies
had anything to do with the South losing the war (pp. 458–481). Recent scholarship
questions the very basis of the essentially Victorian concept of a "Celtic" preference
for the offense as opposed to, say, the more "phlegmatic" Anglo-Saxon's stolidity,
consigning it to the dustbin of historiography along with other quaint nineteenth-
century enthusiasms like phrenology. For more on this, see Bryan Sykes, *Saxons,
Vikings and Celts: The Genetic Roots of Britain and Ireland*, (New York: W. W.
Norton, 2006); Nicholas Wade, "A United Kingdom? Maybe.," in *The New York
Times*, 6 March 2007; and Alexander McCall Smith, "A Wee Identity Crisis," in *The
New York Times*, 11 March 2007.
2. Quoted in James I. Robertson, Jr., *Soldiers Blue and Gray* (Columbia, SC: U. of
South Carolina Press, 1988), p. 56.
3. Ibid., pp. 55–56.
4. Thomas B. Marbaker, *History of the Eleventh New Jersey Volunteers*,
(Hightstown, NJ: Longstreet House, 1990 reprint), p. 175.
5. Berry Benson (ed. Susan Williams Benson), *Berry Benson's Civil War Book:
Memoirs of a Confederate Scout and Sharpshooter* (Athens, GA: U. of Georgia Press,
1992), p. 33.
6. Quoted in Earl J. Hess, *The Union Soldier in Battle: Enduring the Ordeal of
Combat* (Lawrence, KS: U. Press of Kansas, 1997), p. 80.
7. John Gibbon, *The Artillerist's Manual* (New York: D. Van Nostrand, 1860), pp.
221–222; Berkeley R. Lewis, *Small Arms and Ammunition in the United States
Service, 1776–1865* (Washington: Smithsonian, 1956), p. 99.
8. John William DeForest, *A Volunteer's Adventures: A Union Captain's Record of
the Civil War* (Hamden, CT: Archon, 1970), p. 64.
9. Griffith, *Battle Tactics of the Civil War*, p. 147. In another work, Griffith establish-
es the average engaged musketry range of British troops in Spain at 75.5 yards, but
this was part of a deliberate defensive tactic involving taking a reverse slope concealed position until the enemy was at point blank range. Griffith, *Forward into
Battle*, p. 39.
10. John Y. Foster, *New Jersey and the Rebellion: A History of the Services of the
Troops and People of New Jersey in Aid of the Union Cause* (Newark, NJ: Martin R.
Dennis & Co., 1868), p. 168.
11. Griffith, *Battle Tactics*, p. 149.
12. Joseph G. Bilby, "The Keystone Travelers: A Regimental History of the 104th
Pennsylvania," *Military Images Magazine* (March–April 1992).
13. Bailey, *British Military Flintlock Rifles*, p. 173.
14. Myatt, *19th Century Firearms*, 31; British army "Annual Target Practice Return"
form, courtesy Bill Adams collection.
15. William Howard Russell, "Malta, March 17 [1854]," in Andrew Lambert &
Stephen Badsey, *The War Correspondents: The Crimean War* (London: Bramley
Books, 1997), p. 17.
16. Major F. V. Longstaff and A. Hilliard Atteridge, *The Book of the Machine Gun*
(London: Hugh Rees Ltd., 1917), pp. 2–3.
17. Hans Busk, *The Rifle and How to Use It*, (London: Routledge, Warnes and

Routledge, 1859, 4th ed.), p. 133.

18. Ibid., p. 168.

19. Lieutenant Colonel Viscount Bury, "The Volunteer Course at Hythe School of Musketry," *Fraser's Magazine* 62, no. 367 (July 1860).

20. Silas Casey, *Infantry Tactics . . .* (Dayton, OH: Morningside Press, 1985 reprint), p. 47.

21. *Richmond Daily Dispatch*, 1 November 1860; Ibid., 4 June 1861; Griffith, *Forward into Battle*, pp. 64–65.

22. *Military Gazette* 2, no. 14 (July 15, 1859): 214.

23. Casey, *Infantry Tactics*, p. 6.

24. Henry I. Smith, *History of the Seventh Regiment, Iowa Volunteer Infantry During the Civil War* (Mason City, IA: E. Hitchcock, 1903), p. 6; Robert McAllister to wife, September 19, 1862, in James I. Robertson, Jr., ed., *The Civil War Letters of General Robert McAllister* (New Brunswick, NJ: Rutgers University Press, 1965), p. 209.

25. Joseph G. Bilby, *Remember Fontenoy: The 69th New York and the Irish Brigade in the Civil War*, (Hightstown, NJ: Longstreet House, 1995), p. 101; Joseph G. Bilby, "First Blood: A New Jersey Brigade at Williamsburg," *Military Images Magazine* 12, no. 2 (September–October 1990).

26. Albert William Mann, *History of the Forty-fifth Regiment, Massachusetts Volunteer Militia* (Jamaica Plain, MA: Brookside Print, 1908), p. 66; cited in Griffith, *Battle Tactics*, p. 88; Ben R. Maryniak, "Shooting Practice," *Buffalo Civil War Round Table Newsletter* (May 1990).

27. Bell Irvin Wiley, *The Life of Billy Yank: The Common Soldier of the Union* (New York: Bobbs-Merrill Company, 1951), pp. 26–27.

28. *The Charleston Mercury*, 1 January 1861.

29. Robert O. Neff, "The Enfield Rifle," *Muzzle Blasts* (July 1979); Ich B to dear parents, May 1, 1862, copy courtesy Bill Adams; Quoted in Bell Irwin Wiley, *Billy Yank*, p. 63.

30. William O'Grady, "88th New York," in New York Monuments Commission for the Battlefield of Gettysburg and Chattanooga, *Final Report on the Battlefield of Gettysburg* [New York at Gettysburg] (Albany, NY: J. B. Lyon Co., 1900, 1902), p. 513.

31. John C. Thompson, *History of the Eleventh Regiment, Rhode Island Volunteers, in the War of the Rebellion* (Providence, RI: Providence Press, 1881), p. 107; Cyrus Morton Cutler, *Letters From the Front.* (San Francisco: A. D. Cutler, 1892), p. 14.

32. *New York Herald*, 23 February 1862; *Newark* (NJ) *Journal*, 30 November 1863.

33. John Harrison Mills, *Chronicles of the Twenty-first Regiment, New York State Volunteers* (Buffalo, NY: 21st Regiment Veteran Association, 1887), pp. 143–144.

34. Ann Hartwell Britton and Thomas J. Reed (eds.), *To My Beloved Wife and Boy at Home: The Letters and Diaries of Orderly Sergeant John F. L. Hartwell* (Teaneck, NJ: Fairleigh Dickinson University Press, 1997), pp. 55, 58–59; Quoted in James M. Greiner, *Subdued by the Sword: A Line Officer in the 121st New York Volunteers* (Albany, NY: SUNY Press, 2003), p. 45; Joseph Bilby, *Three Rousing Cheers: A History of the Fifteenth New Jersey from Flemington to Appomattox* (Hightstown, NJ: Longstreet House, 2nd ed., 2001), p. 43.

35. Griffith, *Battle Tactics*, p. 86; Letter and Correspondence Book, Fifteenth New Jersey Infantry, U.S. National Archives.

36. George L. Willard (William C. Goble, ed.), *Comparative Value of Rifled and*

Smooth-Bored Arms (Hightstown, NJ: Longstreet House, 1995 reprint), pp, 3, 11–12.

37. D. A. Tisdale, *Soldiers of the Virginia Colony, 1607–1699* (Author, n.d.), pp. 58, 136.

38. Author's discussion with Archeologist Dr. David Orr of Temple University, November 11, 2006; Fredricksen, *Green Coats and Glory*, p. 17.

39. "The Tenth Regiment of Infantry," at http://www.army.mil/cmh-pg/books/R&H/R&H-10IN.htm; McChristian, *An Army of Marksmen*, p. 11.

40. McChristian, *An Army of Marksmen*, p. 13.

41. Ibid., pp. 13–16.

42. Gerard A. Patterson, *From Blue to Gray: The Life of Confederate General Cadmus M. Wilcox* (Mechanicsburg, PA: Stackpole Books, 2001), pp. 9–10.

43. Fred Ray, *Shock Troops of the Confederacy: The Sharpshooter Battalions of the Army of Northern Virginia* (Ashville, NC: CFS Press, 2006), pp. 16–19.

44. U.S. War Department, *A System of Target Practice for the Use of Troops When Armed with the Musket, Rifle Musket, Rifle or Carbine, Prepared Principally from the French.* (Washington, D.C.: 1862), p. 9.

45. George L. Willard, *Manual of Target Practice for the United States Army* (Philadelphia: J. B. Lippincott & Co., 1862), p. 71.

46. U.S. Government, *Report of the Joint Committee on the Conduct of the War* (Washington, D.C.: Government Printing Office, 1863), p. 230.

47. Henry Lee, Jr., *The Militia of the United States: What It Has Been, What it Should Be.* (Boston: T. R. Marvin & Son, 1864), pp. 100–101.

48. Purdue, Howell, and Elizabeth, *Pat Cleburne; Confederate General* (Hillsboro, TX: Hillsboro Jr. College Press, 1973), p. 187; Bromfield L. Ridley, *Sketches and Battles of the Army of Tennessee* (Mexico, MO: Mexico Printing and Publishing, 1906), p. 488.

49. *O.R.*, ser. 1, vol. X, pt. 2, pp. 368–369.

50. Ray, *Shock Troops*, pp. 26–28.

51. William Y. W. Ripley, *A History of Company F, 1st United States Sharp Shooters* (Rutland, VT: Tuttle & Com. 1883), p. 4.

52. Ray, *Shock Troops*, pp. 42–46.

53. Ibid., pp. 46–48.

Chapter 4: The Rifle-Musket, Part III

1. Dean S. Thomas, *Ready, Aim, Fire: Small Arms Ammunition in the Battle of Gettysburg* (Gettysburg, PA: Thomas Publications, 1993 ed.), p. 11.

2. Ibid., pp. 11–12. The large number of unfired "dropped" Minié balls recovered by relic hunters would suggest that this might well have been the fate of much ammunition. A document of April 25, 1863, states that a loaded cartridge weighed 575 grains. With 7,000 grains to the pound, sixty cartridges would weigh 4.928 pounds.

3. Josiah Gorgas, "Contributions to the History of the Confederate Ordnance Department," *Southern Historical Society Papers* 12 (January–December 1884); Thomas, *Ready, Aim, Fire*, pp. 11–12. Even as late as Appomattox, Lee's Confederate infantry had access to around seventy-five rounds per man. Captain Scott Glass, "Confederate Status of Class V, VII and IX at Appomattox," *Ordnance: The Professional Bulletin of the Ordnance Soldier* (August 1992).

4. *O.R.*, ser. 1, vol. XXV, p. 819.

5. *O.R.*, ser. 1, vol. XXVII, pt. 1, pp. 617–618.

6. Dean S. Thomas, *Round Ball to Rimfire: A History of Civil War Small Arms*

Ammunition, Part One (Gettysburg: Thomas Publications, 1997), p. 137.

7. Ibid., p. 140.

8. Penrose to Major General John Sedgwick, June 24, 1863, Regimental Correspondence Book, Fifteenth NJ Infantry, n.a.

9. Lt. Jonathan R. Edie to General George D. Ramsay, October 9, 1863, reproduced in Thomas, *Round Ball to Rimfire, Part One*, p. 138; *O.R.*, ser. 1, vol. XXVII, pt. 1, p. 624.

10. Ibid.

11. Ibid.

12. Lewis, *Small Arms and Ammunition*, p. 193. The complete story of the Augusta Powder Works is comprehensively told in C. L. Bragg, Charles D. Ross, Gordon A. Blaker, Stephanie A. T. Jacobe, and Theodore P. Savas, *Never for Want of Powder: The Confederate Powder Works in Augusta, Georgia* (Columbia, SC: U. of South Carolina Press, 2007).

13. Bragg, et al., *Never for Want of Powder*, p. 139. While powder made at Augusta was shipped around the Confederacy for local manufacture into cartridges, most Augusta manufactured and repackaged ammunition was sent west, not to the Army of Northern Virginia.

14. *O.R.*, ser. 1, vol. XXX, pt. 2, p. 277.

15. Vandiver, *Ploughshares into Swords*, p. 190.

16. For a comprehensive review of all of this ammunition at Gettysburg, see Thomas, *Ready, Aim, Fire.*

17. Thomas, *Round Ball to Rimfire, Part One*, pp. 211–214.

18. Ibid., pp. 217, 227–228.

19. Ibid., pp. 233–234.

20. Augusta *Daily Constitutionalist*, 17 July 1864.

21. Thomas, *Round Ball to Rimfire, Part One*, p. 183.

22. Lewis, *Small Arms and Ammunition*, pp. 126–127; Fremantle, *Book of the Rifle*, pp. 46–47.

23. Thomas, *Round Ball to Rimfire, Part One*, p. 184.

24. Ibid., p. 187.

25. Ibid.

26. Martin A. Haynes, *History of the Second Regiment, New Hampshire Volunteers: Its Camps, Marches and Battles* (Manchester, NH: Charles F. Livingston, 1865), p. 139; Thomas, *Round Ball to Rimfire, Part One*, pp. 188–189; Lewis, *Small Arms and Ammunition*, p. 128.

27. Thomas, *Round Ball to Rimfire, Part One*, pp. 188–189; Lewis, *Small Arms and Ammunition*, p. 128; Horace Edward Hayden, "Explosive or Poisoned Musket Balls,— Were they authorized and Used by the Confederate States Army, or by the United States Army during the Civil War?—A Slander Refuted," *Southern Historical Society Papers* 8 (January–December 1880), pp. 20, 26. Hayden, whose righteous indignation taints his objectivity, seems to have confused the Williams and Shaler bullets with "poisoned" bullets.

28. Quoted in Martin, *Gettysburg, July 1*, p. 100.

29. Samuel P. Bates, *History of Pennsylvania Volunteers, 1861–1865: Prepared in Compliance with Acts of the Legislature* (Harrisburg, PA: R. Singerly, 1869, vol. 2), p. 220.

30. Ibid.; Martin, *Gettysburg, July 1*, p. 108; James L. McLean, Jr., *Cutler's Brigade at Gettysburg* (Baltimore: Butternut and Blue, 1994), p. 67 (map); E-mail correspon-

dence with Dr. David Martin, May 13, 2007. The Fifty-sixth's battlefield monument,
erected in 1888, is surmounted by stacked Model 1863 rifle-muskets. Their rear
sights may, like the Model 1861 Springfield, be elevated to 500 yards maximum distance.
31. Bates, *History of Pennsylvania Volunteers,* vol. 2, p. 220.
32. Ibid.
33. *O.R.,* ser. 1, vol. XXVII, pt. 1, p. 285; Martin, *Gettysburg, July 1,* p. 110; B. E.
Parkhurst, "Co. F. 147th N.Y. At Gettysburg: Heroism of the 147th N.Y.," *National
Tribune* (January 1, 1888), in Sauers (ed.), *Fighting Them Over,* p. 99. A rod was 16.5
feet, or 5.5 yards, in length.
34. Busey and Martin, *Regimental Strengths,* pp. 24, 224.
35. Martin, *Gettysburg, July 1,* pp. 118–119.
36. Howard Michael Madaus, "The Uniform of The Iron Brigade at Gettysburg July
1, 1863," appendix to Lance J. Herdegen and William J. K. Beaudot, *In the Bloody
Railroad Cut at Gettysburg* (Dayton, OH: Morningside Press, 1990), pp. 363–367.
37. Herdegen and Beaudot, *Bloody Railroad Cut,* p. 183. Dawes' horse was hit in the
breast by a ball that drove fourteen inches through muscle before halting. She made
her way back to the baggage train and survived the war and lived for many years
afterward. Dawes recalled that the bullet "could be felt under the skin behind the left
shoulder blade—but woe to the man who felt it, as her temper had been spoiled."
Ibid.; *O.R.,* ser. I, vol. XXVII, pt. 1, p. 276. This, and other engagement range measurements at Gettysburg noted in the text, were taken by the author on June 5, 2007,
using a Leica Rangemaster CRF 900 range finder. The measurement of the Sixth
Wisconsin's distance from the railroad cut was an average of five sightings taken
starting from the position of the regiment's left flank marker by the railroad cut and
moving down an approximation of what would have been the regimental front, to the
north side of the existing road.
38. Herdegen and Beaudot, *Bloody Railroad Cut,* p. 184.
39. William J. K. Beaudot and Lance J. Herdegen (eds.), *An Irishman in the Iron
Brigade: The Civil War Memoirs of James P. Sullivan, Sergt., Company K, 6th
Wisconsin Volunteers* (New York: Fordham University Press, 1993), p. 95.
40. Martin, *Gettysburg, July 1,* pp. 126–127.
41. Herdegen and Beaudot, *Bloody Railroad Cut,* p. 188.
42. Ibid., p. 211.
43. Ibid., p. 195; *O.R.,* ser. I, vol. XXVII, pt. 1, p. 264; Quoted in Herdegen and
Beaudot, *Bloody Railroad Cut,* p. 207. The complete list of captured arms reads as follows: Springfield rifled muskets—174; Enfield rifled muskets—2,402; Austrian rifled
muskets—64; English rifled muskets [P51s?]—26; Harper's Ferry smoothbore muskets—212; total—2,958.
44. *O.R.,* ser. 1, vol. XXVII, pt. 1, p. 279; Martin, *Gettysburg, July 1,* p. 156.
45. *O.R.,* ser. 1, vol. XXVII, pt. 1, p. 493. Range estimates are averages of figures
obtained by the author on June 5, 2007.
46. Ray, *Shock Troops,* p. 65. Iverson's skirmishers, who may have been trained
sharpshooters or at least been employed as such, appear to have been on another mission nearer to Oak Hill, increasing his brigade's vulnerability to an ambush.

CHAPTER 5: THE SMOOTHBORE MUSKET
1. Wiley, *Billy Yank,* pp. 50–51.

2. *The Richmond Daily Dispatch*, 2 November 1860.

3. Russel S. Gilmore, "New York Target Companies: Informal Military Societies in a 19th Century Metropolis," *Military Collector and Historian* 35, no. 2 (Summer 1983): 61–65.

4. Quoted in David F. Harding, *Small Arms of the East India Company, 1600–1856, Vol. III: Ammunition and Performance* (London: Foresight Books, 1999), p. 291. Harding cites the original source of the quote as Hanger's *A Letter to Lord Castlereagh* (1808).

5. Ibid., p. 292.

6. Ibid., p. 263; Haythornthwaite, *Weapons and Equipment*, p. 21.

7. G. Cunnington, "L'entrainement au tir, a' l'epoque des armes a' silex," *Gazette des Armes* 96, Aout 1981 (translation by Dr. Jan Hamier for the author); Griffith, *Forward into Battle*, p. 38.

8. Blackmore, *British Military Firearms*, p. 226; Lewis, *Small Arms and Ammunition*, p. 113.

9. Harding, *Small Arms, Vol. III*, pp. 416–417; Lewis, *Small Arms and Ammunition*, p. 99.

10. Shooting conducted with Steven Garratano as marksman; E-mail correspondence with Dr. John Jenkins, July 7, 1999.

11. Haythornthwaite, *Weapons and Equipment*, pp. 19-20; Jean Boudriot, "Un aboutissement, mais une fin: Le fusil d'infanterie modele 1822," *Gazette des Armes* 96, Aout 1981 (translation by Dr. Jan Hamier for the author); Sir John Fox Burgoyne, *The Employment of Riflemen at Sieges* (London: 1859).

12. Willard, *Rifled and Smooth-Bored Arms*, p. 4.

13. Francis Rawdon Chesney, *Observations on the Past and Present State of Firearms . . .* (London: Longman, Brown, Green, and Longmans, 1852), p. 263.

14. Christopher Hibbert, *Wolfe at Quebec* (Cleveland: World, 1959), p. 152; Guy Chet, *Conquering the American Wilderness: The Triumph of European Warfare in the Colonial Northeast* (Amherst, MA: U. of Massachusetts Press, 2003), p. 57.

15. Albert Stillman Batchellor, *The Ranger Service in the Upper Valley of the Connecticut and the Most Northerly Regiment of the New Hampshire Militia in the Period of the Revolution* (Concord, NH: The Rumford Press, 1903), p. 22; Charles Knowles Bolton, *The Private Soldier Under Washington* (New York: Charles Scribner's Sons, 1902), p. 122; Lewis, *Small Arms and Ammunition*, p. 108; Harold Peterson, *Book of the Continental Soldier* (New York: Bonanza Books, 1977), pp. 60–61; discussion with Dr. Garry W. Stone, Historian, Monmouth Battlefield State Park, June 20, 2007.

16. Bolton, *Private Soldier*, p. 6; Peterson, *Continental Soldier*, p. 61.

17. Lewis, *Small Arms and Ammunition*, p. 115.

18. Ned H. Roberts, *The Muzzle-loading Cap Lock Rifle* (Harrisburg, PA: Stackpole, 1940), p. 185.

19. Griffith, *Forward into Battle*, p. 38.

20. Davis, *Arming the Union*, p. 41.

21. *The Daily Richmond Dispatch*, 19 November 1860.

22. Robert Matteson Johnston, *Bull Run, Its Strategy and Tactics* (Boston: Houghton Mifflin, 1913), p. 4.

23. Baumann, *Arming the Suckers*, pp. 83, 72. As late as the end of 1862, the Eighth carried a wide variety of arms, including smoothbore and rifled .69 caliber muskets. Joseph G. Bilby, ed., "Memoirs of Carlos W. Colby," *Military Images Magazine*

(September/October 1981).

24. *The Richmond Daily Dispatch*, 19 November 1860.

25. Bilby, *Remember Fontenoy*, p. 147.

26. Willard, *Rifled and Smoothbore Arms*, p. 3.

27. *Sussex* (NJ) *Register*, 15 May 1863.

28. Newark (NJ) *Advertiser*, 21 May 1862; Willard, *Rifled and Smooth-Bored Arms*, p. 13.

29. St. Clair A. Mulholland, *The Story of the 116th Regiment, Pennsylvania Infantry: War of Secession, 1862–1865* (Gaithersburg, MD: Old Soldier Books, 1992 reprint), p. 33.

30. Benjamin D. Coley diary, New Jersey Historical Society; Garavaglia and Worman, *Firearms of the American West*, p. 115.

31. Eugene Fitch Ware, *The Lyon Campaign in Missouri, Being a History of the First Iowa Infantry* (Topeka KS: Crane and Company, 1907), p. 86.

32. Ray, *Shock Troops*, pp. 48–49.

33. Edward G. Longacre, *To Gettysburg and Beyond: The Twelfth New Jersey Volunteer Infantry, II Corps, Army of the Potomac, 1862–1865* (Hightstown, NJ Longstreet House, 1988), p. 57.

34. Warren Olney, *Shiloh as Seen by a Private Soldier*, California MOLLUS papers, 1889.

35. Nosworthy, *Bloody Crucible*, p. 7.

36. Alfred Seely Roe, *Monocacy: A Sketch of the Battle of Monocacy, MD., July 9th, 1864* (Worcester, MA: 9th New York Heavy Artillery Veterans' Organization, 1894), p. 14; O'Grady, "88th Regiment," in *New York at Gettysburg*, p. 513.

37. Mordecai, *Military Commission*, p. 157.

38. Ibid., pp. 157, 163.

39. Augusta *Daily Constitutionalist*, 19 March 1862.

40. Ibid., (22 March 1862); Cadmus Wilcox, *Rifles and Rifle Practice* (New York: 1859), p. 157.

41. Dean S. Thomas, *Ready, Aim, Fire! Small Arms Ammunition at the Battle of Gettysburg* (Gettysburg, PA: Thomas Publications, 1993), p. 43; Statistics from Griffith, *Battle Tactics*, p. 76.

42. James N. Duffy, Gottfried Krueger and William H. Corbin, *Final Report of the Gettysburg Battlefield Commission of New Jersey* (Trenton: State of New Jersey, 1891), p. 109; O.R., ser. I, vol. XXVII, pt. 1, p. 465.

43. Busey and Martin *Regimental Strengths*, p. 36.

44. William Corby, C. S. C. (ed. Lawrence F. Kohl), *Memoirs of Chaplain Life: Three Years with the Irish Brigade in the Army of the Potomac* (New York: Fordham University Press, 1992), p. 184.

45. Busey and Martin, *Regimental Strengths*, p. 32; D. Scott Hartwig, "'No Troops on the Field Had Done Better' John C. Caldwell's Division in the Wheatfield, July 2, 1863," in Gary E. Gallagher, ed., *The Second Day at Gettysburg: Essays on Confederate and Union Leadership* (Kent, OH: Kent State University Press, 1993), pp. 141–142; O.R., ser. 1, vol. XXVII, pt. 1, p. 493.

46. Mulholland, *116th Pennsylvania*, p. 137.

47. The Seventh South Carolina lost 115 men killed, wounded, and missing (28.2% of it strength) at Gettysburg. Busey and Martin, *Regimental Strengths*, p. 266.

48. O.R., ser. I, vol. XXVII, pt. 1, p. 380.

49. Richard S. Thompson, "A Scrap at Gettysburg," *Military Essays and*

Recollections, Chicago MOLLUS Papers, vol. 3, 1897, p. 97; Longacre, *Gettysburg and Beyond*, pp. 129–130.

50. Longacre, *Gettysburg and Beyond*, p. 131.

51. Thompson, "A Scrap at Gettysburg."

52. Longacre, *Gettysburg and Beyond*, p. 132; Herdegen and Beaudot, *In the Bloody Railroad Cut*, pp. 190–195. Three measurements taken by the author on June 7, 2007, from the Twelfth New Jersey's position on Cemetery ridge and the current eastern edge of the Emmitsburg Road indicated an average distance of 170 yards.

53. Bruce A. Trinque, "Arnold's Battery and the 26th North Carolina," *Gettysburg Magazine* 12 (January 1995).

54. *O.R.*, ser. I, vol. 27, pt. 1, pp. 373, 453, 470–471; Bilby and Goble, *Remember You Are Jerseymen*, p. 613.

55. David L. and Audrey J. Ladd (ed.), *The Batchelder Papers: Gettysburg in Their Own Words, Vol. III* (Dayton, Ohio, Morningside Press, 1994), p. 1402.

56. *O.R.*, ser. I, vol. 27, pt. 1, p. 176.

57. Bilby and Goble, *Jerseymen*, p. 615; Bilby, *Remember Fontenoy*, pp. 157, 160, 163, 165; Samuel Toombs, *New Jersey Troops in the Gettysburg Campaign* (Orange, NJ: Evening Mail Publishing, 1888), p. 311.

58. Lewis, *Small Arms and Ammunition*, p. 99.

Chapter 6: Repeating Rifles

1. This chapter is based upon Bilby, *A Revolution in Arms*.

2. Herbert G. Houze, *Colt Rifles and Muskets From 1847 to 1870*, (Iola, WI: Krause, 2004), pp. 71–79.

3. "Colt's Revolving Rifle," *Military Gazette* 3, no. 18 (September 15, 1860): 276.

4. John D. McAulay, *Civil War Breechloading Rifles, A Survey of the Innovative Infantry Arms of the American Civil War* (Lincoln, RI: Andrew Mobray, 1991), p. 14.

5. Charles A. Stevens, *Berdan's United States Sharpshooters in the Army of the Potomac: 1861–1865* (Dayton, OH: Morningside Books reprint, 1984), p. 27.

6. Ferdinand Lecomte, *The War in the United States, Report to the Swiss Military Department* (New York: D. Van Nostrand, 1863), p. 103.

7. Bauman, *Arming the Suckers*, p. 53; McAulay, *Civil War Breechloading Rifles*, p. 18.

8. McAulay, *Civil War Breechloading Rifles*, p. 14.

9. Frederick P. Todd, *American Military Equipage, 1851–1871 Vol. II, State Forces* (New York: Chatham Square Press, 1983), p. 115; McAulay, *Breechloading Rifles*, p. 18.

10. Frank C. Barnes, *Cartridges of the World*, (Chicago: Follett, 1965), p. 271; Lugs, *Firearms Past and Present*, p. 78; Raymond Caranta, "Louis Nicolas Auguste Flobert: His Rimfire Rifles and Cartridges," in *Gun Digest* (Northfield, IL: Digest Books, 1973), pp. 122-123.

11. John E. Parsons, *The First Winchester: The Story of the 1866 Repeating Rifle* (New York: Winchester Press, 1969), p. 9.

12. Roy M. Marcot, *Spencer Repeating Firearms* (Rochester, NY: Rowe, 1990), p. 189.

13. Ibid., p. 28.

14. Nosworthy, *Bloody Crucible of Courage*, p. 618.

15. *O.R.*, ser. I, vol. XVI, pt. 1, p. 864.

16. Edwards, *Civil War Guns*, p. 146.

17. Marcot, *Spencer Repeating Firearms.* p. 50.
18. L. S. Satterlee, comp. *Ten Old Gun Catalogs, New Haven Arms Catalog* (Chicago: Gun Digest Company, 1957), p. 16.
19. Wiley Sword, *The Historic Henry Rifle* (Lincoln, RI: Andrew Mobray, 2002), p. 24.
20. Glenn W. Sunderland, *Wilder's Lightning Brigade and its Spencer Repeaters* (Washington, IL: Book Works, 1984), p. 19.
21. Christopher Spencer to James H. Kennedy, March 26, 1912, C. M. Spencer papers, Windsor (CT) Historical Society.
22. Satterlee, *Spencer Catalog*, p. 11.
23. Bilby, *A Revolution in Arms*, pp. 102–106.
24. Coddington, *Gettysburg Campaign*, p. 254; *O.R.*, ser. I, vol. XCVII, pt. 2, p. 63.
25. Satterlee, *New Haven Arms Catalog*, p. 19.
26. Eric J. Wittenberg, *Protecting the Flank: The Battles of Brinkerhoff's Ridge and East Cavalry Field* (Celina, OH: Ironclad Publishing, 2002), p. 104.
27. Bill Adams, "Weapons of the 34th," www.34thvacav.org/weapons.heml. An inventory of the battalion's arms ten months after the battle described them as "principally rifles, long and short, and of all sizes." *O.R.*, vol. XLIV, Pt, I, p. 843. A significant number of the conical rifle projectiles that have been found over the ensuing years at the site of the Rummel Farm fight have been .54 caliber. Thomas, *Ready, Aim, Fire*, pp. 45–46.
28. Busey & Martin, *Regimental Strengths*, p. 104.
29. Ibid.
30. Vincent Witcher to "Hon. Jno. Daniels," January 26, 1906; Witcher to General Lunsford Lomax, August 30, 1908, copies courtesy Bill Adams.
31. Vincent Witcher to "my Dear Gen.," April 6, 1886, courtesy Bill Adams; Busey and Martin, *Regimental Strengths*, p. 108.
32. Robert J. Driver, *14th Virginia Cavalry* (Lynchburg, VA: Howard Publications, 1998), p. 23.
33. John A. Bigelow, "Draw Saber, Charge!" in Sauers, *Fighting them Over*, pp. 466–467.
34. Vincent Witcher to "my Dear Gen.," April 6, 1886, copy courtesy Bill Adams.
35. Busey & Martin, *Regimental Strengths*, p. 145.

Chapter 7: Sharpshooters

1. Gary Yee, "The Longest Shots Ever—and Walter Cline's Attempt to Validate the Feat," *Muzzle Blasts* (November 2003); Walter M. Cline, *The Muzzle-Loading Rifle . . . Then and Now* (Huntington, WV: Standard Publishing, 1942), p. 63.
2. Wiley Sword, *Sharpshooter: Hiram Berdan, His Famous Sharpshooters and their Sharps Rifles* (Lincoln, RI: Andrew Mobray, 1988), pp. 18–22.
3. Ibid., pp. 10–12.
4. Charles A. Stevens, *Berdan's Sharpshooters*, p. 205.
5. Ibid. Theoretically, at least, a shooter could put all of his bullets in the same hole and still have a ten-inch string, providing the hole was ten inches from the center.
6. Sword, *Sharpshooter*, p. 14.
7. Stevens, *Berdan's Sharpshooters*, pp. 5, 18–20.
8. Sword, *Sharpshooter*, p. 37.
9. Edwards, *Civil War Guns*, p. 214; Sword, *Sharpshooter*, p. 75.
10. McAulay, *Civil War Breechloading Rifles*, pp. 73–74.
11. Sword, *Sharpshooter*, pp. 83–84.

12. Ibid., p. 87.

13. Stevens, *Berdan's Sharpshooters*, pp. 41, 64.

14. William F. Fox, *Regimental Losses in the American Civil War, 1861–1865* (Albany, NY: Brandow, 1898), p. 419.

15. White, *Civil War Diary of Wyman S. White*, pp. 323–324.

16. Stevens, *Berdan's Sharpshooters*, p. 205; *O.R.*, ser. 1, vol. XIX, pt. I, pp. 310–312; Sword, *Sharpshooter*, p. 84; Robert Goldthwaite Carter, *Four Brothers in Blue, or Sunshine and Shadows of the War of the* Rebellion (Austin, TX: U. of Texas Press, 1978 reprint of 1913 original ed.), pp. 112–114.

17. George D. Moller, *Massachusetts Military Shoulder Arms, 1784–1877* (Lincoln, RI: Andrew Mobray, 1988), p. 94.

18. McAulay, *Civil War Breechloading Rifles*, pp. 62–63.

19. Busey and Martin, *Regimental Strengths*, pp. 151, 152, 153.

20. John M. Murphy and Howard M. Madaus, *Confederate Rifles & Muskets: Infantry Small Arms Manufactured in the Southern Confederacy 1861–1865* (Newport Beach, CA: Graphic Publishers, 1996), p. 637.

21. John Anderson Morrow, *The Confederate Whitworth Sharpshooters* (Atlanta, GA: Author, 1989), pp. 26, 55.

22. Benjamin M. Powell to wife, November 21, 1907, Fredericksburg and Spotsylvania National Military Park; Benson, *Civil War Book*, pp. 45–48, 68–70. As in the case of the death of Reynolds, Powell's claim that he shot Sedgwick is one of several. The fact that his battalion was nowhere near where the incident happened casts some doubt on his assertion.

23. Sword, *Firepower from Abroad*, p. 108; E-mail correspondence with Bill Adams, March 1, 2007.

24. Benson, *Civil War Book*, p. 45.

25. George Mongtomery, Jr., (ed.), *Georgia Sharpshooter: The Civil War Diary and Letters of William Rhadamanthus Montgomery* (Macon, GA: Mercer University Press, 1997), p. 83; Busey & Martin, *Regimental Strengths*, p. 182.

26. The account of Reynolds' actions and death are based upon the most comprehensive modern account, provided in Martin, *Gettysburg, July 1*, pp. 140–149.

27. Martin, *Gettysburg, July 1*, p. 146. A survey of the Historical Data System consolidated North Carolina roster reveals no "Frank Wood" in a North Carolina regiment. There was a Sergeant Francis Wood who served at various times in Company G of the 16th North Carolina Infantry but who did not serve at Gettysburg. From http://www.civilwardata.com/.

28. Martin, *Gettysburg, July 1*, pp. 147–148.

29. Ibid., pp. 147–148.

30. Ibid., p. 149.

31. Benson, *Civil War Book*, p. 45.

32. Ibid.

33. Ibid., pp. 48–49.

34. Ray, *Shock Troops*, pp. 68–69.

35. Ibid., p. 70.

36. Ibid., pp. 70–71; William Plumer to John B. Bachelder, March 20, 1885, in Ladd (ed.), *Bachelder Papers*, p. 1097.

37. Harry W. Pfanz, *Gettysburg: The Second Day* (Chapel Hill, NC: U. of North Carolina Press, 1987), p. 97.

38. Stevens, *Berdan's Sharpshooters*, p. 303.

39. Busey & Martin, *Regimental Strengths*, p. 235; Pfanz, *Gettysburg: The Second Day*, pp. 98–99.
40. Busey & Martin, *Regimental Strengths*, p. 235.
41. Pfanz, *Gettysburg: The Second Day*, pp. 100–101; "Executive Committee," *Maine at Gettysburg: Report of Maine Commissioners Prepared by the Executive Committee* (Portland, ME: Lakeside Press, 1898), p. 128.
42. O.R., ser. 1, vol. XXVII, pt. 2, p. 617; Stevens, *Berdan's Sharpshooters*, pp. 304, 305, 310.
43. Stevens, *Berdan's Sharpshooters*, p. 305. For a sympathetic, yet critical, view of Sickles' conduct on July 2, see William G. Robertson, "The Peach Orchard Revisited: Daniel E. Sickles and the Third Corps on July 2, 1863," in Gary W. Gallagher (ed.), *The Second Day at Gettysburg: Essays on Confederate and Union Leadership* (Kent, OH: Kent State University Press, 1993).
44. Busey & Martin, *Regimental Strengths*, p. 235; Paterson, *From Blue to Gray*, p. 61.
45. White, *Civil War Diary*, p. 164.
46. Homer Stoughton to John B. Bachelder, December 29, 1881, in Ladd (ed.), *Bachelder Papers*, p. 767; Stevens, *Berdan's Sharpshooters*, p. 325; White, *Civil War Diary*, p. 163.
47. Pfanz, *Gettysburg: The Second Day*, pp. 168–169.
48. Ibid., p. 172.
49. White, *Civil War Diary*, p. 164.
50. William R. Ramsey to John B. Bachelder, April 16, 1883, in Ladd (ed.), *Bachelder Papers*, p. 947.
51. Busey & Martin, *Regimental Strengths*, p. 131.
52. Pfanz, *Gettysburg: The Second Day*, p. 69; O.R., ser. I, vol. XXVII, pt. 1, p. 158.
53. Thompson, "A Scrap at Gettysburg."
54. Obituary transcript posted on The 15th Massachusetts Infantry in the Civil War Web site, http://www.nextech.de/ma15mvi/index.htm; William Plumer to John B. Bachelder, March 20, 1885, in Ladd (ed.), *Bachelder Papers*, p. 1097.
55. Emerson L. Bicknell to John D. Bachelder, August 6, 1883, in Ladd (ed.), *Bachelder Papers*, p. 964.
56. Percival S. Barnes to mother, June 9, 1862, Hennepin History Museum, South Minneapolis, MN; Richard Moe, *The Last Full Measure: The Life and Death of the First Minnesota Volunteers*, (New York: Henry Holt, 1993), p. 267.
57. http://www.bradyssharpshooters.org/; Sword, *Sharpshooter*, p. 83.
58. Pfanz, *Gettysburg: The Second Day*, p. 214; http://www.bradyssharpshooters.org/.
59. Sword, *Sharpshooter*, pp. 83–86; Busey & Martin, *Regimental Strengths*, p. 152; Coates & McCaulay, *Civil War Sharps Carbines & Rifles*, pp. 22, 92.
60. E-mail correspondence with David Powell regarding Fourteenth Connecticut's ordnance reports, March 11, 2007; Charles D. Page, *Fourteenth Regiment Connecticut Vol. Infantry* (Meriden CT: Horton, 1906), pp. 16, 24; "The Fourteenth at Gettysburg," *Harper's Weekly* (November 21, 1863).
61. Page, *Fourteenth Regiment*, p. 155; Philip B. Sharpe, *The Rifle in America* (New York: Funk & Wagnalls, 1947), pp. 198–199; Coates & McAulay, *Civil War Sharps Carbines & Rifles*, p. 22.
62. Pfanz, *Gettysburg, the Second Day*, p. 361; E-mail correspondence on Quarterly Ordnance Reports with David Powell, March 20, 2007.

63. Edwards, *Civil War Guns*, p. 224; William A. Frassanito, *Gettysburg: A Journey in Time* (New York: Charles Scribner's Sons, 1975), pp. 192–192; Stevens, *Berdan's Sharpshooters*, p. 339; Gregory A. Coco, *A Strange and Blighted Land: Gettysburg: The Aftermath of a Battle* (Gettysburg, PA: Thomas Publications, 1995), pp. 35–37. For a comprehensive history of Devil's Den, including its geology, role in the battle, and postwar story, see Garry E. Adelman & Timothy H. Smith, *Devil's Den: A History and Guide* (Gettysburg, PA: Thomas Publications, 1997).

64. Elijah Walker to John B. Bachelder, January 5, 1885, in Ladd (ed.), *Bachelder Papers*, pp. 1094–1095; Elijah Walker, "The 4th Me. at Gettysburg," in Sauers (ed.), *Fighting Them Over*, p. 244.

65. Stevens, *Berdan's Sharpshooters*, pp. 339–341; O.R., ser. I, vol. XXVII, pt. 2, p. 406. Measurements are an average of sightings taken by the author on June 5, 2007.

66. Nosworthy, *Bloody Crucible of Courage*, pp. 57–58.

67. Thomas Scott, "On Little Round Top: A Batteryman's Reminiscences of Gettysburg," in Sauers (ed.), *Fighting them Over*, p. 257.

68. Adelman & Smith, *Devil's Den*, pp. 56, 63–68; William A. Frassanito, *Early Photography at Gettysburg* (Gettysburg, PA: Thomas Publications, 1995), pp. 266–278.

69. Measurements taken by author on June 5, 2007. For the story of the "sharpshooter" see Frassanito, *Journey*, pp. 187–192. The rock barricade in the picture inferentially erected by Confederates could well have been built by members of the Fourth Maine as they awaited the Confederate attack in the late afternoon of July 2.

70. Cited in Coco, *A Strange and Blighted Land*, p. 35; Stevens, *Berdan's Sharpshooters*, p. 341.

71. W. S. Dunlop, *Lee's Sharpshooters: Or, the Forefront of Battle* (Dayton, OH: Morningside, 1988 reprint), pp. 17–23; Bilby, *A Revolution in Arms*, pp. 187–190, 205. The best source for the complete history of the Army of Northern Virginia's sharpshooters is Ray, *Shock Troops*.

CHAPTER 8: SIXGUNS AND SABERS

1. Quoted in Michael McIntosh, *Shotguns and Shooting* (Camden, ME: Countrysport Press, 1995), p. 137.

2. Blackmore, *British Military Firearms*, pp. 92–93.

3. Ibid., p. 251.

4. Ibid.

5. Houze, *Colt Rifles & Muskets*, pp. 11–13.

6. Garavaglia and Worman, *Firearms of the American West*, pp. 100–101.

7. Houze, *Colt Rifles and Muskets*, pp. 16–17.

8. Herbert G. Houze, *Samuel Colt: Arms, Art and Invention* (New Haven: Yale University Press, 2006), p. 20.

9. John D. McAulay, *Civil War Pistols* (Lincoln, RI: Andrew Mobray Inc., 1991), p. 64.

10. Coates & McAulay, *Sharps Carbines & Rifles*, p. 21; Donald L. Ware, *Remington Army and Navy Revolvers, 1861–1888* (Albuquerque, NM: U. of New Mexico Press, 2007), pp. 77–78.

11. McAulay, *Civil War Pistols*, p. 18.

12. David Paul Smith, *Frontier Defense in the Civil War* (College Station, TX: Texas A&M, 1992), p. 31; Photocopy of document "Number and character of arms of 1st Regt. Texas Rangers (8th Tex Cav) at Bowling Green Kentucky, Oct 30, 1861," NARA M323, roll 53; copy by Dean Thomas courtesy of Bill Adams; *The Charleston*

Mercury, 26 June 1861. Of course, it is remotely possible that the "five shooters" were old Paterson Model Colts.

13. E-mail correspondence with Bill Adams, April 27, 2007; "A Sampling of Issues from the Richmond Armory, 1861, from April 1 to June 13, 1861," Courtesy Bill Adams.

14. Douglas Hale, *The Third Texas Cavalry in the Civil War* (Norman, OK: U. of Oklahoma Press, 1993), p. 49.

15. William A. Albaugh III, Hugh Benet, Jr., and Edward N. Simmons, *Confederate Handguns* (New York: Bonanza Books, 1963), p. 23.

16. Ibid.; Sword, *Firepower from Abroad*, pp. 109–110.

17. Norm Flayderman, *Flayderman's Guide to Antique American Firearms and Their Values 7th Edition* (Iola, WI: Krause Publications, 1998), pp. 521–523.

18. Albaugh, Benet, and Simmons, *Confederate Handguns*, p. 84.

19. Sword, *Firepower from Abroad*, pp. 96–97; *The Charleston Mercury*, 10 October 1862.

20. Sword, *Firepower from Abroad*, pp. 50–51, 101.

21. Albaugh, Benet, and Simmons, *Confederate Handguns*, pp. 130–133.

22. *The New York Herald*, 20 April 1861; Jersey City (NJ) *Standard*, 8 May 1861; Frederick T. Farrier to James Lynch, June 26, 1861, James Lynch Papers, New Jersey Historical Society.

23. Ellis Hamilton to father, September 21, 1862, Hamilton Papers, Rutgers University Library Special Collections.

24. John P. Crater Diary, November 18, 1862, in the possession of Everett H. Hatton III; Copy courtesy Neal Friedenthal; Bilby, *Three Rousing Cheers*, pp. 17, 64; Fremantle, *Three Months in the Southern States*, p. 226.

25. Busey and Martin, *Regimental Strengths*, pp. 122, 56; Maine Adjutant General's Report for 1861 (Bangor, ME: 1862); Bilby and Goble, *Remember You Are Jerseymen*, pp. 642–643.

26. De Forest, *A Volunteer's Adventures*, p. 2; Robert Hunt Rhodes (ed.), *All For the Union: The Civil War Diary and Letters of Elisha Hunt Rhodes* (New York: Orion Books, 1991), p. 217.

27. Stephen B. Oates, *Confederate Cavalry West of the River* (Austin, TX: U. of Texas, 1961), p. 70; McAulay, *Civil War Pistols*, p. 43.

28. Bauman, *Arming the Suckers*, p. 41.

29. John Esten Cooke, *Wearing of the Gray, Being Personal Portraits, Scenes and Adventures of the War* (New York: E. B. Treat & Company, 1867), p. 39; Sarah Woolfolk Wiggins (ed.), *The Journals of Josiah Gorgas, 1857–1878* (Tuscaloosa, AL: U. of Alabama Press, 1943), p. 128.

30. Harold L. Peterson, *The American Sword, 1775–1945* (Philadelphia: Ray Riling Arms Books, 1973), pp. 32–35.

31. Bilby and Goble, *Remember You are Jerseymen*, pp. 646–647; Baumann, *Arming the Suckers*, pp. 52, 61; Vandiver, *Ploughshares into Swords*, p. 160.

32. Whittaker, *Volunteer Cavalry*, pp. 5–6.

33. Philip St. George Cooke, *Cavalry Tactics, or Regulations for the Instruction, formation and Movements of the Cavalry of the Army and Volunteers of the United States* . . . (Philadelphia: J. P. Lippincott & Co., 1862), pp. 52–65; Stephen Z. Starr, "Cold Steel: The Saber and the Union Cavalry," *Civil War History* 11 (1965).

34. Dee Brown, *Morgan's Raiders*, p. 50

35. Starr, "Cold Steel."

36. Ibid.
37. John S. Mosby, *Mosby's War Reminiscences and Stuart's Cavalry Campaigns* (Boston: George A. Jones & Co., 1887), p. 30; Williamson, *Mosby's Rangers* (New York: Ralph B. Kenyon, 1896), p. 21.
38. Cited in Alonzo Gray, *Cavalry Tactics as Illustrated by the War of the Rebellion, Together With Many Interesting Facts Valuable for Cavalry to Know* (Fort Leavenworth, KS: U.S. Cavalry Assn., 1910), p. 23; Starr, "Cold Steel."
39. Francis James Lippitt, *A Treatise on the Tactical Use of the Three Arms: Infantry, Artillery and Cavalry* (New York: Francis J. Nostrand, 1865), p. 110.
40. Whittaker, *Volunteer Cavalry*, p. 10.
41. John N. Edwards, *Noted Guerillas, Or the Warfare of the Border* (Dayton, OH: Morningside, 1976 reprint), pp. 144, 51. Younger's revolvers were most likely not the large prewar Colt Dragoons. The term "dragoon" was often used to describe a .44 caliber as "navy" was used to describe any .36 caliber revolver. Youngers' guns were probably Model 1860 Army Colts. Joseph Edwards' guns remained in the family until the 1930s, when they were, unfortunately, sold. Interview with Steve DesMarais, April 30, 1995.
42. *O.R.*, ser. I, vol. XLI, pt. III, p. 348; Ibid., pt. IV, pp. 727, 608.
43. Gray, *Cavalry Tactics*, p. 15; John W. Munson, *Reminiscences of a Mosby Guerilla* (NY: Moffat, Yard and Co., 1906), p. 23.
44. Dean S. Thomas, *Round Ball to Rimfire: A History of Civil War Small Arms Ammunition, Part Three: Federal Pistols, Revolvers & Miscellaneous Essays* (Gettysburg, PA: Thomas Publications, 2003), pp. 1, 9. Thomas offers in evidence an excavated loaded cylinder found *in situ* unassociated with the rest of a handgun, and this must be considered, although it was not unknown to disassemble and scatter gun parts when capture was imminent.
45. Henry Deeks, "Civil War Images," *The Civil War News* (November 1995).
46. Herbert B. Nelson and Preston E. Onstad (ed.), *A Webfoot Volunteer: The Diary of William M. Hilleary, 1864–1866* (Corvallis, OR: Oregon State University, 1965), p. 119; Gravaglia and Worman, *Firearms in the American West: 1803–1865*, p. 216.
47. Edwards, *Noted Guerillas*, p. 15.
48. Ridley, *Battles and Sketches*, p. 486.
49. Thomas, *Round Ball to Rimfire, Part Three*, pp. 2–3.
50. Ibid., pp. 3–4. Eight caps, one for each chamber and two extra, were included in each packet.
51. Ibid., p. 5.
52. Ibid. This would be the cavalry "jounce effect" previously noted with carbine cartridges applied to revolver ammunition. Cited in Ware, *Remington Army and Navy Revolvers*, p. 18.
53. Ibid., pp. 25, 49–52.
54. For a detailed examination of all the revolver cartridges purchased by the Union during the war, see Thomas, *Round Ball to Rimfire, Part Three*. Ware, *Remington Army and Navy Revolvers*, pp. 157–159.
55. Cited in Gray, *Cavalry Tactics*, p. 23; Cooke, *Cavalry Tactics*, p. 117.
56. Edwards, *Noted Guerillas*, p. 134, 123; cited in Gray, *Cavalry Tactics*, p. 23.
57. Cited in Ware, *Remington Army and Navy Revolvers*, p. 110; *O.R.*, ser. I, vol. XXVII, pt. I, p. 894.
58. Mulholland, *The Story of the 116th Regiment*, p. 125; cited in Jorgensen, *Gettysburg's Bloody Wheatfield*, pp. 97–98.

59. New York: Carroll and Graph, 2008.
60. Busy and Martin, *Regimental Strengths*, p. 244.
61. Ibid., pp. 247, 113.
62. Wittenberg, *Protecting the Flank*, p. 86; Bilby, *A Revolution in Arms*, p. 116; Luther S. Trowbridge, "The Operations of the Cavalry in the Gettysburg Campaign," Michigan MOLLUS *War Papers* 1 (1886): 12–13; Henry B. McClellan, *The Life and Campaigns of Major-General J. E. B. Stuart* (Boston, Houghton Mifflin & Co., 1883), p. 340.
63. Ibid., quoted on p. 97.
64. Ibid., quoted on pp. 103–105.
65. Ibid., pp 113–116.
66. Longacre, *The Cavalry at Gettysburg*, pp. 240–244.
67. Ray, *Shock Troops*, pp. 187–189.
68. Peterson, *American Sword*, pp. 37–38.

Conclusion

1. The definitive (to date) account of Gettysburg after the battle, covering burials, hospitals, cleanup activities, souvenir hunters, and more, is Gregory Coco, *A Strange and Blighted Land: Gettysburg, the Aftermath of a Battle* (Gettysburg, PA: Thomas Publications, 1995).
2. Dayton Flint to sister, July 6, 1863, reprinted in the *Washington* (NJ) *Star*, 9 February 1911; copy courtesy John Kuhl.
3. Dayton Flint to sister, July 6, 1863; Paul Kuhl to sister, July 11, 1863, Paul Kuhl letters, courtesy John Kuhl; Ellis Hamilton to mother, July 9, 1863, Hamilton papers, Special Collections, Rutgers University Library; *Hunterdon Republican*, 24 July 1863. Similar fates awaited most of them. Kuhl and Voorhees were killed at Spotsylvania and Hamilton was mortally wounded in the Wilderness. Only Flint survived the war unscathed. For more on the regiment, see Joseph G. Bilby, *Three Rousing Cheers: A History of the Fifteenth New Jersey Infantry from Flemington to Appomattox* (Hightstown, NJ: Longstreet House, 1993).
4. Bilby, *Three Rousing Cheers*, p. 337; Carter, *Four Brothers in Blue*, p. 324; Frassanito, *Early Photography*, p. 89.
5. Penrose to Major General John Sedgwick, June 24, 1863, Regimental Correspondence Book, Fifteenth NJ Infantry, n.a.; *Hunterdon* (NJ) *Republican*, 24 July 1863; Alanson Haines, *History of the Fifteenth Regiment, New Jersey Volunteers* (NY: Jenkins & Thomas, 1883), p. 94.
6. *Doylestown* (PA) *Democrat*, 12 July 1863; copy courtesy Bill Adams; *O.R.*, ser. 1, vol. XXVII, pt. 1, p. 624.
7. Coco, *Strange and Blighted Land*, p. 334.
8. Coco, *Strange and Blighted Land*, pp. 333–336; *O.R.*, ser. 1, vol. XXVII, pt. 1, pp. 225–226; Vandiver, *Ploughshares into Swords*, p. 196.
9. *Report of the Adjutant General of the State of New Jersey for the Year Ending October 31st, 1913* (Trenton: MacCrellish & Quigley, 1913), p. 46.

BIBLIOGRAPHY

MANUSCRIPTS

Bill Adams Collection:
  "A Sampling of Issues from the Richmond Armory, 1861, from April 1 to June 13, 1861," courtesy Paul Davies and Bill Adams.
  British army "Annual Target Practice Return" form.
  Copies of Vincent Witcher letters.
Fredericksburg and Spotsylvania National Military Park:
  Benjamin M. Powell to wife, November 21, 1907.
Neal Friedenthal Collection:
  Copy of John P. Crater Diary, November 18, 1862, in the possession of Everett H. Hatton III.
Hennepin History Museum, South Minneapolis, MN:
  Percival S. Barnes to mother, June 9, 1862.
John Kuhl Collection:
  Paul Kuhl letters.
National Archives:
  Regimental Correspondence Book, Fifteenth New Jersey Infantry, National Archives.
New Jersey Historical Society:
  Benjamin D. Coley diary.
  Canfield/Pickerson family papers.
  James Lynch papers.
  Ryerson family papers.
  Rutgers University Library Special Collections:
  Ellis Hamilton papers.
Windsor (CT) Historical Society:
  Christopher M. Spencer papers.
Other:
  Brannen Sanders, "The Georgia Armory Rifle," unpublished paper.

BOOKS

Adelman, Garry E., and Timothy H. Smith. *Devil's Den: A History and Guide*. Gettysburg, PA: Thomas Publications, 1997.

Albaugh, William A. III, Hugh Benet, Jr., and Edward N. Simmons. *Confederate Handguns*. New York: Bonanza Books, 1963.

Alexander, Edward Porter. *Military Memoirs of a Confederate*. New York: 1907.

Bailey, De Witt. *British Military Flintlock Rifles, 1740–1840*. Lincoln, RI: Andrew Mobray, 2002.

Barnes, Frank C. *Cartridges of the World*. Chicago: Follett, 1965.

Batchellor, Albert Stillman. *The Ranger Service in the Upper Valley of the Connecticut and the Most Northerly Regiment of the New Hampshire Militia in the Period of the Revolution*. Concord, NH: The Rumford Press, 1903.

Bates, Samuel P. *History of Pennsylvania Volunteers, 1861–1865: Prepared in Compliance with Acts of the Legislature* (8 vols.). Harrisburg PA: R. Singerly, 1869.

Bauer, K. Jack. *Soldiering: The Civil War Diary of Rice C. Bull, 123rd New York Infantry*. San Rafael, CA: Presidio Press, 1977.

Baumann, Ken. *Arming the Suckers, 1861–1865: A Compilation of Illinois Civil War Weapons*. Dayton, OH: Morningside Press, 1989.

Bellard, Alfred (ed. David Herbert Donald). *Gone for a Soldier: The Civil War Memoirs of Private Alfred Bellard*. New York: Little, Brown, 1975.

Bellesisles, Michael A. *Arming America: the Origins of a National Gun Culture*. New York: Alfred A. Knopf, 2000.

Beaudot, William J. K., and Lance J. Herdegen. *An Irishman in the Iron Brigade: The Civil War Letters of James P. Sullivan, Sergt. Company K, 6th Wisconsin Volunteers*. New York: Fordham University Press, 1993.

Benson, Berry (ed. Susan Williams Benson). *Berry Benson's Civil War Book: Memoirs of a Confederate Scout and Sharpshooter*. Athens, GA: University of Georgia Press, 1992.

Berringer, Richard E., Herman Hattaway, Archer Jones, and William N. Still, Jr. *Why the South Lost the Civil War*. Athens, GA: University of Georgia Press, 1986.

Bilby, Joseph G. *Three Rousing Cheers: A History of the Fifteenth New Jersey from Flemington to Appomattox*. Hightstown, NJ: Longstreet House, 2nd ed., 2001.

_____. *Remember Fontenoy: The 69th New York and the Irish Brigade in the Civil War*. Hightstown, NJ: Longstreet House, 1995.

_____. *A Revolution in Arms: A History of the First Repeating Rifles*. Yardley, PA: Westholme, 2005.

Bilby, Joseph G. and William C. Goble. *Remember You Are Jerseymen: A Military History of New Jersey's Troops in the Civil War*. Hightstown, NJ: Longstreet House, 1998.

Blackmore, Howard L. *British Military Firearms, 1650–1850*. London: Herbert Jenkins, 1961.

Boatner, Mark M. *Encyclopedia of the American Revolution*. New York: David McKay Company, 1966.

Bolton, Charles Knowles. *The Private Soldier Under Washington*. New York: Charles Scribner's Sons, 1902.

Boritt, Gabor, ed. *The Gettysburg Nobody Knows*. New York: Oxford Press, 1997.

Bragg, C. L., Charles D. Ross, Gordon A Blaker, Stephanie A. T. Jacobe, and Theodore P. Savas. *Never for Want of Powder: The Confederate Powder Works in Augusta, Georgia*. Columbia, SC: University of South Carolina Press, 2007.

Bright, Leslie S. *The Blockade Runner Modern Greece and Her Cargo*. Raleigh, NC: NC Dept. of Cultural Resources, 1977.

Britton, Ann Hartwell, and Thomas J. Reed, eds. *To My Beloved Wife and Boy at Home: The Letters and Diaries of Orderly Sergeant John F. L. Hartwell*. Teaneck, NJ: Fairleigh Dickinson University Press, 1997.

Brown, Dee. *Morgan's Raiders*. Portland, OR: Smithmark Publishers, reprint ed., 1995.

Bruce, Robert V. *Lincoln and the Tools of War*. Urbana, IL: University of Illinois Press, 1989.

Burgoyne, Sir John Fox. *The Employment of Riflemen at Sieges*. London: 1859.

Bury, Lieut. Col. Viscount M. P. *Manual of Rifling and Rifle Sights for the National Rifle Association, 1864*. London: Longman & Co., 1864.

Busey John W., and David Martin. *Regimental Strengths and Losses at Gettysburg, 4th Ed.* Hightstown, NJ: 2005.

Busk, Hans. *The Rifle and How to Use It*. London: Routledge, Warnes and Routledge, 4th ed., 1859.

Carman, W. Y. *A History of Firearms from Earliest Times to 1914*. London: Routledge & Kegan Paul Ltd., 1955.

Carr, Caleb. *The Devil Soldier*. New York: Random House, 1992.

Carter, Robert Goldthwaite. *Four Brothers in Blue, or Sunshine and Shadows of the War of the Rebellion*. Austin, TX: University of Texas Press, 1978 reprint of 1913 original ed.

Casey, Silas. *Infantry Tactics . . .* Dayton, OH: Morningside Press, 1985 reprint.

Catton, Bruce. *Mr. Lincoln's Army*. New York: Doubleday, 1951.

Cheney, Newell. *History of the Ninth Regiment, New York Volunteer Cavalry, War of 1861 to 1865*. Jamestown, NY: Martin Merz & Son, 1901.

Chesney, Francis Rawdon. *Observations on the Past and Present State of Firearms* . . . London: Longman, Brown, Green, and Longmans, 1852.

Chet, Guy. *Conquering the American Wilderness: The Triumph of European Warfare in the Colonial Northeast*. Amherst, MA: University of Massachusetts Press, 2003.

Cline, Walter M. *The Muzzle-Loading Rifle* . . . *Then and Now*. Huntington, WV: Standard Publishing, 1942.

Coates, Earl J., and John D. McAulay. *Sharps Carbines & Rifles*. Gettysburg, PA: Thomas Publications, 1996.

Coates, Earl J., and Dean S. Thomas. *An Introduction to Civil War Small Arms*. Gettysburg, PA: Thomas Publications, 1990.

Coco, Gregory A. *A Strange and Blighted Land: Gettysburg: The Aftermath of a Battle*. Gettysburg, PA: Thomas Publications, 1995.

Coddington, Edwin B. *The Gettysburg Campaign: A Study in Command*. New York: Charles Scribner's Sons, 1968.

Cooke, Philip St. George. *Cavalry Tactics, or Regulations for the Instruction, formation and Movements of the Cavalry of the Army and Volunteers of the United States* . . . Philadelphia: J. P. Lippincott & Co., 1862.

Cooke, John Esten. *Wearing of the Gray, Being Personal Portraits, Scenes and Adventures of the War*. New York: E. B. Treat & Company, 1867.

Corby, William, C. S. C. (ed. Lawrence F. Kohl). *Memoirs of Chaplain Life: Three Years With the Irish Brigade in the Army of the Potomac*. New York: Fordham University Press, 1992.

Cutler, Cyrus Morton. *Letters From the Front*. San Francisco: A. D. Cutler, 1892.

Dalton, Pete, and Cyndi Dalton. *Into the Valley of Death: The Story of the 4th Maine Volunteer Infantry at the Battle of Gettysburg, July 2, 1863*. Union, ME: Union Publishing, 1984.

Daniel, Larry J. *Soldiering in the Army of Tennessee: A Portrait of Life in a Confederate Army*. Chapel Hill, NC: University of North Carolina Press, 1991.

Davies, Paul J. C. S. *Armory Richmond*. Carlisle, PA: Author, 2000.

Davis, Carl L. *Arming the Union: Small Arms in the Union Army*. Port Washington, NY: Kennikat Press, 1973.

Davis, Charles E. *Three Years in the Army: The Story of the Thirteenth Massachusetts Volunteers*. Boston: Estes & Lauriat, 1894.

Davis, William H. *History of the One Hundred and Fourth Pennsylvania Regiment from August 22, 1861 to September 30, 1864*. Philadelphia: J. B. Rodgers, 1866.

DeForest, John William. *A Volunteer's Adventures: A Union Captain's Record of the Civil War*. Hamden, CT: Archon, 1970.

Driver, Robert J. *14th Virginia Cavalry*. Lynchburg, VA: Howard Publications, 1998.

Duffy, James N., Gottfried Krueger, and William H. Corbin. *Final Report of the Gettysburg Battlefield Commission of New Jersey*. Trenton: State of New Jersey, 1891.

Dunlop, W. S. *Lee's Sharpshooters: Or, the Forefront of Battle*. Dayton, OH: Morningside Press, 1988 reprint.

Edwards, John N. *Noted Guerillas, Or, the Warfare of the Border*. Dayton, OH: Morningside Press, 1976 reprint.

Edwards, William B. *Civil War Guns*. Harrisburg, PA: Stackpole, 1962.

Executive Committee. *Maine at Gettysburg: Report of Maine Commissioners Prepared by the Executive Committee*. Portland, ME: Lakeside Press, 1898.

Flayderman, Norm. *Flayderman's Guide to Antique American Firearms and Their Values 7th Edition*. Iola, WI: Krause Publications, 1998.

Foster, John Y. *New Jersey and the Rebellion: A History of the Services of the Troops and People of New Jersey in Aid of the Union Cause*. Newark, NJ: Martin R. Dennis & Co., 1868.

Fox, William F. *Regimental Losses in the American Civil War, 1861–1865*. Albany, NY: Augustus S. Brandow, 1898.

Frassanito, William A. *Gettysburg: A Journey in Time*. New York: Charles Scribner's Sons, 1975.

_____. *Early Photography at Gettysburg*. Gettysburg, PA: Thomas Publications, 1995.

Fredrickson, John C. *Green Coats and Glory: The United States Regiment of Riflemen, 1808–1821*. Youngstown, NY: Old Fort Niagara Association, 2000.

Fremantle, T. F. *The Book of the Rifle*. London: Longmans, Green and Co., 1901.

Fremantle, Lt. Col. Arthur J. L. *Three Months in the Southern States*. Lincoln, NE: Bison Books ed., 1991.

Fuller, Claud E. *The Rifled Musket*. New York: Bonanza Books, 1958.

Gallagher, Gary E., ed. *The Second Day at Gettysburg: Essays on Confederate and Union Leadership*. Kent, OH: Kent State University Press, 1993.

Galloway, George Norton. *The Ninety-fifth Pennsylvania Volunteers (Gosline's Pennsylvania Zouaves) in the Sixth Corps*. Philadelphia: 1884.

Garavaglia, Louis A., and Charles G. Worman. *Firearms of the American West: 1803–1865*. Albuquerque, NM: University of New Mexico Press.

Gibbon, John. *The Artillerist's Manual*. New York: D. Van Nostrand, 1860.

Gottfried, Bradley M. *Roads to Gettysburg: Lee's Invasion of the North, 1863*. Shippensburg, PA: White Mane Books, 2001.

Gray, Alonzo. *Cavalry Tactics as Illustrated by the War of the Rebellion, Together With Many Interesting Facts Valuable for Cavalry to Know*. Fort Leavenworth, KS: U.S. Cavalry Assn., 1910.

Greiner, James M. *Subdued by the Sword: A Line Officer in the 121st New York Volunteers*. Albany, NY: State University of New York Press, 2003.

Griffith, Paddy. *Forward into Battle: Fighting Tactics from Waterloo to the Near Future, 2nd Ed.* San Francisco: Presidio, 1990.

_____. *Battle Tactics of the Civil War*. New Haven, CT: Yale University Press, 1987.

Haines, Alanson. *History of the Fifteenth Regiment, New Jersey Volunteers*. New York: Jenkins & Thomas, 1883.

Hale, Douglas. *The Third Texas Cavalry in the Civil War*. Norman, OK: University of Oklahoma Press, 1993.

Harding, David F. *Small Arms of the East India Company, 1600–1856, Vol. III: Ammunition and Performance*. London: Foresight Books, 1999.

Harrison, Kathy Georg, comp. *The Location of the Monuments, Markers, and Tablets on Gettysburg Battlefield*. Gettysburg, PA: Thomas Publications, 1993.

Haynes, Martin A. *History of the Second Regiment, New Hampshire Volunteers: Its Camps, Marches and Battles*. Manchester, NH: Charles F. Livingston, 1865.

Haythornthwaite, Philip. *Weapons & Equipment of the Napoleonic Wars*. London: Arms and Armour, 1996.

Hess, Earl J. *The Union Soldier in Battle: Enduring the Ordeal of Combat*. Lawrence, KS: University Press of Kansas, 1997.

Hibbert, Christopher. *Wolfe at Quebec*. Cleveland: World, 1959.

Hoole, W. Stanley. *Confederate Foreign Agent: The European Diary of Major Edward C. Anderson*. University, AL: Confederate Publishing, 1976.

Houze, Herbert G. *Colt Rifles and Muskets From 1847 to 1870*. Iola, WI: Krause, 2004.

_____. *Samuel Colt: Arms, Art and Invention*. New Haven, CT: Yale University Press, 2006.

Johnston, Robert Matteson. *Bull Run, Its Strategy and Tactics*. Boston: Houghton Mifflin, 1913.

Jorgenson, Jay. *Gettysburg's Bloody Wheatfield*. Shippensburg, PA: White Mane, 2002.

_____. *The Wheatfield at Gettysburg: A Walking Tour*. Gettysburg, PA: Thomas Publications, 2002.

Katcher, Philip. *The Army of Robert E. Lee*. London: Arms and Armor, 1994.

Ladd, David L., and Audrey J., eds. *The Batchelder Papers: Gettysburg in their Own Words* (3 vols.). Dayton, OH: Morningside Press, 1994.

Lambert, Andrew, and Stephen Badsey. *The War Correspondents: The Crimean War*. London: Bramley Books, 1997.

Lecomte, Ferdinand. *The War in the United States: Report to the Swiss Military Department*. New York: D. Van Nostrand, 1863.

Lee, Henry, Jr. *The Militia of the United States: What It Has Been, What it Should Be*. Boston: T. R. Marvin & Son, 1864.

Lewis, Berkeley R. *Small Arms and Ammunition in the United States Service, 1776–1865*. Washington, DC: Smithsonian, 1956.

_____. *Notes on Cavalry Weapons of the American Civil War*. Washington, DC: The American Ordnance Association, 1961.

Lippitt, Francis James. *A Treatise on the Tactical Use of the Three Arms: Infantry, Artillery and Cavalry*. New York: Francis J. Nostrand, 1865.

Longacre, Edward G. *The Cavalry at Gettysburg*. Lincoln, NE: University of Nebraska Press.

_____. *To Gettysburg and Beyond: The Twelfth New Jersey Volunteer Infantry, II Corps, Army of the Potomac, 1862–1865*. Hightstown, NJ: Longstreet House, 1988.

Longstaff, Major F. V., and A. Hilliard Atteridge. *The Book of the Machine Gun*. London: Hugh Rees Ltd., 1917.

Lugs, Jaroslav. *Firearms Past and Present: A Complete Review of Firearm Systems and their Histories, Vol. I*. London: Greenville, 1975.

Luvaas, Jay. *The Military Legacy of the Civil War: The European Inheritance*. Lawrence, KS: University Press of Kansas, 1988.

Luvaas, Jay, and Harold W. Nelson. *The U.S. Army War College Guide to the Battle of Gettysburg*. Carlisle, PA: South Mountain Press, 1986.

Mann, Albert William. *History of the Forty-fifth Regiment, Massachusetts Volunteer Militia*. Jamaica Plain, MA: Brookside Print, 1908.

Marbaker, Thomas B. *History of the Eleventh New Jersey Volunteers*. Hightstown, NJ: Longstreet House, 1990 reprint.

Marcot, Roy M. *Spencer Repeating Firearms*. Rochester, NY: Rowe, 1990.

Martin, David G. *Gettysburg, July 1*. Conshohocken, PA: Combined Books, 1995.

McAulay, John D. *Carbines of the Civil War, 1861–1865*. Union City, TN: Pioneer Press, 1981.

_____. *Civil War Breechloading Rifles, A Survey of the Innovative Infantry Arms of the American Civil War*. Lincoln, RI: Andrew Mobray, 1991.

_____. *Civil War Pistols*. Lincoln, RI: Andrew Mobray, 1991.

McChristian, Douglas C. *An Army of Marksmen.* Ft. Collins, CO: The Old Army Press, 1981.

McIntosh, Michael. *Shotguns and Shooting.* Camden, ME: Countrysport Press, 1995.

McClellan, Henry B. *The Life and Campaigns of Major-General J. E. B. Stuart.* Boston: Houghton Mifflin & Co., 1883.

McWhiney, Grady, and Perry D. Jamieson. *Attack and Die: Civil War Military Tactics and the Southern Heritage.* Montgomery, AL: University of Alabama Press, 1982.

Mills, John Harrison. *Chronicles of the Twenty-first Regiment, New York State Volunteers.* Buffalo, NY: 21st Regiment Veteran Association, 1887.

Moe, Richard. *The Last Full Measure: The Life and Death of the First Minnesota Volunteers.* New York: Henry Holt, 1993.

Moller, George D. *Massachusetts Military Shoulder Arms, 1784–1877.* Lincoln, RI: Andrew Mobray, 1988.

Montgomery, George, Jr., ed. *Georgia Sharpshooter: The Civil War Diary and Letters of William Rhadamanthus Montgomery.* Macon, GA: Mercer University Press, 1997.

Mordecai, Alfred. *Military Commission to Europe in 1855 and 1856: Report of Major Albert Mordecai of the Ordnance Department.* Washington, D.C: U.S. Government, 1860.

Morrow, John Anderson. *The Confederate Whitworth Sharpshooters.* Atlanta, GA: Author, 1989.

Mosby, John S. *Mosby's War Reminiscences and Stuart's Cavalry Campaigns.* Boston: George A. Jones & Co., 1887.

Mulholland, St. Clair A. *The Story of the 116th Regiment, Pennsylvania Infantry: War of Secession, 1862–1865.* Gaithersburg, MD: Old Soldier Books, 1992 reprint.

Murphy, John M., and Howard M. Madaus. *Confederate Rifles &Muskets: Infantry Small Arms Manufactured in the Southern Confederacy 1861–1865.* Newport Beach, CA: Graphic Publishers, 1996.

Myatt, Frederick. *The Illustrated Encyclopedia of 19th Century Firearms.* New York: Crescent Books, 1994.

Nafziger, George. *Imperial Bayonets: Tactics of the Napoleonic Battery, Battalion and Brigade as Found in Contemporary Regulations.* London: Greenhill Books, 1996.

Nelson, Herbert B. (ed. Preston E. Onstad). *A Webfoot Volunteer: The Diary of William M. Hilleary, 1864–1866.* Corvallis, OR: Oregon State University, 1965.

Newell, Joseph Keith. *"Ours." Annals of 10th Regiment, Massachusetts Volunteers, in the Rebellion.* Springfield, MA: C. A. Nichols, 1875.

New Jersey Adjutant General Reports for 1856–1866. Trenton: State of New Jersey, 1857–1867.

New Jersey Quartermaster General's Annual Reports for 1857–1866. Trenton: State of New Jersey, 1858–1867.

New York Monuments Commission for the Battlefield of Gettysburg and Chattanooga. *Final Report on the Battlefield of Gettysburg (New York at Gettysburg).* Albany, NY: J. B. Lyon Co., 1900, 1902.

Nolan, Alan T. *The Iron Brigade: A Military History.* Madison, WI: The State Historical Society of Wisconsin, 1975.

Norton, John. *A List of Captain Norton's Projectiles.* Gravesend: Caddel and Son, 1860.

Nosworthy, Brent. *The Bloody Crucible of Courage: Fighting Methods and Combat Experience of the Civil War.* New York: Carroll & Graf, 2003.

Oates, Stephen B. *Confederate Cavalry West of the River.* Austin, TX: University of Texas, 1961.

O'Connell, Robert. *Of Arms and Men: A History of War, Weapons, and Aggression.* New York: Oxford University Press, 1989.

Parsons, John E. *The First Winchester: The Story of the 1866 Repeating Rifle.* New York: Winchester Press, 1969.

Page, Charles D. *Fourteenth Regiment Connecticut Vol. Infantry.* Meriden, CT: Horton, 1906.

Patterson, Gerard A. *From Blue to Gray: The Life of Confederate General Cadmus M. Wilcox.* Mechanicsburg, PA: Stackpole Books, 2001.

Peterson, Harold. *Book of the Continental Soldier.* New York: Bonanza Books, 1977.

_____. *The American Sword, 1775–1945.* Philadelphia: Ray Riling Arms Books, 1973.

Pfanz, Harry W. *Gettysburg: The Second Day.* Chapel Hill, NC: University of North Carolina Press, 1987.

_____. *Gettysburg, Culp's Hill and Cemetery Hill.* Chapel Hill, NC: University of North Carolina Press, 1993.

Pullen, John J. *The Twentieth Maine: A Volunteer Regiment in the Civil War.* Dayton, OH: Morningside, 1980 reprint.

Purdue, Howell, and Elizabeth Purdue. *Pat Cleburne; Confederate General.* Hillsboro, TX: Hillsboro Jr. College Press, 1973.

Ray, Fred L. *Shock Troops of the Confederacy: The Sharpshooter Battalions of the Army of Northern Virginia.* Ashville, NC: CFS Press, 2006.

Rhodes, Robert Hunt, ed. *All For the Union: The Civil War Diary and Letters of Elisha Hunt Rhodes.* New York: Orion Books, 1991.

Ridley, Bromfield L. *Sketches and Battles of the Army of Tennessee.* Mexico, MO: Mexico Printing and Publishing, 1906.

Ripley, William Y. W. *A History of Company F, 1st United States Sharp Shooters*. Rutland, VT: Tuttle & Co. 1883.

Roads, C. H. *The British Soldier's Firearm From Smoothbore to Smallbore, 1850–1864*. Livonia, NY: R&R Books, 1994.

Roberts, Ned H. *The Muzzle-loading Cap Lock Rifle*. Harrisburg, PA: Stackpole, 1940.

Robertson, James I., Jr. *The Stonewall Brigade*. Baton Rouge, LA: LSU Press, 1963.

_____, ed. *The Civil War Letters of General Robert McAllister*. New Brunswick, NJ: Rutgers University Press, 1965.

Roe, Alfred Seely. *Monocacy: A Sketch of the Battle of Monocacy, MD., July 9th, 1864*. Worcester, MA: 9th New York Heavy Artillery Veterans' Organization, 1894.

Rosenblatt, Emil, and Edith, eds. *Hard Marching Every Day: The Civil War Letters of Private Wilbur Fisk, 1861–1865*. Lawrence, KS: University Press of Kansas, 1992.

Satterlee, L. S., comp. *Ten Old Gun Catalogs*. Chicago: Gun Digest Company, 1957.

Sauers, Richard A., ed. *Fighting Them Over: How the Veterans Remembered Gettysburg in the Pages of the National Tribune*. Baltimore: Butternut and Blue, 1998.

Sharpe, Philip B. *The Rifle in America*. New York: Funk & Wagnalls, 1947.

Smith, Henry I. *History of the Seventh Regiment, Iowa Volunteer Infantry During the Civil War*. Mason City, IA: E. Hitchcock, 1903.

Smith, David Paul. *Frontier Defense in the Civil War*. College Station, TX: Texas A&M, 1992.

Starr, Steven Z. *The Union Cavalry in the Civil War: Vol. I. Fort Sumter to Gettysburg*. Baton Rouge: LSU Press, 1979.

Stevens, Charles A. *Berdan's United States Sharpshooters in the Army of the Potomac: 1861–1865*. Dayton, OH: Morningside Books, 1984 reprint.

Stillwell, Leander. *The Story of a Common Soldier of Army Life in the Civil War 1861–1865*. Chicago: Franklin Hudson, 1920 2nd ed.

Sunderland, Glenn W. *Wilder's Lightning Brigade and its Spencer Repeaters*. Washington, IL: Book Works, 1984.

Sword, Wiley. *Firepower from Abroad: The Confederate Enfield and the LeMat Revolver*. Lincoln, RI: Andrew Mobray, 1986.

_____. *The Historic Henry Rifle*. Lincoln, RI: Andrew Mobray, 2002.

_____. *Sharpshooter: Hiram Berdan, His Famous Sharpshooters and their Sharps Rifles*. Lincoln, RI: Andrew Mobray, 1988.

Sykes, Bryan. *Saxons, Vikings and Celts: The Genetic Roots of Britain and Ireland*. New York: W. W. Norton, 2006.

Tate, Thomas K. *From Under Iron Eyelids: The Biography of James Henry Burton, Armorer to Three Nations.* Bloomington, Indiana: Author House, 2005.

Thomas, Dean S. *Ready, Aim, Fire: Small Arms Ammunition at the Battle of Gettysburg.* Gettysburg, PA: Thomas Publications, 1993 ed.

_____. *Round Ball to Rimfire: A History of Civil War Small Arms Ammunition, Part One.* Gettysburg, PA: Thomas Publications, 1997.

_____. *Round Ball to Rimfire: A History of Civil War Small Arms Ammunition, Part Two, Federal Breechloading Carbines & Rifles.* Gettysburg, PA: Thomas Publications, 2002.

_____. *Round Ball to Rimfire: A History of Civil War Small Arms Ammunition, Part Three: Federal Pistols, Revolvers & Miscellaneous Essays.* Gettysburg, PA: Thomas Publications, 2003.

Thompson, John C. *History of the Eleventh Regiment, Rhode Island Volunteers, in the War of the Rebellion.* Providence, RI: Providence Press, 1881.

Tisdale, D. A. *Soldiers of the Virginia Colony, 1607–1699.* Author, n.d.

Todd, Frederick. P. *American Military Equipage, 1851–1871 Vol. II, State Forces.* New York: Chatham Square Press, 1983.

Toombs, Samuel. *New Jersey Troops in the Gettysburg Campaign.* Orange, NJ: Evening Mail Publishing, 1888.

Trench, Charles Chenevix. *A History of Marksmanship.* Chicago: Follett, 1972.

U.S. Government. *Report of the Joint Committee on the Conduct of the War.* Washington, DC: Government Printing Office, 1863.

U.S. Government. *The War of the Rebellion: A Compilation of the Official Records of the Union and Confederate Armies.* Washington, DC: Government Printing Office, 1880–1901.

U.S. Government. *Reports of Experiments with Small Arms for the Military Service by Officers of the Ordnance Department, U.S. Army, Published by Authority of the Secretary of War.* Washington, DC: A. O. P. Nicholson, Public Printer, 1856 (Gettysburg, PA: Thomas Publications, 1984 reprint).

U.S. War Department. *A System of Target Practice for the Use of Troops When Armed with the Musket, Rifle Musket, Rifle or Carbine, Prepared Principally from the French.* Washington, D.C.: 1862.

Vandiver, Frank E. *Ploughshares into Swords: Josiah Gorgas and Confederate Ordnance.* College Station, TX: Texas A&M, 1952.

Walker, Francis A. *History of the Second Army Corps in the Army of the Potomac.* New York: Charles Scribner's Sons, 1887.

Ware, Donald L. *Remington Army and Navy Revolvers, 1861–1888.* Albuquerque: University of New Mexico Press, 2007.

Ware, Eugene F. *The Lyon Campaign in Missouri, Being a History of the First Iowa Infantry*. Topeka, KS: Crane and Company, 1907.
_____. *The Indian War of 1864*. Lincoln, NE: University of Nebraska, 1994 reprint.
White, Russell C., ed. *The Civil War Diary of Wyman S. White, First Sergeant, Company F, 2nd United States Sharpshooters*. Baltimore: Butternut and Blue, 1993.
Whittaker, Frederick. *Volunteer Cavalry: The Lessons of the Decade*. New York: Author, 1871.
Wilcox, Cadmus. *Rifles and Rifle Practice*. New York: 1859.
Wiley, Bell Irvin. *The Life of Billy Yank: The Common Soldier of the Union*. New York: Bobbs-Merrill Company, 1951.
Willard, George L. *Manual of Target Practice for the United States Army*. Philadelphia: J. B. Lippincott & Co., 1862.
Willard , George L. (ed. William C. Goble). *Comparative Value of Rifled and Smooth-Bored Arms*. Hightstown, NJ: Longstreet House, 1995 reprint.
Wittenberg, Eric, J. *Protecting the Flank: The Battles of Brinkerhoff's Ridge and East Cavalry Field*. Celina, OH: Ironclad Publishing, 2002.
Woolfolk Wiggins, Sarah, ed. *The Journals of Josiah Gorgas, 1857–1878*. Tuscaloosa, AL: University of Alabama Press, 1943.
Wray, William J. *History of the Twenty-third Pennsylvania Volunteer Infantry, Birney's Zouaves*. Philadelphia: Survivor's Assn., 1904.

ARTICLES
Adams, Bill. "The Model 1854 Austrian Lorenz." *The Unconquered Banner: Newsletter of the 34th Virginia Battalion* (1996).
Bilby, Joseph G. "Memoirs of Carlos W. Colby." *Military Images Magazine* (September–October 1981).
_____. "First Blood: A New Jersey Brigade at Williamsburg." *Military Images Magazine* 12, no. 2 (September–October 1990).
_____. "The Keystone Travelers: A Regimental History of the 104th Pennsylvania." *Military Images Magazine* (March–April 1992).
Boudriot, Jean. "Un aboutissement, mais une fin: Le fusil d'infanterie modele 1822." *Gazette des Armes* 96 (Aout 1981).
Bury, Lieutenant Colonel Viscount. "The Volunteer Course at Hythe School of Musketry." *Fraser's Magazine* 62, no. 367 (July 1860).
Caranta, Raymond. "Louis Nicolas Auguste Flobert: His Rimfire Rifles and Cartridges." *Gun Digest* (1974).
Carrington, Henry B. "Familiar Hints to Indiana Soldiers Taking to the Field." Undated newspaper clipping from the Greencastle, Indiana, *Putnam Republican Banner*.

"Colt's Revolving Rifle." *Military Gazette* 3, no. 18 (September 15, 1860).

Cunnington, G. "L'entrainement au tir, a' l'epoque des armes a' silex." *Gazette des Armes* 96 (Aout 1981).

Deeks, Henry. "Civil War Images." *The Civil War News* (November 1995).

Gilmore, Russel S. "New York Target Companies: Informal Military Societies in a 19th Century Metropolis." *Military Collector and Historian* 35, no. 2 (Summer 1983).

Glass, Captain Scott. "Confederate Status of Class V, VII and IX at Appomattox." *Ordnance: The Professional Bulletin of the Ordnance Soldier* (August 1992).

Gross, John. "A War Fought and Won with 'Inferior' Firearms." *The Gun Report* 47, no. 10 (March 2002).

Hayden, Horace Edward. "Explosive or Poisoned Musket Balls,—Were they authorized and Used by the Confederate States Army, or by the United States Army during the Civil War?—A Slander Refuted." *Southern Historical Society Papers* 8 (January–December 1880).

Mallet, John W. "Work of the Ordnance Bureau." *Southern Historical Society Papers* 37 (January–December 1919).

Maryniak, Ben R. "Shooting Practice." *Buffalo Civil War Round Table Newsletter* (May 1990).

McCall Smith, Alexander. "A Wee Identity Crisis." The *New York Times*, 11 March 2007.

Neff, Robert O. "The Enfield Rifle." *Muzzle Blasts* (July 1979).

Olney, Warren. *Shiloh as Seen by a Private Soldier*. California MOLLUS papers (1889).

Starr, Stephen Z. "Cold Steel: The Saber and the Union Cavalry." *Civil War History* 11 (1965).

Thompson, Richard S. "A Scrap at Gettysburg." *Military Essays and Recollections* (1897).

Trinque, Bruce A. "Arnold's Battery and the 26th North Carolina." *Gettysburg Magazine* 12 (January 1995).

Trowbridge, Luther S. "The Operations of the Cavalry in the Gettysburg Campaign." Michigan MOLLUS papers (1886).

"The How and Why of Long Shots and Straight Shots." *The Cornhill Magazine* (April 1860).

Wade, Nicholas. "A United Kingdom? Maybe." The *New York Times*, 6 March 2007.

Yee, Gary. "The Longest Shots Ever—and Walter Cline's Attempt to Validate the Feat." *Muzzle Blasts* (November 2003).

Newspapers and Periodicals

Augusta (GA) *Daily Constitutionalist*
Charleston Mercury
Doylestown (PA) *Democrat*
Harper's Weekly
Hunterdon (NJ) *Republican*
Jersey City (NJ) *Standard*
Military Gazette
Newark (NJ) *Advertiser*
New York Herald
New York Times
Newark (NJ) *Journal*
Richmond Daily Dispatch
Sussex (NJ) *Register*
Scientific American
Washington (NJ) *Star*

Internet Sources

Bill Adams, "Weapons of the 34th," www.34thvacav.org/weapons.html.
Eric Wittenberg, "John Buford's Defense in Depth at Gettysburg."
    http://www.bufordsboys.com/WittenbergBufordDefense.htm.
The Tenth Regiment of Infantry," http://www.army.mil/cmh-
    pg/books/R&H/R&H-10IN.htm.
http://www.civilwardata.com/.
The 15th Massachusetts Infantry in the Civil War Web site, http://www.nex-
    tech.de/ma15mvi/index.htm.
http://www.bradyssharpshooters.org/.

ACKNOWLEDGMENTS

As WITH ANY EXTENSIVE PROJECT, especially concerning Gettysburg, this book was made possible by those who came before. Without books like Edwin B. Coddington's The Gettysburg Campaign: A Study in Command, David G. Martin's Gettysburg, July 1, and Harry W. Pfanz's Gettysburg: The Second Day and Gettysburg, Culp's Hill and Cemetery Hill and others to provide a historical framework, this would have been a much more difficult task. In addition, the numerous secondary studies, particularly the specialized studies by Thomas Publications of Gettysburg that highlight different aspects of the battle, proved invaluable. I am particularly indebted to Dean Thomas' comprehensive three-volume work on Civil War small arms projectiles in general and his older work on those found at Gettysburg in particular.

A number of people, including Bill Adams, David Martin, Brent Nosworthy, Dave Powell, Fred Ray, Bruce Trinque, and Jeff Williams offered valuable comment on and constructive criticism of this work while it was in progress, and through their knowledge, expertise, and careful critical reading, suggested improvements and supplied sources I had overlooked. Last, but my no means least, I would like to thank my wife Patricia Bilby for her proof reading, and my designated marksman, Steve Garratano, who is a far better shot than I, for assisting me in shooting tests of original small arms.

Needless to say, if I have forgotten anyone, I apologize and the usual caveat applies: any errors in this book are entirely my own.

INDEX